Let's Go Stag!

T0407271

Global Exploitation Cinemas

Series Editors
Johnny Walker, Northumbria University, UK
Austin Fisher, Bournemouth University, UK

Editorial Board
Tejaswini Ganti, New York University, USA
Joan Hawkins, Indiana University, USA
Kevin Heffernan, Southern Methodist University, USA
Ernest Mathijs, University of British Columbia, Canada
Constance Penley, University of California, Santa Barbara, USA
Eric Schaefer, Emerson College, USA
Dolores Tierney, University of Sussex, UK
Valerie Wee, National University of Singapore, Singapore

Also in the Series:
Disposable Passions: Vintage Pornography and the Material Legacies of Adult Cinema, by David Church
Grindhouse: Cultural Exchange on 42nd Street, and Beyond,
edited by Austin Fisher & Johnny Walker
Exploiting East Asian Cinemas: Genre, Circulation, Reception,
edited by Ken Provencher and Mike Dillon
The Politics of Nordsploitation: History, Industry, Audiences,
by Tommy Gustafsson and Pietari Kääpä
The Mad Max Effect: Road Warriors in International Exploitation Cinema,
by James Newton

Let's Go Stag!

*A History of Pornographic Film from the
Invention of Cinema to 1970*

Dan Erdman

BLOOMSBURY ACADEMIC
NEW YORK • LONDON • OXFORD • NEW DELHI • SYDNEY

BLOOMSBURY ACADEMIC
Bloomsbury Publishing Inc
1385 Broadway, New York, NY 10018, USA
50 Bedford Square, London, WC1B 3DP, UK
29 Earlsfort Terrace, Dublin 2, Ireland

BLOOMSBURY, BLOOMSBURY ACADEMIC and the Diana logo
are trademarks of Bloomsbury Publishing Plc

First published in the United States of America 2022
This paperback edition first published in 2023

Cover design by Johnnie Walker and Eleanor Rose
Cover image: [Untitled Stag Film], from the personal collection of the author

Library of Congress Cataloging-in-Publication Data
Names: Erdman, Dan, author.
Title: Let's go stag! : a history of pornographic film from the invention
of cinema to 1970 / Dan Erdman.
Description: New York, NY : Bloomsbury Academic, 2021. | Series: Global exploitation
cinemas | Includes bibliographical references and index.
Identifiers: LCCN 2021023809 (print) | LCCN 2021023810 (ebook) |
ISBN 9781501333019 (hardback) | ISBN 9781501333026 (epub) |
ISBN 9781501333033 (pdf) | ISBN 9781501333040
Subjects: LCSH: Pornographic films–History and criticism. | Erotic films–History and
criticism. | Motion pictures–History–20th century.
Classification: LCC PN1995.9.S45 E67 2021 (print) | LCC PN1995.9.S45 (ebook) |
DDC 791.43/6538–dc23
LC record available at https://lccn.loc.gov/2021023809
LC ebook record available at https://lccn.loc.gov/2021023810

ISBN: HB: 978-1-5013-3301-9
        PB: 978-1-5013-8647-3
        ePDF: 978-1-5013-3303-3
        eBook: 978-1-5013-3302-6

Series: Global Exploitation Cinemas

Typeset by Integra Software Services Pvt. Ltd.

To find out more about our authors and books visit www.bloomsbury.com
and sign up for our newsletters.

Contents

Acknowledgments

Dan Kanemoto came up with the title of this book, so it's only appropriate to put him at the head of the queue here. Thanks, Dan. A far greater number helped in some way with the stuff in between the covers, and I will mention them here.

My editors at Bloomsbury, Johnny Walker, Austin Fisher, and Erin Duffy, have done yeoman's work in getting all of this into readable shape; if this book makes sense at all it is due to their efforts. Thanks to them for their diligence and patience.

This project originated as my master's thesis at New York University's Moving Image Archiving and Preservation program. I received invaluable advice, criticism, and direction from my advisor Howard Besser, and an equal measure of the same from Ann Harris, Mona Jimenez, and Dan Streible. I was very lucky to have the classmates that I did during those years, and will always remember the indispensable moral support they gave and continue to give. Here are their names: Chris Banuelos, Laurie Duke, Rebecca Fraimow, Kathryn Gronsbell, Kelly Haydon, Julia Kim, Federica Liberi, Kristin MacDonough, Pawarisa Nipawattanapong, Shira Peltzman, Juana Suarez, and Erica Titkemeyer.

Researching this book led me to make the acquaintance of many scholars whose primary field of study is adult films; getting to know them has been an unexpected but happy consequence of my work. Thanks to all of these for their expertise, advice, and fellowship: Peter Alilunas, Brandon Arroyo, Robin Bougie, Michael Bowen, David Church, Lynn Comella, Finley Freibert, Elena Gorfinkel, Kevin Heffernan, Laura Helen Marks, Ryan Powell, Joe Ruben, Eric Schaefer, Russell Sheaffer, Whit Strub, and Tom Waugh. I must make a special mention here of Casey Scott, whose tenacious research on and advocacy for adult films have been personal inspirations; I doubt I would have even begun this project absent his example.

Many others have left their mark on this work, even if they didn't realize that's what they were doing at the time. Julian Antos, Snowden Becker, Brian Belak, Douglas Charles, Liz Coffey, Sebastian del Castillo, Stefan Elnabli, Skip Elsheimer, Stacey Jones Erdman, Walter Forsberg, Rebecca Hall, Genevieve Havermeyer-King, Dan Kanemoto (him again!), John Kostka, Japeth Mennes,

Matt Messbarger, Yuki Nakamura, Lars Nilsen, Bono Olgado, Stephen Parr, Samuel Prime, Katie Risseeuw, Jay Schwartz, Bobby Smiley, Bill Stamets, Albert Steg, Jackie Stewart, Dwight Swanson, Steven Toushin, Andy Uhrich, Robert Vazari, Nancy Watrous, Anne Wells, and Bryan-Mitchell Young have all favored me with their insights, film recommendations, reference suggestions, willingness to share PDFs, and conversation. I've learned a lot from all of you.

Special thanks to Sara Chapman and Tom Weinberg at Media Burn Archive (my real job) for many, many things, the most relevant to the present purpose being their tolerance of my periodic truancies for research trips and writing marathons. The reader is strongly urged to visit mediaburn.org at their earliest opportunity—you're not up to anything right now, are you?—and lose yourself in our collection of thousands of documentary videos created by artists, activists, and community groups, from the 1970s to the present day. A fascinating alternative record of the last fifty years awaits you!

Speaking of research trips, I was fortunate to be the recipient of a Moody Research Grant from the LBJ Foundation, which was a great help to me when I went down for an extended visit to Lyndon Baines Johnson Library in 2016; I very much appreciate the Foundation's generosity, and the extensive use I have made of materials from the Library's collection in the pages that follow attest to that trip's importance to my project. Thanks also to the archives staff at the LBJ Library, particularly Brian McNerney, for making the visit a fruitful and fascinating one (and thanks to Clay and Marijane Billington for hosting me at their place!). I also made several trips to the Kinsey Institute during my work on this book, and their staff went beyond the call of duty to answer some truly obscure requests for material. And, speaking of writing marathons, thanks to Tom Colley and Ann Hruby for letting me sequester in their remote wilderness cabin for a week while I willed myself into writing a first complete draft.

It is surely the dream of every parent to find their names in their son's book about the history of pornographic films; this happy moment has arrived at last for Tom and Barb Erdman. Because of them I know how to read, write, research, and revise; they are my first and best teachers.

I can hardly imagine where I'd be, or who I'd be, without Kristin MacDonough. Her kindness, encouragement, and love have made all of this possible.

Introduction

On Friday, February 5, 1954, in Milwaukee, Wisconsin, the Hayloft Tavern would play host to an uncommonly rowdy screening.

Spectators began gathering by the scores at 8:00 p.m. for the show, which was scheduled for 9:00 p.m. Most bought drinks at the first floor bar before going to the second floor dance hall to sit around tables covered with blue checkered cloths.

The audience ranged from grandfathers, some near the tottering stage, to pink cheeked youths. Some wore expensive camel hair overcoats, some overalls. As the hall filled, latecomers took seats in balconies at each end or hung over the railings. A small space in a corner near the piano was left clear for the entertainers.

A balding man bustled about, collecting tickets. If spectators had none, they paid $5 apiece. Managers of the affair began pinning red-checked curtains over the frosted windows.

"The cops could never raid this place," one customer confided to a companion. "How would they ever haul everybody away?"

… At 9pm the audience began clapping and stamping for the show to start. A male singer with a guitar appeared and opened with: "I know you didn't come here to see me."

"You ain't kiddin'!" somebody yelled.

"Bring on the women!" another shouted.

The projectionist, who confided to a helper that he had brought some of his "own equipment tonight," called for "lights out."

Two indecent films were shown with obscene dialog added by spectators. One film involved two women and a man. The man had a hole in one sock. The women had dirty feet. The second film starred a couple cast away on a Pacific island.

"Five years in the navy," a man yelled, "and I never saw anything like that on an island!"

The film, seemingly as old as "The Great Train Robbery," broke every few minutes and had to be spliced as spectators, many hunched in overcoats in the cold loft, screamed.

After the screening had finished, the live entertainment portion of the program commenced; it seemed to exceed the standard of ribaldry set by the films.

A drunken Negro girl staggered into the spotlight and "danced" in nothing but a large pair of earrings. As she tried to leave, walking nude through the audience, she was pushed back to the corner to perform again. Spectators showered her with coins.

A Negro man and woman performed without clothing. Some yelled that they couldn't see, so tables were brought to the corner and pushed together into an impromptu stage. Answering a call for "volunteers" for the show, a drunken white youth stripped and took part.

A drunk clambered to a rafter and staggered precariously in a "tight wire" act to get a better look. He fell and crashed on the floor.

Just as the mania reached a kind of crescendo, the police arrived; fear and confusion rippled through the crowd.

"It's the cops!" somebody yelled.
There were cries of:
"The joint's raided!"
"What'll my wife say!"
"Let's get out of here!"
Several men tried to escape through a window of the women's washroom.

Two climbed to the roof through a "hatch" and sat in the biting wind, with no chance of escaping until deputies heard footsteps on the shingles and seized them.

"Everybody stay where you are," [the police] told the throng through a portable public address system.

Milling spectators stampeded for exits blocked by deputies. Officers soon brought about order.

268 people were sent to jail that night; the head of the city's vice squad claimed that "the show was so revolting that one young officer was 'very upset emotionally' over it." Among those to be charged were Daniel Schramka, the tavern's proprietor, who, afterwards, appeared shell-shocked over the whole incident.

Schramka said: "I rent to a hundred parties a year. These men came to me and told me the bar trade would be good, so I gave them the hall for nothing."

"Did you know what kind of party it was going to be?" a Milwaukee Journal reporter asked.

"I knew it was going to be a stag party," Schramka said, "but we've had other stag parties for fellows getting married and things like that, but I never had a party where things like this went on."[1]

Throughout most of the twentieth century, from nearly the debut of cinema to the 1960s, the kinds of films shown at the Hayloft were being screened on a regular basis somewhere in the United States. Hardcore pornographic films were produced, distributed, and exhibited throughout the country to audiences at secret screenings in bars, clubs, private homes, or other non-theatrical settings. Very often other kinds of performances were there to supplement the film, usually including, at the very least, a striptease act. Compared with most other contemporary accounts of these kinds of events, the Hayloft incident was only unusual in the degree to which it descended into drunken riotousness, even before the arrival of the police. The intrusion of the law into this event is also, unfortunately for the organizers and audience, something of a regular occurrence at these screenings; though laws relating to pornographic films varied by state, and sometimes by municipality, possession and screening of such material was almost always legally banned, or at the very least heavily restricted.

In the course of my research for this project, I found hundreds of accounts in newspapers and magazines, over a period of nearly seventy years, of events very similar to this one. Yet, despite the apparent prevalence of these kinds of screenings, despite the existence of an extensive underground exhibition culture serving these audiences, surprisingly little research and analysis has been done on these films, their creators, or their audiences. Incidents like the one at the Hayloft should be the catalyst for research questions from the historically minded writer: Who arranged this event? How was it publicized? Where did the films come from? The answers to queries about a specific incident may be found in the further investigations of the local press, but the presence of so many similar screenings occurring across the decades in so many different parts of the United States should give rise to questions posed at a more general level: How were these films produced, and by whom? How did they circulate? Where were they shown, and under what circumstances? And, as such films were produced, distributed, and exhibited over the course of several decades, did these practices change over time, if so how so, and in response to what factors? These are the questions I will

---

[1] *Milwaukee Journal*, February 6, 1954, 1–2.

address in the present work. Before proceeding with my inquiry, however, it will be necessary to address the most basic question of all: What, exactly, is a stag film?

The term "stag film" has, through the years, become a kind of shorthand for almost any kind of moving image pornography. (I will explore some of the word's etymological origins and the history of its use in a later chapter, but for now I will use it as my preferred term simply as a convenience.) Instead of one pithy definition, I offer two complementary ones. It is only fitting that the first is from Linda Williams, who all but inaugurated the serious study of pornographic cinema with her book *Hard Core: Power, Pleasure, and the Frenzy of the Visible* in the late 1980s. "Stag films are anonymously made, short, undated silent films displaying one or more hard-core sex acts."[2] Already a significant amount of material has been excluded, with each term doing its share of the work. The meaning of "anonymously made" is obvious, but it also situates these films at some point in the fairly distant past, before federal regulations mandated that the identities of all on-screen performers in adult films be kept on file by the producers, and thus in a time when association with this sort of production meant not just social disapproval, but the legal sort as well. "Short" removes feature-length films from consideration, "undated" reinforces the secretive nature of these productions, as their creators had no incentive to link their work to a particular year (such as the assignment of a copyright date, something which was forgone in every case). "Silent" gives a clue to the cut-rate nature of the productions, which tended (with some exceptions) not to bother with the extra cost or technical hurdle required for synchronized sound; "hard-core sex acts" should require no further elaboration.

While this is probably sufficient in a general sense, the arguments I will be making in the following chapters will require a bit more precision; for this I will turn to another milestone of pornography scholarship, this one by a corporate author: the compilers of the *1970 Report of the President's Commission on Obscenity and Pornography*, which will figure prominently in what follows. Naturally enough, they preferred the somewhat less-colloquial "'under-the-counter' or 'hard-core' 'pornography'" to "stag film," but I think that their definition, though a bit labored, has the advantage of being more exhaustive.

---

[2] Linda Williams, "'White Slavery' versus the Ethnography of 'Sexworkers': Women in Stag Films at the Kinsey Archive," *The Moving Image*, Vol. 5, No. 2 (2005), 108.

The characteristics of hard-core materials are as follows:

1. The sexual activity depicted is certain. That is, photographs of human sexual intercourse (including bestiality) leave nothing to the imagination. The viewer has no doubt that the activity being depicted is real, not simulated, intercourse.
2. The photographic depiction of the sexual activity focuses upon the sexual contact of the genitals. The male genital organ is shown erect, rather than in the flaccid state depicted in "borderline" material.
3. Intromission, or penetration, whether oral, vaginal, or anal, is clearly shown with particular emphasis on oral–genital contact.
4. The materials are not openly sold but are distributed in an under-the-counter manner.[3]

These definitions describe the films themselves, and also summarize some of the problems native to their study. Encountering a stag film, the content on screen is as obvious as the Johnson commission's definition itself; to paraphrase the obligatory Potter Stewart quote, you know it when you see it. But if Williams's definition doesn't get into as much detail about the content of these movies, her other terms say a lot about the other, equally essential quality, which is the secret nature of the films' origins.

Film scholars and archivists have developed a range of methods for researching and identifying orphaned films. Jan-Christopher Horak's narrative of his efforts to identify the film now known as *The Fall of Jerusalem* provides a veritable instruction manual of the strategies available to the film detective. Besides some scant notes written on reel bands, Horak found himself with no information whatsoever about the film in his possession, forcing him to investigate sources of documentation ancillary to the item itself—"looking for actors, researching producers, distributors, copyright records, national filmographies, trade periodicals, distribution patterns, genres, publicity materials, and any other documentation tangentially connected with the object in question."[4] Though he ultimately met with success, it seems clear that the methods Horak is advocating here rely on the existence of a certain bureaucratic infrastructure which arose to accommodate the circulation of commercial feature films; while these are

---

[3] *Technical Report of the Commission on Obscenity and Pornography, Volume* III (Washington, DC: U.S. Government Printing Office, 1971), 180.
[4] Jan-Christopher Horak, "The Strange Case of *The Fall of Jerusalem*: Orphans and Film Identification," *The Moving Image*, Vol. 5, No. 2 (2005), 8.

undoubtedly sound for the kind of projects he describes, they are of little use to researchers of certain other types of moving images. Horak acknowledges this, honestly if discouragingly admitting that "film history will always remain a patchwork," and acknowledging that the situation is especially dire for "smaller films, independent productions, shorts, and ephemeral genres such as industrials."[5]

Though not mentioned by name, stags definitely fall among those "ephemeral genres"; indeed, they're more ephemeral than most. At least the other varieties of non-theatrical films he mentions existed within some manner of public space. Industrial and instructional films advertised to potential clients, producing catalogs and other publicity materials in significant quantities, and were produced by recognized companies which owned office space, paid taxes, and left something of a public footprint. Even home movies often feature content clues which appear in passing, giving the dedicated researcher at least a chance of assigning a provisional history to the item.[6] None of these conditions apply to the stag film, which was defined by deliberate secrecy surrounding its production, distribution, and exhibition. For most of these films, nearly all identifying details were deliberately suppressed by their creators at every stage of its life cycle in order to avoid a paper trail and the threat of legal action.

Supporting documentation does not exist for stag films. As near as my research has been able to determine, no stag film was ever submitted for copyright registration, therefore any dates which might be linked to a title are suspect. Similarly, there is no conceivable reason why a producer would have bothered to submit a film to any of the regional censorship boards which existed during the heyday of the stag, rendering that often-illuminating source of information useless. Likewise the trade press, which did not exist for pornographic films produced during the period under consideration. Limited amounts of promotional material from stag distributors and sellers do exist, but the information that would link this ephemera to a particular film is often quite vague, typically including only a title at best. These tidbits might reveal something about a distributor, such as an address or possibly the specific years during which they were active, but will very often say nothing about their wares; even flyers advertising the films will only refer them in the vaguest terms, in an effort to attract just enough attention, but not too much.

---

[5] Ibid., 45.
[6] See Snowden Becker, "Family in a Can: The Presentation of Home Movies in Museums," *The Moving Image*, Vol. 1, No. 2 (Fall 2001). 88–106.

The information found in the films themselves, such as they are, is notorious for unreliability, typically having been designed specifically to obfuscate and frustrate any efforts at locating the creators. The credits of the ancient stag movie *A Free Ride*, for example, cheekily attribute A. Wise Guy with direction, Will B. Hard with photography and Will She as the author of the titles; those of *Wonders of the Unseen World*, for another, name Ima Cunt as that film's director and features cinematography by R. U. Hard (presumably a relative of Will B.).

Matters are little better with regard to names of cast members. The definitive crack in Horak's case was the serendipitous identification of an actor, but this is much less likely in the case of stags. Obviously, credits are as reliable for this group as they are for the rest of the crew (which is to say not at all), but even the apparent advantage of being able to refer to visible faces (as well as much else) has produced very little in terms of historical information. *Smart Aleck*, a film from the 1950s, features a young (and possibly juvenile) Candy Barr, a stripper who later achieved some notoriety for, among other things, having been in the employ of Jack Ruby. Jack Stevenson has claimed that a woman named "Blondie Blondell" "used the same pseudonym and created a recognizable character over a series of films"[7] (though he neglects to provide her given name and only credits her with one movie) but, even if this is true, she was decidedly in the minority. In fact, the uncertainty of the performers' identities is the source of the persistent urban legend that certain notable actors (Joan Crawford and Chuck Connors are perennials here) participated in stag films in their earlier, leaner years.

As with so much else about these films, even titles are not entirely consistent. A single film may have had several titles assigned to it over the course of its life; whether this occurred due to damage to the head of the reel necessitating replacement of identifying information, efforts at differentiating a pirated film, unsavory attempts to sell the same movie twice to the same party, or some other unknowable reason, Arthur Knight and Hollis Alpert hint at the annoying persistence of this practice:

> *While the Cat's Away* was sold again under the imaginative second title *The Mice Will Play* and—to confuse things further—*Play Girl*. A recent film from Detroit has appeared with three different titles: *Scroungy Truck Driver* and, for those who don't care for that image, *Clean Cut Truck Driver*, as well as *Scroungy Turned Chicken* for good measure. As various times, the stag classic *Pricking*

Cherries has also been sold as *The Dream Salesman, Sock Salesman, Office Girl's Dream* and *Secret Dreams*.[8]

The opposite problem has occurred as well, in which one title may encompass several discrete works; in an industry as diffuse as the one which produced stag films, there would be no way to keep track of titles of other films in circulation, and it is unlikely that this would have mattered to anyone with the wherewithal to do anything about it in the first place. Knight and Alpert claim to have discovered in their survey "of 1000 film titles [that] there are two of *Picnic*, two of *Sleep Walker*, three called *Strip Poker*, three *Call Girls* and no fewer than five entitled *The Lovers*. Two different films have been called *Unexpected Company*, and one of these has been sold as *Love Bug*, but two other and quite different films have been titled *Love Bug*, too."[9]

The problem of identification is an unfortunately common one for pornography researchers. Subject to varying degrees of social and legal opprobrium for their actions, those responsible for producing pornographic works—at all levels of participation, and in all media, not only film—generally did what they could to distance themselves from their creations. Those scholars with an interest in sexually explicit material have, as a result, had to hone their detective skills, sometimes several decades removed from the object under examination.

The most complete and careful archeological work has probably been done in the field of pornographic literature and publishing. Although often produced in different historical and legal contexts from those I am addressing here, erotic literature faced a degree of sanction at least as severe as that meted out to moving images, with similar risks to authors, printers, and publishers. In the face of this, the steps they took to protect themselves anticipate those of their descendants in the stag film world. In his bibliography of what he calls "clandestine erotic fiction in English," Peter Mendes defines his subject as "books whose publishers and printers attempted to hide their identities, either by offering no information or, more frequently, misleading information as to date and/or place of publication. In effect, this usually involved a title page whose aim may have been to shock and/or amuse, but which always intended to mystify."[10] Henry Spencer Ashbee,

---

[8]   Arthur Knight and Hollis Alpert, "The History of Sex in Cinema, Part Seventeen: The Stag Film," *Playboy*, November 1967, 172.

[9]   Ibid., 172.

[10] Peter Mendes, *Clandestine Erotic Fiction in English, 1800–1930: A Bibliographical Study* (Aldershot: Scholar Press, 1993), vii.

undoubtedly the greatest collector and investigator of pornographic literature, describes a situation remarkably similar to the one above with regard to stags:

> The author writes, for the most part, anonymously, or under an assumed name; the publisher generally affixes a false impress with an incorrect date; and the title is not infrequently worded so as to mislead with regard to the real contents of the book. To discover these authors is frequently impossible … [and] in English literature nothing has been done, and the task is now almost hopeless.[11]

Despite this pessimistic note (perhaps literary history, too, is destined to remain a patchwork?), these and other bibliographers have accomplished much in the way of determining both the content and authorship of many of these mysterious volumes. Mendes devised a particularly intriguing strategy involving the association of certain typefaces with particular printers which were known to exist at the time of a book's publication. Reasoning that no printer would be able to stay in business by handling forbidden volumes alone, his strategy compares the elements of the banned works with those of the legitimate book trade.

> The principal internal evidence linking clandestine books to particular printers (and, more problematically, publishers), derives from the openly published books that most of them also produced (with a helpful imprint) for "official" above-board publishers, in some cases the *same* publishers who published openly *and* clandestinely. Typographical and other technical bibliographical comparisons between a clandestine mystification and an openly published work which announces its publisher and printer can build a strong case for attribution of clandestine books.

This is admittedly something of a needle-in-a-haystack approach, and Mendes recognized that typefaces alone would not do as the sole identifying element. However, "although it may have severe limits in establishing *definite* links between 19th century books, typographical comparison can be important in building a conjectural case along with other comparisons—of paper, layout, imposition, etc."[12] Nevertheless, his attention to the technical details of the item, as opposed to its content or its (likely bogus) stated bibliographical information, has helped him to identify and classify several volumes.

---

[11] Henry Spencer Ashbee, *Forbidden Books of the Victorians, Volume I* (London: Odyssey Press, 1970), 19.

[12] Mendes, *Clandestine Erotic Fiction*, 53.

To replicate something like this kind of strategy for movies would be very difficult indeed. Motion picture film obviously brings to bear vastly different technical issues than does the printed page, but dedicated archeologists of film technology have conducted research which might make such investigations at least possible in principle. Historian of amateur cinema Alan Kattelle has produced several diagrams of the various distinct identification marks left on the film frame by aperture plates in certain models of motion picture cameras.[13] These charts include the earliest Cine-Kodak cameras, as well as models of those from competitors such as Bell and Howell. If the model of camera used to shoot a particular stag film could be determined by the historian, a rough span of dates during which production might have happened may be inferred. A film shot with, say, a Bell and Howell Filmo 141 cannot have been made any earlier than that model's debut year of 1937, and its origins would likely have been within some years of that date. Furthermore, the type of camera can lead to other clues about production which may be useful for identification. The hypothetical Filmo 141 movie would have had to have been shot on 50 ft lengths of film, as that model was only able to shoot with 50 ft Eastman magazines;[14] this fact could be useful in generating inferences about the length and completeness of the finished work, as well as the way in which the footage was cut together.

A look at the actual film itself could provide invaluable data which may be useful in placing a movie's production at a particular time. Edge code markings on Kodak film give a precise year of the reel's manufacture (which is, admittedly, distinct from the date on which the content would have been shot), and various other proprietary identification marks on film of all types often carry the name of a particular type of stock, which will further situate the production within history.[15] Once again Kattelle has provided a potentially vital resource here in his "Compilation of Motion Picture Film Formats" chart, which collates information on a particular format's width, base, brand name, perforation location, manufacturer, and years produced.[16] While this is by no means a complete inventory of all such formats ever produced, it does somewhat simplify the process of forensic examination of various edge codes and other markings distinct to one type of film.

---

[13] See Alan Kattelle, *Home Movies: A History of the American Industry, 1897–1979* (Nashua: Transition Publishing, 2000), 367–79.

[14] Ibid., 341.

[15] Paul Read and Mark-Paul Meyer, *The Restoration of Motion Picture Film* (Oxford: Butterworth-Heinemann, 2000), 60.

[16] Katelle, *Home Movies*, 363–6.

But stag films present roadblocks to even these efforts. Because of their clandestine nature, stags tended to be haphazardly copied throughout their lives, often many years after their initial production and without the knowledge (or, probably, interest) of their makers, and, in every case, with no record of the event. This persistent copying proved to be a major stumbling block for the efforts of law enforcement groups, notably the FBI, to trace individual films back to their makers and distributors, as we shall see in later chapters. Even some of the major archival collections of pornographic films had underestimated the prevalence of this practice, and only became fully aware of it as their holdings grew. In a recorded conversation from 1965, George Huntington and Eugene Slabaugh, of the Kinsey Institute for Sex, Gender, and Reproduction, discussed the protocols for acquiring new films for their archive. They would borrow reels of particular interest from the various stag dealers they were in contact with, make their own film-to-film copies on site using the campus's own optical printer, and then return the originals to the dealers once they were done.[17] This may have seemed like a sensible approach at the time—if for no other reason than that it provided the archive with brand new copies—but this also disregarded much of the contextual information that might have been present on the original films themselves. Potentially revelatory data was sent back to the stag dealers, and it disappeared along with them.

Most of the Kinsey Institute's efforts to identify films depended on an analysis of content. Initial notes taken by Slabaugh for what would eventually become the official catalog records for the films were written in an intricate code denoting the type of sexual behavior included in the film, as well as the number, gender, and (apparent) race of the participants; also included were granular descriptions of the action of the film, as well as notes about items visible in the background of the shot which might stand as a clue to the time period of the production (furniture in particular is recorded with great fastidiousness). This is a standard strategy for attempting to date orphaned films—Read and Meyer's textbook *Restoration of Motion Picture Film*, to pick a representative example, suggests that by "observing the hairstyles, clothing, automobiles etc., it is possible to acquire circumstantial evidence" of the period during which the content was produced[18]—but a difficult one to apply productively to stags. Outside of a very few examples, stags tended not to feature any more elements of the outside

---

[17] Eugene Slabaugh audio notes, 1965, Kinsey Institute.
[18] Read and Meyer, *The Restoration of Motion Picture Film*, 55.

world than necessary, generally staging the main action indoors or, if any of the performers were to venture outside, at a remote enough spot that no regional landmarks would be visible. Hairstyles and clothing may give a rough indication as to the time period, but this can give a hopelessly broad window within which the events of the film occurred, at best informing other, more definite evidence; in any case, it is inconsistent and insufficient on its own. Though one is loathe to gainsay Kevin Brownlow on any matter relating to film history, his oddly specific assertion that "judging by the fashion," *A Free Ride*—long suspected to be one of the earliest surviving stags produced in the United States—was produced in 1923 (as opposed to nearly every other resource, including the Kinsey Institute, which pegs the film at 1915) can be taken no more seriously than can his (unsubstantiated) claim that the film's "locale is Southern California."[19] In short, the visible content of a stag film can only say so much about its historical circumstances.

This leaves the historian of the twenty-first century in a delicate position, as very little is or can now be definitively known about this field of moving image culture. For the first three quarters of the twentieth century, very little serious historical or documentary work had been done on pornographic film. The handful of serious scholars addressing sexuality in cinema (Parker Tyler probably being the most prominent) tended to ignore stag films altogether. Up through the 1960s, the only scholarship to address actual pornography were a pair of French works, Ado Kyrou's 1964 *Positif* article "Amour-Erotisme et Cinema" and Lo Duca's three-volume 1957 *L'Erotisme au Cinema*.

This changed in the late 1960s and early 1970s, after the legal fetters on pornography in the United States loosened up. Almost on the eve of the *Stanley* decision—the 1969 Supreme Court case which greatly weakened restrictions on the possession of moving image pornography—books began to appear which purported to finally illuminate the heretofore dusky world of pornographic cinema. Often these were simply cash-grabs meant to take advantage of the relaxed censorship, slim volumes which were heavy on illustration and light on text. Donald H. Gilmore's *Sex and Censorship in the Visual Arts Volume II* is a representative example, containing a potted general history on eroticism in films, a summary of recent legal debates on obscenity, some breezy pages on the characteristics of the stag film, and several plates of color stills from recent stags from Scandinavia. The final page of the book consists entirely of the following

---

[19] Kevin Brownlow, *Behind the Mask of Innocence* (New York: Knopf, 1990), 28.

words posted beneath the headline "FINAL NOTICE": "Film portions shown and described in Sex and Censorship in the Visual Arts, Vols. I & II have been compiled into 200 feet of breathtaking eroticism, 100' of which are in living color! This 8mm sexual study film is available through the Erotica Book Club (See inside back cover for details)."[20] Huckersterism is sometimes as much a feature of pornography scholarship as it is of its ostensible object of study.

Somewhat more serious in its purpose, or at least less blatantly mercenary, is Al Di Lauro and Gerald Rabkin's *Dirty Movies*, which styles itself as (per its subtitle) "An Illustrated History of the Stag Film, 1915–1970." It also features many excellent illustrations, and makes some arguments that, whatever their actual merits, actually attempt to address historical questions, for example suggesting that pornographic films were distributed mostly by itinerant projectionists during the 1920s and 1930s, and that this system was replaced by mailorder films being sold directly to solo home-viewers after the Second World War.[21]

The most useful aspect of their book is probably their observations of particular films. They provide an extensive filmography, drawn from "(1) films seen by the authors in the United States and abroad; (2) significant titles from the ISR [Kinsey Institute for Sex Research] collection; (3) Ado Kyrou's invaluable *Positif* filmography; (4) films from Scandinavian catalogues of the late 1960s, early 1970s; and (5) the catalogue listings of one of the United States' most extensive private stag collections (the owner of which must remain anonymous)."[22]
The titles are supplemented by estimated year and location of production, combination of performers, and cross-indexed by common alternative names.

Unfortunately, they limit the usefulness of this list by neglecting to note which film is associated with which collection, giving the researcher no way to check their references or follow up with different research questions; furthermore, they provide no explanation for the method behind their assignment of dates and countries of origin. For these and other reasons, such as its refusal to cite any of its claims directly, *Dirty Movies* is somewhat deficient as a work of history. It does feature a bibliography, but the references devoted to pornographic film tend to rely on secondary sources. As Di Lauro and Rabkin present a superficially

[20] Donald H. Gilmore, *Sex and Censorship in the Visual Arts, Volume II* (San Diego, CA: Greenleaf Classics, 1970), 416.
[21] Al Di Lauro and Gerald Rabkin, *Dirty Movies: An Illustrated History of the Stag Film, 1915–1970* (New York: Chelsea House, 1976), 55.
[22] Ibid., 125.

plausible account of stag films' production, distribution, and exhibition in the underground era, this is especially disappointing. Even more disconcertingly, their book initiates what seems to be a common split in attempts at stag histories, which is a separation between the individual films themselves and the historical context in which they existed; the book includes sections devoted to both historical overview and close readings of certain movies that they find significant or typical, but these two approaches almost never overlap. The main advantage of Di Lauro and Rabkin's book—and this could be said also of Arthur Knight and Hollis Alpert's long *Playboy* article on stag films, which makes similarly broad historical claims with similarly thin support—is that it includes a great deal of interesting commentary on individual titles, even if, for them, these films exist in a social and historical vacuum.

Many subsequent attempts at histories of early pornography dutifully make the same mistakes as Di Lauro and Rabkin, and Knight and Alpert. Dave Thompson's *Black and White and Blue*, published a considerable time after these, is a much longer, quasi-narrative treatment, but it too is inconsistent in its citations, making claims about the world of pornographic films that are all-too-frequently free of evidence (and those that are cited are often linked to secondary sources). The most intriguing aspect of Thompson's book is a handful of interviews with people who are alleged to have been participants in the production of stag films. However, the subjects are kept completely anonymous. If these are genuine, then reticence from what would have been a group of senior citizens is somewhat understandable, and Thompson is right to respect their wishes, but he could still have presented proof of their involvement and credibility while still preserving their privacy—the most obvious way to do this would have been to associate them with particular films, which he never does. Plausible though some of these accounts may be, the general lack of detail in any of their stories severely limits their evidentiary value. Like the aforementioned authors, he devotes many pages to description and analyses of groups of films, explicating them in terms of theme and motif, mostly.

Probably the most thorough historical treatment of the stag movie has come from the various works of Joseph Slade. Slade has never written a long work addressing the subject, but has rather dealt with it in smaller portions. He's devoted considerable space to the topic in a pair of reference works, *Pornography in America: A Reference Handbook*, and the massive, three-volume *Pornography and Sexual Representation: A Reference Guide*. His fullest engagement with stag films is probably his article "Eroticism and Technical Regression: The Stag Film," which tries to establish a relationship between pornography and representational technology (with an extended consideration of what he considers to be the generally shoddy stylistic and narrative qualities of the classic stag). A decent brief history of pornographic cinema from the birth of the medium can be found here,[23] functioning as a basis for the longer philosophical argument he wishes to make, and it's worth mentioning that this example is in many ways superior to the longer works referenced above.

The excellent details found in Slade's writings are a testament to the considerable amount of time he's spent at the Kinsey Institute (much of what he says about difficult-to-quantify topics, such as the total number of stags produced in the United States, or the viability of the distribution network is linked to some evidence from that collection), and to the wide net of his research, which covers not only pornography in other media but also the evolution of amateur film technology, and a host of sources in German, French, or Spanish.

But even this generally accomplished body of work often displays errors, and is marred by a tendency to "print the legend," reporting stories with shaky factual foundations as straightforwardly true. At one point, for example, he sneakily implies that the playwright Eugene O'Neill was directly involved in the stag trade in Buenos Aires, citing a long biography by Louis Sheaffer; checking up on this reference, I found nothing in Sheaffer's book to back up this claim.[24] On other occasions he inadvisedly follows the lead of the other historians I've discussed and simply asserts things without even attempting to prove them, such as his insistence that the 1924 film *The Casting Couch* had not only been shot by an "anonymous American professional," but that this occurred "in an actual Hollywood studio"[25]—why Slade believes this to be true is left as an exercise for the reader. Other times he simply gets well-established facts wrong, such as

---

[23] Joseph W. Slade, "Eroticism and Technological Regression: The Stag Film," *History and Technology*, Vol. 2, No. 1 (March 2006), 32–5.

[24] Slade's assertion can be found in his *Pornography and Sexual Repression: A Reference Guide, Volume I* (Westport, CT: Greenwood Press, 2001), 80; Sheaffer's O'Neill biography quotes the playwright saying he frequented "theaters so-called but actually ramshackle structures that showed pornographic movies made in France and Spain," but never so much as even implies that his subject participated in the wider trade in stags in any other way.

[25] Slade, "Eroticism and Technological Regression," 38.

when he puts the invention of acetate film stock at 1926[26] (which is three years after it became commercially available as 16mm film, although its invention and development occurred even before that date). I don't want to spend too much time finding fault with his articles, since he intends more here than to simply make a historical sketch, but it is enough to point out that even this generally good take on the subject is too brief, and too prone to error.

The overall deficiencies of those attempts to write the history of the stag film would have consequences for academic and scholarly analysis of these movies; left without any previously established links to build on, these analyses routinely ignore issues of historical context. This is, in some sense, an entirely appropriate response to the limited work that has been done to establish that kind of background; Linda Williams can hardly be faulted when, in the introduction to *Hard Core*, she admits that a later chapter on stag films will, by necessity, simply disregard the question of specifically when, where, and for whom any particular film would have been made.

> In the less acceptable realm of silent, illegally and anonymously made stag films ... for which no identifiable information exists on exhibition history, I have restricted myself to a near-random sample of films in the large collection at the Kinsey Institute ... In this area I make no claim to thoroughness or to an extensive knowledge of all the texts. I simply hope that this initial examination will encourage further discussion about a genre that previously has evoked either so much hostility or so much ridicule as to seem beyond the pale of any analysis.[27]

Williams's willingness to own up to doubt, rather than pretend to write from a false certainty, is commendable. But even in the chapter which follows this caveat, she grounds much of her argument upon received notions about how stags were distributed, shown, and appreciated by their audience. For example, she claims, crediting Di Lauro and Rabkin, that stag films' "primary pleasure seems to involve forming a gender-based bond with other male spectators"[28] (a plausible hypothesis to be sure, but does not acknowledge that the solo, home-viewing audience was significant in this period as well), and also that stopping obscene film was not a priority for the post office in the way that literature was because "purveyors [of films] would have been too careful to send by mail in any

---

[26] Ibid., 32.
[27] Linda Williams, *Hard Core: Power, Pleasure, and the Frenzy of the Visible* (Berkeley: University of California Press, 1989), 8.
[28] Ibid., 73.

case"[29] (stag films were in fact sent via US mail in massive quantities once 16mm film had been perfected, as I shall demonstrate in a later chapter).

Much more egregiously, the lack of solid information on the way these films were shown leads her to repeat incorrect assertions about exhibition practices, which then form the bases of many of her theoretical arguments. The most serious misstep comes when she assumes that every visual element of the film was the result of conscious formal decisions on behalf of the filmmakers, carefully calibrated to the viewing situation of the typical stag crowd. Included among these are what she describes as instances of "temporal discontinuity" during certain films' hard-core sex scenes, which are more likely to have been a result of deteriorating film than a deliberate aesthetic choice; and the allegedly deliberate "amateurism" of the films—conceived of here as a kind of brute authenticity, circumventing the artificiality of mainstream narrative cinema with certain visual assurances that *"this* is no act"—functions as "compensation for the spectator's physical and temporal separation from the sexual performance he observes."[30] But, as seen in the example which opened this chapter, stag film screenings were very often accompanied by live striptease shows, and sometimes, as seems to be implied in the report from the Hayloft, live sex performances, which would seem to obviate the need to compensate the spectator for his distance from a real act.

This is not to pick on Williams, or to suggest that her approach cannot produce useful insights—these specific criticisms aside, I agree with the scholarly consensus that holds *Hard Core* in very high regard. She is not attempting a full historical treatment of pornographic cinema, and doesn't present her work as such. But even so, relying on urban legends and half-truths found in earlier, less-rigorous histories have led her and subsequent scholars down some blind alleys. Here, I think, it is useful to remember the principle best articulated by Robert Sklar, who suggested that film theory works best when wedded to film history;[31] "film history" in the sense that he's using the term in this context means much more than simple trainspotting, and I of course aim to provide more than simply that. But I do think it's beyond dispute that the study of the early days of pornography on film suffers from a general lack of understanding of the most prosaic, everyday aspects—production, distribution, and exhibition—and it is

---

[29] Ibid., 85.
[30] Ibid., 78.
[31] Robert Sklar, "Oh! Althusser!: Historiography and the Rise of Cinema Studies," in *Resisting Images: Essays on Cinema and History*, eds Robert Sklar and Charles Musser (Philadelphia, PA: Temple University Press, 1990), 31.

my hope that, in what follows, I can at least plow the field for those who would try to reach a higher-level understanding of this mysterious genre.

In the interest of filling in the parts of the history of stag films which have either been ignored or insufficiently explained by previous historians, I plan to rely as much as possible on primary sources. This isn't going to be to the exclusion of other kinds of evidence or information, but I feel that much of the contemporary documentation has been underutilized in scholarship to this point. As one adds a new spice to an old recipe to discover how it alters the flavor of the whole dish, I would like to see how the introduction of these materials into the standard stag historical narrative changes the overall conception of that story. Furthermore, digital scholarship now allows me to delve into this material in a way that wouldn't have been practical for Di Lauro and Rabkin, Slade, or Williams to attempt.

The largest part of this is going to come from contemporary journalism. As Dan Streible, in a study of early boxing films which drew from similar sources, cautioned, such stuff "must be read with great skepticism."[32] He was reading tabloids, overly effusive showbiz press, and other types of yellow journalism; I will be doing the same, but also including wire reports, mid-century newspapers from both big cities and small towns, amateur film club magazines, trade journals, and other such records of daily life. Much of this will be used to construct a broader context, but the vast majority will be news reports on arrests of those directly involved with pornographic films.

Of the hundreds of news articles I have read which report on actual, identifiable screenings of pornographic film, all but a handful concern themselves with those that were raided by the police, post office inspectors, FBI, liquor control board, or some other type of law enforcement. Pointing this out is almost tautological—had there been no raid, the papers would have had nothing to write about. Stag screenings that went off without incident didn't make the news. However, it may be worth it to consider that this moves the vast majority of my evidence into another conceptual category, from simply "stag film screenings" to "stag film screenings interrupted by the police." It cannot be discounted that there may have been some important, unique quality to those gatherings that did make it through the night unmolested, even if it must finally be admitted that that ingredient will forever be out of our reach. Perhaps

---

[32] Dan Streible, *Fight Pictures: A History of Boxing and Early Cinema* (Berkeley: University of California Press, 2008), 21.

an ambitious researcher can uncover some first-hand evidence of this. At any rate, I point it out only to remind the reader that there is much that will never be known about these decades of pornographic film, and that the best we can do in many cases is to try to identify what some of these missing links might be, if only to take them into account for whatever inferences may be necessary later on.

With some exceptions, the mainstream press of the period I am covering tended to err on the side of discretion when covering these kinds of incidents. The story which opens this chapter is in many ways an outlier in that it describes fairly straightforwardly all the decadence on offer for the evening. Much more common are reports consisting of a small paragraph mentioning only that someone was arrested for screening an "obscene film." The precise nature of the obscenity under review is almost never explored by any of these papers, and certainly never described in detail sufficient for the reader to make up their own mind. I bring this up not so much as a philosophical point but simply to note that, due to journalistic reticence, it is not often clear exactly what is objectionable about a particular forbidden film in a particular case. It is likely that not all of the films which landed their creators, or sales agents, or projectionists in jail were pornographic by the definition I offered above. Some of them may have been striptease films, some nudist films, some rather mild burlesques featuring nothing racier than a dancing woman in a bustier. Lack of precision on this matter is, in most cases, impossible to avoid; I have labored to include what few descriptions of the films I could find in my own text, but the comparative salaciousness of any one movie will remain a mystery.

Nevertheless, I think the words of William Uricchio (writing in this case about the difficulty of establishing the number of nickelodeon theaters in early-twentieth-century New York) could be relevant here:

> The "incompleteness" of this particular evidence base need not necessarily restrict historical interpretation, since considering discursive evidence concerning the period's dominant perceptions of the new moving picture medium proves far more profitable than searching for definitive "facts." I would argue that portrayals of moving picture exhibition originating from the press and pulpit had far greater import than the numbers or even locations of the actual theatres. Indeed, if one wishes to understand the mobilization of public sentiment, the passing of legislation, and the film industry's responses, the period's own depictions tell us more than a futile attempt to reconstruct a historical "reality." Of course, some sense of "empirical reality" provides a necessary reference point by which we can

appraise press reports and other such data, but documenting perceptions gets us far closer to understanding the implementation of cultural policy.[33]

Of course, I will be trying to use the news reports as both a means of accessing some part of "empirical reality," and "the period's dominant perceptions" of this area of film culture. To the extent that I find a news story useful for the latter purpose, it could be argued that the exact nature of an objectionable film's content isn't all that important—it was regarded by those in authority as pornographic, and my project is concerned not with the work itself, but the social and bureaucratic structures that grew around it, and the way in which some sought to work around these (activating social structures of their own— all-male clubs, secret networks of pornography peddlers, film collectors, and others—to accomplish this). Given the difficulty of placing any one film in a specific time or place, and that the object of my study is on the "industry" which allowed stag movies to be shown, I will not have much to say about any films per se—no formal breakdown, no analysis of gendered behavior or performance, no political critiques. This is not because I think these things aren't worth doing, or haven't been done well in the past; David Church, for one, has written a fine book on "vintage" pornography—stags included—that takes up the challenge to "explore what kind of cultural histories about gender and sexuality these surviving materials can tell, and how the very telling of those histories can be a profoundly embodied experience."[34] Rather, I'm choosing to focus my attention on the state of the historical knowledge about how these films were made and circulated, which I think is (still) far too thin. Not only is this worth pursuing on its own merits, but I hope that, once this aspect is better understood, it may perhaps serve as a spur to better and deeper textual analysis in the future.

The design of this book is roughly chronological, though it doesn't follow a strict narrative. Chapter 1 will briefly consider what is known about the very earliest days of pornographic film. This by necessity means that I will be exclusively considering films from outside of the United States, since this seems to be where the earliest examples have been placed. Much of this will involve following up on specific claims made about these films by some of the other historians, though I will be investigating some European and Latin American

---

[33] William Uricchio, "Archives and Absences," *Film History*, Vol. 7, No. 3 (Autumn 1995), 62.

[34] David Church, *Disposable Passions: Vintage Pornography and the Material Legacies of Hardcore Cinema* (New York: Bloomsbury Academic, 2016), 20.

sources, albeit in a limited way. From there, I will begin the investigation of production, distribution, and exhibition of pornographic films in the United States in earnest. Again, I will be using the writings of the historians mentioned previously (however much I may take issue with them overall) as the ground of my own work, using them as basis for research questions. Is it true that, as rumored, professionals involved in the mainstream film industry (such as it existed at the time) participated in the production of stag films? To what extent can that even be established? How were showings of stag films related to the mainstream of film exhibition at this time? Did stag films have any other sort of antecedents, particularly in pre-cinematic forms of entertainment?

Chapter 2 addresses the period from 1923, when 16mm safety film became available from Kodak, to the Second World War. The debut of the smaller gauge is often credited with giving a crucial boost to the activities of amateur filmmakers, resulting in, among other things, increased production of home movies and establishment of various social networks for these budding cinematographers. In what way was stag film production related to this kind of activity? From a theoretical standpoint, is there anything to be gained conceptually from considering pornography as a type of amateur film? What are the consequences of this? Additionally, in what way did the stag film scene change from the previous period, and why did it do so?

Chapter 3 deals with the Second World War years, and will investigate the degree to which the relatively young market for moving image pornography adapted to this. Were stags ever found in a military setting? Was the production, distribution, or exhibition of stags on the homefront affected by the contingencies of the war, such as rationing, relocation of a large part of the male population, and redirection of the industrial base toward manufacture of military necessities?

Chapter 4 will take on the remaining part of the story, up to approximately 1970. This will cover twenty-five years, the longest single period in the book, and as such will attempt to address a wide range of themes. How did stags eventually come to be legalized, along with all other types of pornography? In what way did the old networks established by distributors evolve in this era? Did the audience for stag films change in any way? What was the basis of the broad social concern over pornography, and how did that change from previous eras? Finally, what is the relationship of the new kinds of pornography on film that emerged from the 1960s—including public, theatrical exhibition—to the old stag films that had dominated the twentieth century up to that point? Can they be said to have served the same social function?

Taking on this project, I have experienced many thrilling moments of discovery, found at least provisional answers to many of my research questions, and done all that I could to move the general understanding of this period forward. But a great deal cf work remains to be done on this topic, and my greatest hope is that the present work will inspire other researchers to pursue some of the same lines of inquiry, as well as to revisit some of the trails of evidence that I wasn't able to follow to their conclusion. I hope that my mistakes will be corrected, and that the investigation into this subject expands in directions I have not considered, and could not have considered. I certainly don't imagine that this book will stand as the final word on its subject; rather, my ambition is that it inspires further research, enriches historical arguments, and revises received assumptions to such an extent that it may properly be regarded as the first.

1

The Earliest Stag Films: To 1923

Though the focus of this project will be the production of, traffic in, and screening of pornographic films in the United States, a few words about how pornography was received elsewhere will be necessary. First, because it seems as though the earliest stag films were produced outside of North America, and thus I think are deserving of some special consideration. The two oldest films in the collection of the Kinsey Institute, according to their records, are *Am Abend* (1910) and *El Satario* (*c.* 1907–12), from Germany and Argentina, respectively. Furthermore, it seems as though distinctive regional practices were developed for the exhibition of these films, based on the particular state of a given local economy, legal climate, and various other social factors. These I offer as a contrast to what I have found in the United States, simply as a way to illustrate the variance in the ways that different societies treated sexually explicit cinema. All of them tended to restrict it in various ways, or to at least allow them to be shown only under certain circumstances, and I think that the examples here can add some kind of perspective to my main story.

The consensus among most historians is that the earliest stags were European productions. We cannot attribute dates to the earliest screenings of pornographic films there with any precision, a matter which is complicated somewhat by the fact that some overzealous chroniclers confuse merely risque films with the early hard-core reels. For example, *Le Bain*, an 1896 short showing dancer Louise Willy taking a bath while purportedly in the nude (she in fact wears a fairly obvious body stocking) is often cited as an early example of a hard-core stag film. Another short starring Willy, *Le Coucher de la Marie*, is supposed to have been a filmed record of her striptease act. Many sources seem at pains to prove that these works are the earliest examples of a nascent craze for pornography in the early cinema. Stephen Bottomore, in *Who's Who of Victorian Cinema: A Worldwide Survey*, has tried to insinuate that Albert Kirschner, allegedly the director of both films, and known professionally as Lear, was involved in the trade in pre-cinematic pornography (he doesn't record the titles of any other of Kirschner's films that might have qualified for this designation, but he optimistically writes that "it is just possible that this is the man behind a company called Lear and Co. in Cairo which was prosecuted in 1901 for exporting pornographic pictures to Europe."[1]), and thus establish guilt by association. Elsewhere in the same volume, he writes that *Le Coucher*'s producer, Eugene Pirou, inaugurated "an entire genre of risque films, known in France as *scènes grivoises d'un caractere piquant*. Such films were not always welcomed, and one of them (probably *Le Coucher de la Marie*) had to be withdrawn from a London music hall in January 1897 after protests from the more respectable clientele."[2] Predictably, mass-market newspapers have been the most eager to brand these works as stag films; the opening sentences of a 1996 *Observer* report on the then-recent discovery of a fragment of *Le Coucher* reads: "Amid the hullabaloo over the first hundred years of cinema, one crucial aspect has been forgotten. The first public film screening took place in December 1895. Before the year was up, man was making porn."[3]

In fact the kinds of films mentioned above are wholly separate from the ones which will be the main focus of discussion in this chapter. Even at the time, the very legal reasoning that gave rise to the earliest movie censorship was based on an implicit distinction between hard-core stag films showing unsimulated, clearly visible sexual acts and the merely provocative. This latter kind of spectacle is what Slade is referring to when he writes:

> Major cities in America and most countries in Europe passed regulations forbidding "immoral" or "indecent" films, [but] these laws were directed at the legitimate or mainstream industry. Various films were prosecuted for revealing a naked breast or including suggestive situations, although they were much more likely to be charged with depicting a prize fight or gambling or some other social rather than sexual transgression.[4]

By contrast, true stag films were an entirely different class of cinema, so outside of the mainstream as to be beneath the notice of authorities. "Official censorship

[1]　Stephen Bottomore, "Lear (Albert Kirschner)," in *Who's Who of Victorian Cinema: A Worldwide Survey*, eds Stephen Herbert and Luke McKernan (London: British Film Institute, 1996), 80.
[2]　Stephen Bottomore, "Eugene Pirou," in *Who's Who of Victorian Cinema: A Worldwide Survey*, eds Stephen Herbert and Luke McKernan (London: British Film Institute, 1996), 112.
[3]　"When the French Started Making Dirty Movies," *The Observer*, November 3, 1996.
[4]　Joseph W. Slade, "Eroticism and Technical Regression: The Stag Film," *History and Technology*, Vol. 22, No. 1 (March 2006), 30.

rarely touched, nor was it ever intended to regulate, the truly pornographic film ... Pornographic—rather than merely 'indecent'—films were so clearly 'obscene' by standards of the period that they occupied a realm of their own."[5] As a general rule, if a film from this era features credited performers or personnel, it is overwhelmingly likely to not have been pornographic, whatever contemporary (or even present-day) commentators may have alleged.

Nevertheless, films which did include unsimulated nudity and sex were produced in this period and, although the historical basis for this has never been made clear in anything that I've read, the consensus among scholars is that the earliest examples came from France. Slade estimates that the "first filmed act of intercourse was probably shot in France."[6] Curt Moreck, writing in the 1920s, claims that stag films were being made in France as early as 1904.[7] Di Lauro and Rabkin, surveying two influential early attempts at the history of stags, find agreement on the question of French origin, though not necessarily on that of what the first title might have been.

Lo Duca dates one film, *Le Voyeur*, as early as 1907. Ado Kyrou's filmography of scenarios of "un certain cinema clandestin" in the film journal *Positif* offers a full description of a film called *A l'Ecu d'Or ou la Bonne Auberge* ("At the Golden Shield or the Good Inn"), definitively dated 1908. Kyrou describes it as "the oldest pornographic film having a scenario."[8] (Frank Black and Josh Frank's interesting novel *The Good Inn* takes the production of this film as its subject, though it plays somewhat fast and loose with the historical record).

Also enjoying broad consensus is the notion that these early French stags were screened in brothels. As Tom Waugh explains, such places were "unofficially tolerated by the police and apparently visited by vacationing American bon vivants. In France the films were called 'radiant' and the Madames of both high-class establishments ('maisons closes') and their more grubby counterparts would ceremoniously announce 'les projections.'"[9] Assuming that this claim has basis in fact, this is a somewhat more significant observation than it might first appear to be. The association of stag movies with brothels is the earliest example

[5] Ibid.
[6] Joseph Slade, *Pornography and Sexual Representation: A Reference Guide, Volume I* (Westport, CT: Greenwood Press, 2001), 80.
[7] Curt Moreck, *Sittengeschichte des Kinos* (Dresden: Paul Aretz, 1926), 175.
[8] Al Di Lauro and Gerald Rabkin, *Dirty Movies: An Illustrated History of the Stag Film, 1915–1970* (New York: Chelsea House, 1976), 43–5.
[9] Thomas Waugh, *Hard to Imagine: Gay Male Eroticism in Photography and Film from Their Beginnings to Stonewall* (New York: Columbia University Press, 1996), 310.

of a relationship which will be something of a constant throughout this book, namely, the piggybacking of pornographic exhibition upon already-established performance practices, including not only those established by other types of cinema but also, as in this case, pre- or extra-cinematic forms of entertainment. French stag films did not just migrate to the brothel arbitrarily; for decades, such places had already staged live performances for the delectation of their customers. As Di Lauro and Rabkin point out:

> Brothels have traditionally presented erotic "entertainments" of various kinds to stimulate recalcitrant energies (eighteenth and nineteenth century brothels often staged elaborate erotic spectacles), [thus] it is logical that such films must have been presented as soon as technologically feasible. Indeed, before the Second World War in France and other countries the showing of pornographic films in brothels was customarily and officially permitted.[10]

This dynamic found many different types of expression depending on prevailing local practices. Stag screenings in Germany, for example, appear to have occurred as early as 1904.[11] However, due to a complete absence of exhibition regulations, films in that country were simply screened after the fashion of any other type of cinema, albeit in spaces devoted exclusively to such fare. There is testimony (from journalist Kurt Tucholsky) suggesting that stags were shown in small spaces put to use exclusively for the projection of pornography;[12] "not," as Jack Stevenson puts it, "in a bordello as such but in a secret room attached to one of these fabled dive bars that live in legend."[13]

Far fewer films seem to have been produced in Germany during this period than in France, or at least far fewer survive, either as references in accounts from that time or as reels in an archive. The only film that has been definitively traced to Germany is *Am Abend*, which the Kinsey Institute dates from 1910. This film seems to have been an amateur production, which, if the few accounts of stag screenings from this period are anything to go by, was typical. In one such incident from 1910, four years after the establishment of film censorship in that country, Martina Roepke notes that "Berlin police arrested some 200 men from the upper class for watching films of 'obscene content.' ... While most

[10] Di Lauro and Rabkin, *Dirty Movies*, 46.
[11] Gertrude Koch, "The Body's Shadow Realm," in *Dirty Looks: Women, Pornography, Power*, eds Pamela Church Gibson and Roma Gibson (London: British Film Institute, 1993), 23.
[12] Ibid., 23.
[13] Jack Stevenson, "Blue Movie Notes: Ode to an Attic Cinema," in *Fleshpot: Cinema's Sexual Myth Makers & Taboo Breakers*, ed. Jack Stevenson (Manchester: Headpress/Critical Vision, 2002), 10.

films were said to be of French origin, the rest were identified, on the basis of the 'peculiar width and perforation' of the gauge, as 'amateur productions.'"[14] Note that "French" here is meant to stand in as a synonym for "obscene"; even in 1910, the French film industry had a reputation for excessive eroticism.

As with France, however, figures from the world of "mainstream" (i.e., non-pornographic) production have been alleged to have been involved in the German stag scene; Slade names cinematic pioneer Oskar Messter, who created an early sync-sound system in the first years of the twentieth century, but I haven't been able to unearth any other evidence of his involvement in the making of pornographic films. (He cites as evidence a passage in Wollenberg's *Fifty Years of German Film* to this effect, but the pages in question only credit Messter with some assorted street scenes and news films.[15]) A much stronger link implicates Fridolin Kretzschmar and Otto Dedertscheck, who evidently produced pornographic films, as in the case above, on amateur-grade 17.5mm film. The two men "were sued in 1910 for having produced morally offensive films, of erotic and 'obscene' content. These films had been taken in a forest nearby as well as in their office, then shown in the Dedprophon Theater in Dresden to a male audience. The film list for the Kretzschmar-Kinemetograph contains 12 titles under the heading 'Pikant! Nur für Herrenabende!' (Only for gentlemen's evenings)."[16]

It is also in Europe that we find the beginning of a surprisingly robust urban legend, one that will recur throughout this book, in which one's social betters are said to habitually indulge in a taste for moving image pornography. In Europe, of course, this could only refer to aristocracy and royalty. Roman Gubern claims, for example:

> The Russian aristocracy was among the most avid consumers of French pornographic cinema, according to Jay Leyda, while it has been said that the Barcelona-based production company Royal Films, founded in 1916 by Ricardo de Baños, supplied films of this type to the cinephile Alfonso XIII, a detail that would agree with the anecdote about the monarch recounted by Anita Loos in her memoir *Kiss Hollywood Goodbye*.[17]

---

[14] Martina Roepke, "Tracing 17.5mm Practices in Germany (1902–1908)," *Film History*, Vol. 19, No. 4 (2007), 348–9.
[15] H.H. Wollenberg, *Fifty Years of German Film* (New York: Arno Press & New York Times, 1972), 7–8.
[16] Roepke, "Tracing 17.5mm Practices in Germany (1902–1908)," 49.
[17] Roman Gubern, *La imagen pornografica y otras perversions opticas* (Barcelona: Editorial Anagrama, 2005), 9.

The two figures under discussion to this point—the mischievous professional technician and the bored aristocrat—come together nicely in the person of Count Kolowrat, who was rumored to have opened his own studio in Vienna for the sole purpose of producing his own stag films. (Slade points to two separate Marlene Dietrich biographies for evidence of the Count's involvement in pornographic films, though the pages he points to seem to demonstrate only that he was involved in film production generally, not in this specific niche.[18])

These sorts of rumors would accompany the first stags to the United States, though they would eventually evolve to reflect that country's own cultural biases more accurately. The slightly wounded sense of inferiority that was the animating force of this legend remained, but would be directed not specifically at louche gentry, but Europe as a whole. Although the nineteenth century saw undeniable American contributions to literature, art, philosophy, and technology, there remained a lingering sense that the United States was something of a poor relation, culturally; the salve for this was the notion that Europe, and specifically France, was, despite its pretensions, in a state of decadence, a veil of pompous pretensions serving only to conceal loose sexual behavior. Pornographic material of all sorts was often assumed to be of European origin, as euphemisms such as "French postcards" demonstrate, and films were no different; the earliest reports of stag movies in the United States were frequently said to have been "from Europe." While this may have been strictly true in the very first years of this phenomenon, this designation survived well past the point of having any descriptive utility, into the era when the majority of pornographic films shown in the United States would have been produced there as well.

In the Western hemisphere, Latin America, particularly Argentina, seems to have been both a source of production and a destination for exhibition. We are fortunate to have access to contemporary first-hand testimony on screening practices from this region, albeit from European commentators. During this period, writer Norbert Jacques visited a brothel in Barracas, a suburb of Buenos Aires, at which some stags were playing.

> I arrived at the house with the arc lamp. A big sign said: "CINEMATOGRAFICO PARA HOMBRES SOLO." The pure vices! ... From the ceiling hung a screen. Upon that surface the cinematographic projector played its scenes. For the most part the pretense of a continuous story was abolished ... Every vice of the human

---

[18] Steven Bach, *Marlene Dietrich: Life and Legend* (New York: Da Capo, 2000), 76–7; Charles Higham, *The Life of Marlene Dietrich* (New York: Norton, 1979), 34–5.

race trembled by up there. All versions of the old "Tract about the 150 ways to love" were displayed, every once in a while interrupted by lesbian, pederast and masturbation jokes.[19]

Another visiting European writer, Curt Moreck, detailed his own visit to an Argentine pornographic screening, this time in the port city of Rosario. By his telling, the city itself was a sort of compendium of clichés about the social blight to be found in areas with a too-substantial population of sailors. "It is wild and rough, and filled with frights which last through the bloody evening hours. These hours are marked by the far-off bang of the Browning pistol and hisses of the knife; the struggle rages in all saloons, with only victory or death ending the fierce brawls over women or pesos."[20] Amid this urban squalor, Moreck sought out a makeshift, improvised movie theater showing exclusively pornographic fare; unlike Jacques's experience, the screening was not associated with any kind of brothel (despite there being a surfeit of such places in Rosario, by Moreck's description), and instead seems to have been in a room approximating a regular theater. The movies themselves were hard-core stags, explicit to the point of the author's discernible discomfort. "Although these films are known in Tokyo and Havana, they are regarded as a South American specialty. Their place of manufacture is near Paris or even Buenos Aires. The films are very craftily made and the human material is, especially in the films of South American origin, often very beautiful— nevertheless, nevertheless, it remains a nauseating, lowbrow filthiness."[21]

For all of these accounts from European chroniclers, very little definite knowledge exists about Latin American stag films. No names have been associated with them after the fashion of Kretzschmar or Dedertscheck, and nothing is known about the circumstances of their production or sale. The canon of movies from this period is depressingly slender, even more so than is the case with their European counterparts. Moreck describes the film he sees in great detail, but doesn't note any title, assuming there was one. Very few stag films have been definitely identified as Argentine in origin—only one appears in the film collection of the Kinsey Institute, none in Di Lauro and Rabkin's extensive filmography. The only other titles I am aware of that were produced in Argentina are *Haz bien sin mirar a quien* and *Pepe el verdulero*, which are known among

---

[19] Quoted in Stevenson, "Blue Movie Notes," in *Fleshpot*, 10.
[20] Curt Moreck, "Rosario 1930: The Vintage Porno Journalism of Curt Moreck," in *Cinema Sewer: The Adults-Only Guide to History's Sickest and Sexiest Movies, Volume 5* (Godalming: FAB Press, 2015), 119.
[21] Ibid., 120.

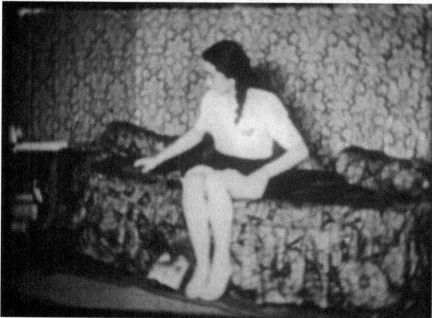

Figures 1.1 and 1.2 Decidedly non-risque frames from the Argentine stag film *Haz bien sin mirar a quien*. (Courtesy of Ariel Castro Ferro.)

South American film collectors.[22] Much better represented in the lore of Latin American pornography are movies from Cuba and Mexico, with eleven and eight films respectively in the Kinsey archives, and several more each in Di Lauro and Rabkin. However, most of these are dated past the early period I'm focusing on here, with the greatest concentration from the 1940s and even 1950s, so while those two countries seem to have eventually found an enthusiasm for stag films, they can't be said to have been active during the earliest years of the medium.

There is much more to be written regarding the early years of pornographic cinema outside of the United States beyond the brief treatment the subject is given in the opening chapters of history books (this one included). Intriguing research questions abound: Was there any significant production outside of Latin America or Europe, particularly in Japan, India, Russia, Hong Kong, Scandinavia? When did obscenity become a legal reason for suppressing a film in each country? Were there any for which it never was? Was homosexual content a feature of any country's pornographic cinema (Waugh contends it was in some of Bernard Natan's work, though this has been disputed)? Was pornography always only shown to sex-segregated audiences? How were these films written about in contemporary journalism, including the trade press?

Addressing these and other questions simply cannot be the work of a single scholar. I have tried here to add some depth to the conventional wisdom on this part of the story, but I am hobbled not only by having to consider the scale and focus of my main topic—pornographic films in the United States—but also by my location in the middle of the country, and my limited proficiency with non-English languages. Consider as well that each region's output would have to be properly contextualized within the histories of the surrounding countries, the local film industry, the economic developments of the twentieth century, and any number of other variables unique to the area, and one is tempted to conclude that specialists on the countries in question, native or otherwise, ought to take the lead on researching and writing about this underserved area of film history (it is hoped as well—by this scholar, at least—that, once this comes to pass, some enterprising translators will take the lead on rendering these studies into English). For the time being, then, this precis of the earliest days of stag films abroad will have to suffice as a prelude to the main story.

That pornographic films were at least shown, and very probably produced in the United States before 1923 is beyond dispute, though the exact date that

---

[22] Ariel Castro Ferro, personal communication, June 9, 2014.

this first occurred will never be known with certainty. But by the middle of the 1920s, it was well and truly understood that these films would find no place on any public, commercial screen within the borders of that country (private, secret screens were another story); after this point, no exhibition situation, even one explicitly designated as private and arranged specifically for adult men, could be certain that, once begun, it could conclude peacefully and free from harassment by the authorities. During the approximately three decades covered in this chapter, cinema would go from a mechanical novelty to a young but mature and energetic segment of the entertainment business. Luck, ambition, and skill made managers of single-screen storefront theaters into captains of industry, but none of these men were able (or, truth be told, willing) to incorporate films featuring this degree of sexual explicitness into their business model. By the end of this period, pornographic films had not been driven out of existence—in fact they would undergo a veritable surge in production—but into a shadow realm which they would occupy for the next fifty years.

This chapter will identify some of the common factors present among different instances of stag film exhibition in the United States in the period before 1923. As I have only been able to find evidence for a handful of screenings (although it is almost certain that many more occurred), the conclusions I will draw from these will be highly provisional. Nevertheless, the incidents share enough similarities between them that I feel like some generalization is not only possible but appropriate. I will demonstrate here the ways in which the first screenings of pornographic films drew from already-existing conventions of the entertainment industry broadly; evidence for this will come from close readings of reports in the trade press, as well as supplementary data from mass market newspapers and the archives of law enforcement agencies. As in the previous section, I am turning my gaze to the furthest horizons of the past— the first decades of the twentieth century are practically pre-history, as far as pornographic cinema is concerned—but, in this case, I will be drawing from a much firmer foundation of evidence.

Every freshman film student learns the story of the 1896 premiere of the Lumiere brothers' *The Arrival of a Train at La Ciotat Station*, during which terrified spectators allegedly dove for the exits as the on-screen train advanced into the foreground of the image. The factual basis of this story has since been undermined[23] but its staying power probably has to do with the way in which this

---

[23] See Martin Loiperdinger, "Lumiere's Arrival of the Train: Cinema's Founding Myth," *The Moving Image*, Vol. 4, No. 1 (Spring 2004), 89–118.

nineteenth-century scenario is (still) immediately relatable for the twenty-first-century viewer. What's familiar here is not the fact of absorption in the image to the point of forgetting one's surroundings, but the surroundings themselves: in this tale, the audience is engaged in the type of viewing situation which survives even into the present day, seated in neat rows in a darkened room before an image projected onto a wall.

Though the technological ingredients necessary for this kind of exhibition had all been perfected by the 1890s, it would actually be some time before this model could survive, commercially, on its own. Edison's peep-show Kinetoscope viewer actually predates the Lumiere's projector as a device capable of both reproducing the moving image and offering an unobstructed view of the same. Though the Kinetoscope arcades did not last long, the first attempts at dedicated spaces for projected film exhibition didn't last much longer, as scholars like Douglas Gomery have shown. Both New Orleans and Washington, DC, to take two typical examples, saw the local debut of "Vitascope Halls" in 1896. None of them would last into 1898.[24]

Film projection would initially flourish not as a stand-alone program, but as one amusement among many in the great variety on offer in the early-twentieth-century urban landscape, akin to a pinball machine or Ferris wheel. The two most prominent outlets for this new medium in these early years were vaudeville theaters and amusement parks. These latter could be found in the fairgrounds which had been built in the suburbs of any city of any size, often in convenient partnership with the companies which operated street cars and light rails. Films were shown here among other, more typical fare, such as "live theatre, circuslike acts, and uplifting sermons,"[25] to name just a few that were mainstays of the fairgrounds.

Amusement parks were seasonal attractions, however. Much more stable were the venues which served as the home base for the great variety of live performers that blossomed in the early part of the twentieth century, referred to by the umbrella term "vaudeville." This was the dominant form of public entertainment in its day, particularly in urban areas, consisting of "a complete matrix of commercialized, popular entertainment in ... every major city from New York to San Francisco."[26] Here, as in amusement parks, films competed for

---

[24] Douglas Gomery, *Shared Pleasures: A History of Movie Presentation in the United States* (Madison: University of Wisconsin Press, 1992), 7–8.
[25] Ibid., 10.
[26] Ibid., 13.

attention with many other acts, and were not necessarily assumed to be the main event. All manner of performers might be found on the stage, including "tenors and sopranos of European origins, trained animal acts, inspirational readings, acrobats or other circus-inspired performers, comics and 'playlets'—condensed versions of popular theatre of the day."[27] At least initially, no particular favor was given to the novelty of the cinema.

Tom Gunning has famously set the films from this era of exhibition apart from the longer, narrative-focused works which were to dominate the 1910s and beyond into a category he called "the cinema of attractions." Rather than creating a cause-and-effect narrative driven by goal-directed characters, films of this vintage traded in a more self-conscious display of showmanship, adapting the expressive features of the cinema to the sort of performances that one might have found on the vaudeville stage. The typical movie of this era, according to Gunning's telling, "directly solicits spectator attention, inciting visual curiosity, and supplying pleasure through an exciting spectacle—a unique event, whether fictional or documentary, that is of interest in itself." Even in the case of films which were more than simply a "passive" record of some act—those which took advantage of the new technology's ability to manipulate the image via editing, optical effects, or other means as were available at the time—the principle of highlighting a spectacular event in and of itself as the source of visual interest remained the form's aesthetic lodestone. "The attraction to be displayed may also be of a cinematic nature ... or trick films in which a cinematic manipulation (slow motion, reverse motion, substitution, multiple exposure) provides the film's novelty." Though moving images were certainly regarded as a novelty by audiences of the time, and likely would have been no matter what specific performer or scene was being depicted, the tendency for many of the individual works was to emulate certain aspects of live performances.

Gunning explicitly links this quality of early cinema to the medium's imbrication within the context of the era's other forms of existing public entertainment; the cinema of this era, for him, is the inheritor of the same "exhibitionist quality of turn-of-the-century popular art that made it attractive to the avant-garde—its freedom from the creation of a diegesis, its accent on direct stimulation." As he tells it, this quality was encouraged by the willingness

---

[27] Ibid., 14.

of the movies to rub shoulders with other types of amusements, and the earliest all-film programs continued this heterogeneous approach.

> Film appeared as one attraction on the vaudeville program, surrounded by a mass of unrelated acts in a non-narrative and even nearly illogical succession of performances. Even when presented in the nickelodeons that were emerging at the end of this period, these short films always appeared in a variety format, trick films sandwiched in with farces, actualities, "illustrated songs," and, quite frequently, cheap vaudeville acts.[28]

However radical film may have been in its technology or presentation, its earliest producers and exhibitors seemed to be content to fit into the entertainment culture of the day, rather than unsettle it.

This is a point worth emphasizing, I think. Rather than attributing cinema's early success to its supposedly disruptive character, it would seem to make more sense to emphasize what Leo Enticknap has called "the ability of that technology to be adapted for compatibility with existing cultural practices."[29] In contrast to the (alleged) existential shock experienced by Lumiere's first audience, subsequent viewers responded to the willingness of exhibitors and producers to serve the new wine of the movies in the old bottles of nineteenth-century popular amusements. Indeed, despite Gunning's implication that this rapid succession of different programs was somehow a consequence of turn-of-the-century industrialization and urbanization, the fact is that such practices had been a mainstay of popular entertainment for a considerable time, pre-dating the film age by decades. Lawrence Levine has documented several examples of this, such as an 1890s tricentennial production of *Taming of the Shrew* in New York, which included on the same bill "the farce, Dumb Belle and featuring 'Mr. Harrison, the Comic and Impromptu Singer, and Mr. Stoepel, with his wood and straw instruments,'" between the acts. This was in addition to Barnum's "Colossal Giants," "Infant Drummer," "Three Albino Children," "Tableaux of Moving Wax Figures," "Monster Serpent," and "Musically-Educated Seal."[30] Had the technology been viable during this time, a short film presentation in between some of these acts would not have felt out of place.

---

[28] Tom Gunning, "The Cinema of Attraction: Early Film, Its Spectator and the Avant-Garde," in *Early Cinema: Space, Frame, Narrative*, ed. Thomas Elsaesser (London: British Film Institute, 1990), 58–9.

[29] Leo Enticknap, *Moving Image Technology: From Zoetrope to Digital* (New York: Wallflower Press, 2005), 11.

[30] Lawrence Levine, *Highbrow/Lowbrow: The Emergence of Cultural Hierarchy in America* (Cambridge, MA: Harvard University Press, 1990), 69.

The cinema of attractions lasted, by Gunning's admittedly imprecise estimate, until approximately 1906, after which point the movies became a lone attraction in their own right and graduated from vaudeville, amusement parks and the like to self-sufficient picture houses. For a variety of reasons, films projected in these buildings would become more and more narratively focused, eventually forming the basis of the Classical Hollywood continuity style which would become the visual lingua franca of world cinema.

I have not been able to find any record of any hardcore pornographic films being produced and projected in the United States during the era of the cinema of attractions. To be sure, there were films from the era which dabbled in some form of mild sensuality to a greater or lesser degree, after the fashion of Pirou's *scenes grivoises d'un caractere piquant* referred to earlier. Gunning himself points out that "erotic display made up an important genre of the cinema of attractions. Pathe produced filmes with frontal female nudity early in the century ... [and] films of erotic exhibition—women in their underwear or wearing body stockings, couples kissing, girls kicking up their legs or dancing in pajamas, and women wrestling—appeared frequently until at least 1906."[31] But none of this comes anywhere near level of explicitness of the hard-core pornography (and Gunning explicitly admits as much). All of the technological ingredients necessary to shoot or show hardcore pornographic movies in this country were in place, and could, in principle, have occurred at any time; however, no exhibition infrastructure existed at this time, and this only was able to develop after the eclipse of the cinema-of-attractions era. It was not a scientific innovation which allowed for the screening of stag films to occur, but a social one.

The researcher needs to tread cautiously through the public record here, as the rhetoric of the period can sometimes seem to be more suggestive to modern readers than it might have been to the intended audience. An error that some pornography scholars have made in the past is to take the howls of early-twentieth-century habitual offense-takers too seriously, especially when complaining about the alleged vulgarity of this or that film. As the local press of the time was reluctant to write about a supposedly licentious film in anything but euphemism, identifying the exact nature of the offense a century hence can be tremendously difficult. An issue of *Moving Picture World* from 1912, for example, castigates a film then in release called *Tracy the Bandit* as "a specially atrocious,

---

[31] Tom Gunning, *D.W. Griffith & the Origins of American Narrative Film: The Early Years at Biograph* (Urbana: University of Illinois Press, 1991), 156.

crude film … which with lurid and offensive posters and highly objectionable 'literature', is going the rounds of certain theaters in New Jersey and New York."[32] Despite this dramatic rhetoric, the publication's complaint seems not to have been shared by others—every other reference to that film found in news and trade papers from the time makes no mention of its supposed crudity, instead reporting on its take at the box office as though it were just another film. Unless complaints such as these are followed up by diligent research, one courts the danger of extending the heckler's veto to the dead.

If we must be cautious about taking the past's ideas about itself too seriously, so too should we conversely be aware of our own tendency to project our understanding onto that world. This habit, if not checked, may lead to misunderstanding and confusion over the documents describing historical events, but also even the very language used to describe them. Certain words and phrases which seem to twenty-first-century English speakers to possess unambiguous meanings may require proper context to be understood and evaluated. Such is the case here, and it is therefore necessary to go into an etymological digression. Russell Sheaffer has pointed out that the very term "stag" has, in fact, evolved in its use over the course of the century. While the sobriquet "stag film" even now has something of an old-timey feel to it, it is still commonly understood to refer to pornography; Sheaffer, reviewing its use in the context of old newspapers and magazines, has found that this hasn't always been the case, credibly suggesting that the term "stag" simply referred, for much of the period of its use, to an all-male gathering.[33] The relevant entry in the Oxford English Dictionary would seem to back this up as well: it finds the earliest use of the term to mean "a man who attends a social function without a female partner" in 1905, though, curiously, "stag party" can be traced to a reference in 1856.

The following story appears in the April 27, 1900 edition of *The Geneva Times* of Geneva, New York, below the headline "A STAG PARTY":

> H. A. Doxsee and G. E. Priest entertained 23 of their male friends last night at a smoker, given in their rooms in the Smith block. Whist was played until midnight, when refreshments were served. Following the refreshments the company was entertained by songs from a male quartette composed of Frank

[32] *Moving Picture World*, January 20, 1912.
[33] Russell Sheaffer, "Smut, Novelty, Indecency: Reworking a History of the Early-Twentieth-Century American 'Stag Film'," *Porn Studies*, Vol. 1, No. 4, 2014, 348–9.

Fairfax, R. A. Weld, L. H. Barth and C. W. Fairfax, and a solo by Mr. Priest. The recipients of prizes were compelled to respond to calls for speeches. Mr. Priest is president of Hydrant hose company and Mr. Doxsee is vice president. A number of their friends from that organization attended in a body, garbed in evening dress, large red neck ties and hit-or-miss cuffs.[34]

Similar stories may be found in countless other newspapers from the era, all of them referring to events substantially identical to the one above as "stag parties." News of similar festivities were frequent items in newspapers large and small, either as notices of upcoming events or, as in the above-quoted portion, reports after the fact. Despite the notoriety with which they would later be associated, the local press would continue to announce these gatherings for many decades, using the same kind of language.

While these examples seem to have been simply a friendly gathering of small-town luminaries, stag parties were not always simple spontaneous affairs. Especially in the cities of the east coast, these very often were professionally arranged events, put together by theatrical agents in concert with working dancers, comedians, and other performers, all of whom were experienced, working members of the popular entertainment industry. At least to a certain extent, the stag party of the early twentieth century can be considered an auxiliary branch of the live theater business.

A 1910 *Variety* article surveying the business of the club agent generously illuminates this relationship. The agents of the era, according to the article, organized entertainment for "clubs, lodges, societies, churches, social functions and other private affairs." At this point, the stag party business had evidently "grown so large that there are any number of acts who like the agent, depend solely upon clubs for their livelihood"; as a useful metric, the article estimated that more than a hundred such agents were operating in New York City at the time. In addition to the drudgery of arranging the schedules of performers and collecting fees owed by clubs, the agent was also tasked with work of a more curatorial function in matching acts and audiences of a similar nature; as the article puts it, the agent must be "capable of knowing just where and when to secure material that will fit the occasion."[35]

Thus a 1904 ad in the *New York Clipper* openly seeks "Sketch Teams, Sister Teams and Single Ladies" for a regular "stag music hall" operating out of

---

[34] *The Geneva Times*, April 27, 1900.
[35] "Clubs and Club Agents," *Variety*, December 10, 1910, 29.

Parkersburg, West Virginia; the hall in question was careful to note that it was only interested in "sober and reliable" performers, presumably for a similarly disposed audience. Although stag performances were, by definition, for a private audience, the variety of acts matched that of the aforementioned types of public amusements; a typical instance of this may be found in another *Clipper* ad, this one from 1907, which offers, under the bold headline "SMOKERS, STAG PARTIES," "The only monologue published for this line of entertainment, and it's a dandy. The price is 50 [cents]. You want this. Also other monologues, Blackface, Irish and Dutch."[36] Like their more famous cousins the vaudeville theater and the amusement park, then, stag parties seem to be the very ideal of Gunning's "mass of unrelated acts in a non-narrative and even nearly illogical succession of performances."[37] It would not be long before film would also come to take its place here among the entertainments on offer.

Thus, long before it became a slang term for moving image pornography (and its exhibition), "stag" referred to a very specific thing, although its operations were very different depending on a particular event's location and connection to the live entertainment business. Absent this crucial context, occasional bouts of confusion have occurred in the work of the less-rigorous scholars of pornography. Di Lauro and Rabkin, for example, note that something called "stag parties" were openly advertised in certain local newspapers; however, they neglect to interrogate or historicize the term, and thus conclude that the relative frequency of these notices can only be taken as evidence of public approval, or at least tolerance, of the exhibition of pornographic films. So they point out that in "Bloomington, Indiana, the local Legion even announced their next stag screening in the hometown newspaper."[38] They don't cite any particular issue or edition in which this was supposed to have appeared (and none of the archivists I consulted at the Bloomington-based Kinsey Institute had any idea what they might have been referring to in this case), but it seems likely that, whatever allusion to "stag screenings" they may have found, it was likely not an advertisement for pornographic exhibition. Obviously, there is no conclusive evidence for my interpretation here, but, given the context I have described above, it seems at least as likely as their reading.

---

[36] *New York Clipper*, October 19, 1907, 971.
[37] Gunning, "The Cinema of Attractions," 60.
[38] Di Lauro and Rabkin, *Dirty Movies*, 54.

Skepticism should greet any mention of "stag films" or "stag parties" found in the archival wilderness. It should not be assumed, for example, that the Rose City Film Company, a film exchange operating out of Portland, Oregon, was looking for hard-core pornography when it ran an ad in the April 8, 1911 edition of *Moving Picture News* soliciting "Stag Films suitable for Smokers, Clubs, etc." Not only must we consider that the "stag parties" reported on by newspapers of that period still tended to involve the rather more innocuous activities of the type mentioned earlier in these pages, but it is significant that Rose City's other solicitations for films are of a uniformly un-salacious sort: the very same ad also seeks a copy of the hit "Pathe Passion Play (hand-colored)," which would seem to indicate either that their business was on the up-and-up, or that they had an uncommonly overdeveloped sense of chutzpah.[39]

To point all of this out is simply another way of making the same argument that Sheaffer has above, which is that scholars have placed too much emphasis on the term "stag," without giving it proper historical consideration. Not only has a fixation on this single word led researchers to hasty conclusions, but it has perhaps also blocked off more productive lines of inquiry by ignoring language which actually had been used to describe the era's movies which, for one reason or another, were thought to have violated middle-class standards of taste— Sheaffer gives as examples words like "stag smokers," "indecent films," "naughty," "frank," "snappy," "novelty," "art," or "blue" movies,[40] which were used throughout the twentieth century to describe films which had run afoul of the law. Each of these was highly context-dependent, however, and, as with "stag," might or might not necessarily describe pornography as it would be understood in the twenty-first century (and maybe not even as it would have been understood at the time). "Smut," "novelty," and "indecent," to take three examples that Sheaffer explicates at some length, were variously used to refer to mainstream films, non-pornographic films for stag parties, and legal definitions of obscenity. My own research has found each of these terms in news stories from various points throughout the century and in various regions of the United States, often used in reports of films seized from distributors or renegade projectionists.

This confusion over the language used to describe stag films (or rather, films projected at stag parties) in the press is something of an unavoidable methodological hazard associated with researching this topic. Since these outlets

---

[39] *Moving Picture News*, April 8, 1911, 19.
[40] Sheaffer, "Smut, Novelty, Indecency," 351.

were reluctant to describe the content of the films in any detail, the scholar is left to try to decipher these euphemisms to the best of their ability. This can be very difficult, as these terms may have had very specific connotations based on the time and place in which they were being used—if the fluid definition of "stag" itself should teach us anything, it is to never assume a stable meaning for any of the words used to describe either these gatherings or the films shown at them, especially the slangier terms. Sheaffer's astute observations here are a side effect of the greatest obstacle to the study of stag films, which is the impossibility of situating a specific film within a specific context. If one could establish exactly which film was being referred to as (say) "indecent" in a particular document, it might be possible to determine exactly what the term was supposed to mean at that time and place.

Ultimately, educated guesses based on incomplete documentation are the only strategy available to us. The reason that this history must be re-assembled from fragments in the first place has nothing to do with anything on film per se—film is inert celluloid, an object with no agency or independent power—but because of the fact of its social proscription. Sheaffer is exactly right when he suggests, at the end of his study, that "there is no category that can simply be defined as the 'stag film' but that there were instead 'smut films,' 'novelty films,' and 'indecent films,' for example, that were screened for 'stag' audiences, at 'stag' parties, or at 'stag' venues."[41] The language used to talk about these films described less their specific content, and more their social use.

Though it may not be possible to claim a stable meaning for such terms across all possible contexts, we may observe trends in the way they were used at different times and places. Thus, the time when "stag" began to take on its familiar connotations may be, if not pinpointed, at least roughly established. Sheaffer contends that the term "stag" didn't become synonymous with obscene or pornographic entertainment until the 1930s, but I have found evidence that suggests this association dates from much earlier. Although many turn-of-the-century stag parties were probably simply good clean fun (or might at least be presumed by the historian to be innocent until proven guilty), there had always been a latent assumption of vague unseemliness about them. Even as far back as 1896, an issue of Huntington, Indiana's *Daily Democrat* printed a short, jokey dialogue in which young Johnny asks "Mamma, why do they call it a stag party?",

---

[41] Ibid., 358–9.

to which she replies "Ask your father—I think it is on account of the horns."[42]
Two decades on, the suspicion lingered: an issue of *The Literary Digest* finds
little Louise asking her mother to define the term; before she can answer, "Sister
Mabel, seven years old who had been listening, with a dignified attitude of
superior wisdom answered instantly: 'It's where they stagger. Don't you know?'"[43]

Allusions of this sort were not confined to the funny pages. Whatever they
may have been called, all-male parties began to take on an aura of suspicion. In
1907, the managers of Brooklyn's New Utrecht Club could convincingly play the
following prank on the audience at a men-only gathering there (which had been
amply stocked with "attractions, mostly of the feminine gender, with a proper
knowledge of the requisites of an all-man party").

> To add to the enjoyment of the evening, it was arranged that a farcical police raid
> was to be made during the course of the evening. Eight policemen, a roundsman
> and sergeant were enlisted for this purpose, and Mr. Gallagher selected an "act"
> on the program during which the "raid" could be made with propriety.
>
> While this "act" in the person of a young woman was giving what is delicately
> described as a "sensational dance," wearing a trifle more than she was born with,
> the officers swooped down on the gathering, causing consternation, and many
> objections from the suburbanites, who were basking in the light of that deviltry
> seldom seen by a commuter so far from New York.[44]

The suburbanites were let in on the gag in due time and the deviltry
resumed, but it is apparent that the promoters and audience (to say nothing
of the journalist and his readers) were operating in an atmosphere where the
possibility of such a raid was no joke at all. While interruptions of this sort
were still relatively rare at this point, there were other signs that the guardians
of morality were losing their patience with the sudden availability of this sort
of fun.

The trade press, in particular, took special umbrage at what they saw as a
rising tide of overly vulgar entertainment, which they tended to characterize
as a sign of desperation on the part of some theaters. A common lament was
that these measures would only result in attracting undesirable crowds—as one
Variety article maintained, "frequenters of these dissolute resorts are usually
of the obnoxious and vulgar sort"—and the combination of low-brow fare and

---

[42] *The Daily Democrat*, June 10, 1896, 8.
[43] "Wise Mabel," *The Literary Digest*, March 2, 1918, 75.
[44] "Stag Burlesque Raid," *Variety*, March 27, 1907, 5.

low-brow patrons would be to the ultimate detriment to the image of live acts in general in the mind of the wider public. "If the authorities would be stringent, and regulate or prohibit the revelry of lasciviousness under the guise of 'vaudeville' and 'burlesque,' there would be no misrepresentations at the expense of the decent theatres. The disreputable dives wrongfully claim 'vaudeville' or 'burlesque' as the style of performance. The regular patrons of vaudeville and burlesque know better; others may be deceived."[45]

Beginning in the latter half of the first decade of the twentieth century, the trade press, probably motivated in equal measures by a desire to maintain moral propriety as well as to convince the civil authorities of the uprightness of the industry as a whole, took it upon itself to call out breeches of decency where they saw fit. Much of their ire was aimed at establishments which allowed "cooch" dancing on stage. That term originated in the name given to the dances performed at the Algerian Village exhibition at the 1893 World's Fair; there, a group of women performers, said to be Algerian, engaged in dances of an allegedly "Oriental" influence, and which included overtones of eroticism that were unusual for late-nineteenth-century America. It was a sensation at the time, but inspired as much consternation as fascination; dance historian Rachel Shteir contends that "the hootchy cootch became not just bizarre and comical, suggesting carnal mischief and folklore, but dangerous. The association of dancing masters denounced it and called for the closing of the exhibit where it was practiced. A minister described the dance as 'a muscular contraction of the abdomen with certain peculiar motions wholly improper.'"[46] By the early 1900s, both the style of dance and the name associated with it had filtered into the more raucous burlesque houses, becoming a shorthand for a genre of sexually charged striptease. Leaving the middle-class (and female dominated) audience to traditional vaudeville, the new style of burlesque was brazen in its appeal to working-class and bachelor men. The variety format of classic vaudeville remained, but the more-or-less innocuous acts that prevailed there were replaced by "raucous skits and the solo female performer. 'Burlesque queens,' 'lady athletic acts,' and cooch dancers … trotted across the burlesque stage. Scenes gave way to male comics' telling ribald jokes. Burlesque of this era boiled

---

[45] "Chicago Police Keeping Watch on Dive Keepers," *Variety*, April 4, 1908, 6.
[46] Rachel Shteir, *Striptease: The Untold History of the Girlie Show* (New York: Oxford University Press, 2005), 42.

down to gags expressing class and sexual anxiety and to a brand of female sexual display that was essential and crude."[47] As mentioned above, the trade press was not pleased.

So, for example, O. M. Samuel's 1907 review of the show "A Self-Made Man," playing at the Greenwall Theatre in New Orleans, lamented that "when managers of the standing of Weber & Rush will stoop so low as to engage a 'cooch' dancer it's about time to call a halt. 'Cooch' dancing should be thrown out of burlesque for good."[48] Six months later, in a follow-up article, Samuel returned to the scene of the crime, and was happy to report that the management of the theater had learned its lesson.

> The shows presented at the Greenwall during the early part of the season seemed to rely upon "cooch" dancing and risque situations in order to garner the shekels of burlesque lovers, and by so doing they caused a journalistic and moral tirade against the Greenwall Theatre, which resulted in the loss of many thousand dollars and drew away from the house a great deal of the patronage that it will take years to bring back. When interviewed regarding the past season Manager Greenwall remarked "All I have to say is that the good shows got the money and the bad shows got what they deserved."[49]

For this theater at least, civic pressure, rather than the legal kind, was enough to force a change in its acts.

(Not everyone who found themselves on the receiving end of these periodic outbursts of morality was quite so contrite. Around 1910, theaters in the "Western Wheel" circuit, serving the cities and towns of the Midwest, banned *Variety* reviewers from attending their shows after a rash of condemnations for excessive ribaldry. Even individual performers took exception; one review— from somewhat later in the period under discussion—records an incident where, for once, a critic was at the mercy of a player: "A performer on stage must have recognized the *Variety* reporter and it became known to the company. When the 'cooch' dancer appeared she walked directly over in front of the reviewer and did the filthiest 'cooch' dance he had ever seen. After finishing she remarked, sotto voce, 'And stick that in *Variety* and see how they like it.'"[50])

---

47 Ibid., 54.
48 O.M. Samuel, "New Orleans, L.A.," *Variety*, December 7, 1907, 31.
49 O.M. Samuel, "New Orleans, L.A.," *Variety*, May 5, 1908, 35.
50 "Burlesque over the Years," *Variety*, January 14, 1925, 47.

But before long, public authorities let it be known that they were not content to allow the entertainment industry to regulate itself. The city of Chicago took the lead, threatening theaters with arrests, fines, and closure if they didn't clean up their acts. In March of 1908, for example, police went after the "Girl in Red" act at the Trocadero in that city, which "was the first to attract the attention of the crusaders through the suggestive nature of the performance."[51] Soon after, the police made a special effort to crack down on "the so-called 'concert halls' on the West Side, [where they] notified the dive keepers to abandon the revelry, which evoked severe criticism. Not since the days of lawlessness has the West Side district been so thickly infested with indecent resorts, which audaciously offer 'burlesque' or 'vaudeville' and are actually nothing more than drinking dives."[52]

While no arrests appear to have been made in these cases—*Variety* only refers to "the most stringent investigation"—the city's other establishments seem to have gotten the message. The very next week saw a notice announcing that "the number of 'cooch' dancers in the city this week has been reduced to one. There is Chooceeta, appearing at the Empire with 'The Cherry Blossoms.' The young woman, aside from her 'Oriental' accomplishments, 'wiggled' in her own unrestrained way, but kept within the 'limit.'"[53] The trades of course approved of this wholeheartedly, and it is during this period that they seem to have discovered—and even encouraged—the salacious dimension of the term "stag." To pick one example which might stand in for the many, many others which can be found, an anonymous *Variety* annalist, commenting on the Trocadero incident, wrote that "if all the burlesque houses here would strengthen the shows, when necessary, with other features than a dancer, fit only for a drunken 'stag' party, the result would be more gratifying to the managers and public."[54] The Chicago campaign against the "cooch dancer" would also ensnare the "stag show" in its net.

Though its most prominent press organ vociferously opposed any engagement with such material, the live entertainment industry readily adapted itself to the audience for off-color and salacious acts, usually female dancers, moving these programs from the public stage to private, all-male gatherings. Given the

---

51 "Police Censor 'Troc's' Bill," *Variety*, March 14, 1908, 4.
52 "Chicago Police Keeping Watch on Dive Keepers," 12.
53 "But One 'Cooch' Dancer," *Variety*, March 14, 1908, 4.
54 "Police Censor 'Troc's' Bill," 4.

atmosphere of the time, the club agent had to tread cautiously here, putting as much trust in his street smarts as in his curatorial acumen.

> When an agent makes a contract to deliver a show for a stag entertainment he is usually approached by some member of the committee who will ask if it is possible for the agent to obtain the services [of] a "cooch."
>
> By the term "cooch dancer" it is mutually understood that a woman is to be secured who will not hesitate to perform a series of terpsichorean postures in the altogether. Most of the agents who book stags to a great extent have any number of these so-called "Oriental dancers" on their list, but unless they are fully satisfied as to who they are doing business with the usual reply is they do not supply that sort of entertainment, but that they will give the committee the addresses of several who will undoubtedly fit the bill.[55]

Although stag shows represent a move away from the vaudeville stage and into the realm of the private performance, these new programs retained much of the older format. Similar to variegated acts at a vaudeville theater, a host of other amusements jostled for a place at a stag program. An especially testy *Variety* article on the topic outlined the essential ingredients—"A girl show of the cheap type consisted of a half dozen painted dolls, a smut slinging comedian and a repertoire of songs and dialog that needed a strong disinfectant"[56]—but this by no means exhausted the possibilities. In addition to "single women in lewd dances," one 1922 gathering is reputed to have featured, among other attractions, "suggestive barking," "paddle wheels," "gambling," and "pick-pockets."[57] Film would fit into this mix as well as it had on the vaudeville stage.

Thus, *Variety* could report in 1916 that "cooch reels" (the earliest American slang term for pornographic films that I have been able to uncover) were "a lucrative business consisting of supplying clubs and stag banquets. Prices of $100 up to $500 are said to have been paid for pictures almost hot enough to ignite celluloid films."[58] By this time, not only the press but also the police were well aware of the phenomenon, and were actively pursuing those engaging in the nascent dirty movie trade.

---

[55] "Clubs and Club Agents," *Variety*, December 10, 1910, 125.
[56] "'Girl Shows', Carnival's Ruination; Not So Many Now but All Must Go," *Variety*, September 8, 1922, 7.
[57] "Carnival Crimes," *Variety*, April 28, 1922, 7.
[58] "Hunting 'Cooch' Reels," *Variety*, January 7, 1916, 27.

The experience of Chicago's Intercollegiate Club, which was visited by police in 1920 for hosting "naughty dances and a very frank film," is a perfect illustration of the "classic stag" format. According to a reporter's paraphrase of court testimony given during the ensuing prosecution, a "very scantily clad woman opened the entertainment by dancing 'what is popularly known as the hoochie-coochie.' She was followed by a danseuse who was 'even more scantily clad than the first.' Then came an innocuous slap-stick comedy, to be succeeded, after a brief announcement, by the nameless and questionable film" in which "women, unhampered by raiment, perform with much dash and vim." A man by the name of S. E. Bryson was allegedly responsible for securing the entertainment for the evening; during cross-examination, he admirably stood up for his program.

> Regarding the dancing, Mr. Bryson was laudatory.
> "What, that Egyptian dance, as interpreted last night, was one of the most beautiful works of art I've ever seen!" he exclaimed.
> "You don't mean to say a hoochie-koochie dance is a work of art?" interposed the judge.
> "But this wasn't hoochie-koochie. It was—er—synthetic, the kind they dance on the sands with these high-priced teachers."[59]

A 1922 stag party in Long Island City, held in the offices of a tire manufacturer, featured a similar lineup. While the relevant news article does not include a description of the event, it does note that the police raid netted not only "a phonograph and films said to be immoral" but also seven men and two women, all vaguely referred to as "performers" (the women presumably dancers, the men possibly comedians, jugglers, or other types of entertainers). Seventy-two members of the audience were arrested en masse; the seven performers found their names and addresses published in the *New York Times*.[60]

These vaudeville-style, classic stag shows were not the only venue for stag films in this era; there is evidence that programs consisting entirely of projected film occurred as well. What is startling here is the fact that these kinds of gatherings featured extensive, documented participation by film industry professionals.

The degree to which members of the nascent, "above-ground" movie industry were involved with any part of early pornographic film has long been a matter of (ultimately unanswerable) speculation. The persistent rumor among historians of pornography claims that the earliest productions were shot, edited, and

[59] "Naughty Dances and Snappy Film End Club's Life," *Chicago Tribune*, June 29, 1920, 1.
[60] "Raid on Film Show Lands 81 in Cells," *New York Times*, December 1, 1922.

printed off the clock by professionals in the movie industry. This is justified by the supposed relative technical sophistication of that era's stags. Di Lauro and Rabkin write that "the extant early films display an expertise that suggests that at the outset the stag film received the attention of professionals, a condition which progressively diminished in subsequent history. The professionalism was understandable in an era in which film equipment was expensive and cumbersome, hence unavailable to the amateur."[61] This line of reasoning was also taken up by the 1970 Report from the President's Commission on Obscenity and Pornography: "Much of the initial stag production apparently was photographed by individuals involved in legitimate movie production."[62] In neither case is evidence brought forth to support these claims; one wishes that the President's Commission had made explicit the reasoning that made their claim so "apparent."

That the brute clumsiness and bulkiness of motion picture equipment as it existed at that time precluded non-professional production is probably broadly true. Films which would have been projected in a public setting during this period would likely have been 35mm reels. They likewise would have been shot on 35mm negative film, requiring a labor- and resource-intensive process to become a projectable print. Most motion picture cameras then being manufactured were large, heavy, and of limited mobility, though smaller models, such as the Wilart News Camera, had recently been marketed to news and documentary producers. Furthermore, the type of film stock used in professional production required a great deal of light to capture an image, therefore shooting had to occur either outside under direct sun or below a fleet of large, hot, power-sucking lights.

Alternatives to this process existed, but only on the economic margins. Most filmmaking equipment marketed to amateurs in the United States would have been inappropriate for the production of even a short stag film. Many of the available consumer models took only non-standard film, such as the short-lived 17.5mm gauge, or were able to handle only very short lengths of 35mm. The first cameras built for the home market at this time were largely taken up by a relatively wealthy or devoted niche. As Leo Enticknap puts it in his technological history of production, "The reality was that non-professional filmmaking before 1923 was sporadic and limited, and most film not intended for revenue-earning

---

[61] Di Lauro and Rabkin, *Dirty Movies*, 59.

[62] *Technical Report of the Commission on Obscenity and Pornography, Volume III* (Washington, DC: U.S. Government Printing Office, 1971), 186.

exhibition was shot by people with some connection to the film industry (which gave them access to equipment and film stock) and on 35mm."[63] Only very late in this period were 35mm cameras, such as the Sept model, developed and marketed to amateurs. Various problems held up the early development of amateur equipment, most notably the difficulties inherent in the manufacture of film which didn't use the flammable nitrate base of most standard gauges.

It is interesting to note, then, that the only professionals found on hand at these earliest stag screenings were technicians who mainly handled not cameras, but projectors. As with production equipment, the earliest projectors were large, heavy, and difficult to move; portable and dependable machines would not appear until after 1923. More importantly for my purposes, the involvement of professional projectionists in the first documented stag screenings is a matter of documented fact, not, as with cameramen and directors, informed speculation. The earliest participation from the official film industry in this era that can be demonstrated, then, came not from producers, but exhibitors.

A glance at the classified ad pages in the December 9, 1911 edition of *The Washington Times* will find this rather vaguely worded item: "NOTICE, Moving Picture Managers / A mass meeting of managers and others interested in moving pictures is called at 714 7th st. N.W., Tuesday at 2 p.m. to take action against the outrage perpetuated by the committee and officers of the Operators Union at their banquet held at National Rifles Armory, Wednesday last / (Signed) A.C. JOY, / Pres. Wash. Photoplay Assn."[64] Curious readers had only to flip back a few pages to discover what Mr. Joy's discretion had hoped to conceal, under the headline "Men Accused of Showing Improper Films Not Tried:" "The three men charged with violating the section of the code forbidding the exhibition of improper pictures did not appear in the United States branch of Police Court today. Assistant United States Attorney Ralph Given stated he has been unable to reach the witnesses of the exhibition in National Rifles Armory on Wednesday."[65] A somewhat fuller account appeared in a contemporaneous issue of *Moving Picture News*.

It is greatly to be regretted that the Washington Moving Picture Operators' Association, which has just begun its career, should have brought discredit upon

---

[63] Enticknap, *Moving Image Technology*, 6.
[64] *Washington Times*, December 9, 1911, 12.
[65] "Men Accused of Showing Improper Films Not Tried," *Washington Times*, December 9, 1911, 5.

itself at its first banquet, which occurred recently. That some of the members had prepared a picture show after the feast was quite in keeping with the organization; but that disgusting, objectionable views should be presented was not the wish of the association, yet such pictures composed the show, and some one secured the reels purposely and some one is to blame. The question is, "Who?" but the answer is not forthcoming. The police, with the further assistance of one of the local papers, have so bungled the affair that it will be no easy matter to place the blame on the responsible parties.[66]

Indeed, five arrests were initially made, but nothing of any legal consequence seems to have come of this. One of those charged, Bernard Spellbring, was the "president and business agent" of the union, and next appears in the local press in July of the following year, in a pedestrian announcement of his departure for the International Alliance of Theatrical Stage Employees national convention in Peoria, suggesting that, despite the consternation of the industry press over the incident, he endured no particular professional setbacks as a result of his alleged involvement. The prosecuting attorney had to resort to charging two members of the group with the making of unlicensed electrical connections, justifying this by reasoning that the men "did the necessary wiring to enable the other defendants to give the alleged exhibition."[67] Even the reels themselves were never found. A local theater manager gamely offered a $100 reward for their recovery, pledging to destroy them in front of the authorities afterward.[68]

The outcome of these investigations, as well as the specific content of the films, is lost to history. The howls of the nascent exhibition industry, however, echo across the gulf. *Moving Picture News* was moved very nearly to panic. "The matter has a serious side, as it reflects discredit on this new industry which is now becoming helpful to humanity. It is to be regretted that there are always in organizations some 'misfits' and 'objectionable parties' who are a drawback to the society, but who somehow get in."[69] At a time when the reputation of cinema as a public amusement was still very much under contestation, exhibitors felt that any hint of bad publicity was unacceptable.

The identity of the misfits was never divulged, at least in the press. If the rogue projectionists escaped personal scandal, the same could be said for those

---

[66] "Operators' Union of Washington D.C.," *Moving Picture News*, December 16, 1911, 6.
[67] "Men Accused of Showing Improper Films Not Tried," 5.
[68] "Operators' Union of Washington D.C.," 6.
[69] Ibid.

further up the chain of production. Who made the film? This question included not only the cameraman and on-screen performers, but also those involved in the actual manufacture of the physical film itself—the ones who procured negative stock, who developed the camera negative after exposure, who created at least one positive projection print, who edited the film together, and who may have written, photographed and spliced in titles (if there were any). Even the production of a short stag film would have been a remarkably labor-intensive process at this time, and at least a small handful of people would have been involved in its creation.

If those present on the scene were not able to establish any of these facts, the odds are hardly better for a scholar at a century's remove. Barring some archival discovery, literally nothing will be known about the film itself—not the title (if it had one), its origin, or specific content. However, even from the bare facts that we do know, a few general suppositions may be made, and these can be an entry point into some broad arguments about the stags of this period.

That the earliest recorded screening of a pornographic film took place in the context of a gathering of film industry professionals—admittedly, professionals in the exhibition sector, not in production—could be taken as circumstantial evidence that both production and circulation of stag movies occurred primarily among those in the industry. Obviously, somebody present had a contact who could supply the film—whether a producer, importer, or other type of rogue distributor. The argument becomes much stronger, however, when a look at the evidence reveals that nearly every screening of an obscene film in this period was, in some way, associated with the film industry, at least tangentially.

For another example, I turn to a much better-documented case from 1917 involving the New York Society for the Suppression of Vice (hereafter the Society). The Society was one of the many reform groups which were formed in the post-Civil War era. Though similar organizations concerned with the fostering of public decency appeared during this time, the Society had the most impressive pedigree, having been founded by former postmaster general Anthony Comstock. Comstock was the most prominent anti-obscenity campaigner of the era, having devoted much of his career in public service to preventing printed information about birth control—just then starting to be disseminated in the form of pamphlets by various feminists and radicals—from traveling via US mail. His last name was for years used as a shorthand for the first package of federal censorship laws to be enacted; the Act for the Suppression of Trade In, and Circulation of, Obscene Literature and Articles of Immoral Use, passed in 1873, was more often referred to as the "Comstock Act." He died in 1915, but his influence was felt for many decades after, and could be properly said to be one of the strongest legacies of the progressive era.

The Society was distinguished from other similar groups in that they were able to assume law enforcement powers within the city, despite the fact that they were ostensibly a private group unaffiliated with municipal government in any official way. The Society will appear with some frequency in the course of this narrative, as it was not only one of the most prominent decency groups in the United States, but, as importantly, it was one of the most well-documented, generating almost fifty years of monthly internal reports on its activities in New York City. Though I am casting my net well beyond the boundaries of the five boroughs, the reports of the Society's chronicler have proven to be a useful archive of the activities not only of the movement for public decency, but of those of the subterranean pornography scene as well.

Though the greatest part of their efforts were directed against the trade in pornographic literature, the Society certainly made efforts against films that they considered to be indecent. This was of course not limited to those movies shown to private audiences; in fact, most of the reports detail their objections to various commercial works projected in public theaters, many of which had already passed the relevant municipal censorship boards. But the organization was clearly concerned about the nascent pornographic film scene even in the 1910s. The report for March of 1916 notes that a "Mr. W. M. P. Mitchell" has passed on information "regarding a proposed dinner at Healy's Restaurant, 6th Avenue, where indecent moving pictures would be shown." The following sentences give a good indication of both the nature of pornographic infiltration of stag shows (which apparently sometimes occurred without the knowledge of the owners of the venue) and the terse, utilitarian style of the reports. "Assigned Mr. McHugh to the case. He visited the restaurant at 6 P. M. Saw the manager and later explained his visit to Mr. Healy the proprietor who, upon investigation, found that the information was correct. He stated that he had not previously known of the contemplated moving pictures, and assured our agent that such an exhibition would not take place."[70] Most of the cases involving supposedly obscene films to be found in these reports consist of a single entry, such as in the example of Healy's Restaurant. Typically, the Society's

---

[70] "Report of the Secretary for the Month of March, 1916," John Saxon Sumner Papers 1901–1961, Box 2, Folder 10 (Wisconsin State Historical Society, Madison, Wisconsin), 5.

further investigations revealed that there was little substance to their suspicions or, if there had been, the offenders were dissuaded after a warning from the group rather than by a visit from the police.

The most detailed description of a stag film screening from this era is not mentioned in any of the Society's reports, but in a later, unpublished reminiscence from one of their most ardent prosecutors, Charles J. Bamberger. In 1917, the organization was clued in to the activities of a man named Sam Efrus. Efrus was the owner and operator of the Sun Projection Room, a screening auditorium and editing suite catering to local filmmakers. A notice in the *Exhibitors Herald* from 1918 describes it thus: "Two projection rooms have been fitted up with the latest model Simplex [projection] machines. In connection with the projection theatre a special cutting room for cutters and directors has been outfitted with all the necessary cutting tables. S. Efrus, proprietor, will give his personal attention to the trade."[71]

Efrus's attention was evidently broad enough to encompass a number of trades; by the next year, word had reached the local chapter of the Society that he had been, in Bamberger's words, "showing obscene moving pictures to parties in his projection rooms. He showed them to private parties who would pay to see them." The Society was bound to investigate this.

Bamberger was sent as an undercover operative to assess the situation. Using an assumed name, he visited Efrus in his office and claimed to be a representative of a group of Long Island businessmen. "I told him that once a month members would come to New York City to have a good time, have a good dinner, and go to a night club. I told him I heard he (Efrus) would show the pictures for a certain sum, and the boys had delegated me to come and see him to make arrangements to see them when they came to town." After some suspicious hesitation, Efrus arranged a screening for Bamberger and his "business associates," actually plainclothes policemen. He "showed us into a projection studio and told us all to be seated and make ourselves comfortable. Then Efrus ran off the pictures on screen. Needless to say they were vile. When he was through, Efrus came to me for the balance of the twenty-five dollars [that he had been promised.] I gave him fifteen dollars marked money; then took it back. He was placed under arrest and the films were seized and later he was fined $150 in Special Sessions Court."[72]

---

[71] "Popular Pictures and Sun Corp Move," *Exhibitors Herald*, May 25, 1918, 34.
[72] Charles J. Bamberger, "E-V-I-C R-O-T-A-C-I-D-A-R-S," July 1943, John Saxon Sumner Papers, 1904–1961, Box 2, Folder 2 (Wisconsin State Historical Society, Madison, Wisconsin), 16–17.

I suspect that these kinds of screenings—seemingly put on by lone wolves of the exhibition sector of the young film industry, working outside of the established live entertainment business—were most likely crimes of opportunity, occurring as a chance for these independent projectionists to make some extra money. It's worth repeating that projectors available to the would-be amateur exhibitor were notoriously expensive, difficult to use, and simply not up to the job of projecting even a short 35mm reel. Hovering over all of this is the fact that safety film stock had not been manufactured or sold on a wide scale at this point. What the club agent could offer in terms of contacts in the world of show business, the professional projectionist could perhaps offer in his access to equipment and technical abilities (the latter being nothing to regard lightly when one considers that sloppy work in the projection booth could, in the nitrate era, be potentially fatal).

This point touches, indirectly, on the development which contributed significantly to the demise of both of these exhibition styles, which is the commercial debut, in 1923, of 16mm safety film stock from Kodak. This new type of film, as well as the cameras and projectors which could handle this new format, were marketed specifically to amateurs, and were wildly successful. 8mm film and equipment followed shortly thereafter in 1932, to similar acclaim. The result of this would be, among other things, a veritable explosion of stag film production, a boom which would more or less sustain itself for the next four decades.

With a sudden abundance of films, and with equipment to project it suddenly cheap, plentiful, and easy to use, the advantages of dealing with the professional entertainment world, either theatrical or cinematic, dwindled to nothing. After this period, the two types of exhibition outlined in this chapter occur as a far smaller proportion of arrests related to stag films. The classic stag party—featuring both a variety of live entertainment in addition to films, and with the involvement of theatrical agents—declines precipitously. It will remain common practice to read of strippers included in screenings of stag films after 1923, as shall be seen in the next chapter, but these would only rarely share the degree or kind of variety on offer at a classic stag party from this early era. However, stag shows in which film was but one of the attractions, even if the main one, would remain popular, and this particular pattern would persist for many decades. In any case, the general decline of the live entertainment industry during the course of the twentieth century meant that much of the professional infrastructure necessary to support classic stag parties had ceased to exist as well; these shows would become ad-hoc events put on by either the attendees themselves or by a self-styled showman who had no, or only incidental, relationship with the mainstream entertainment industry. No longer would events of this kind be put on by theatrical agents who would hire all active personnel, but more often they would be the work of a single person who would himself be responsible for running the projector, transporting the films, and any other necessary tasks.

Professional exhibitors, likewise, would avoid stag films after this point. I have found no indication that anyone involved in the operation of a public movie theater involved themselves with pornographic films in any way after the mid-1920s. This likely has to do with the increasing standardization and centralization of film exhibition within the vertical integration model (both the expansion and refinement of popular cinema and the related change in the fortunes of the live entertainment business will be explained in greater detail in the next chapter). One final incident, late in the era covered by this chapter, illustrates the new attitude among exhibitors.

In December 1923 Raymond Pfeiffer, manager of the Princess Theatre of Chilton, Wisconsin, sent out word of a unique promotional ploy. Not only did he advertise the showing of what seemed to be a stag film, he subsequently wrote the *Exhibitors Herald*, a national trade publication for theatre owners, to brag about having done so. To promote a show that he characterized as a "smoker," he, by his own account, "mailed out several hundred cards (sample enclosed) which brought a good house. This was the only advertising I did. Only a few cards were mailed to neighboring towns but they brought several cars filled with men." As the house filled up, Pfeiffer "passed around good cigars free of charge. Talk about smoke! You'd have thought there was a big fire."

Whatever the card might have implied, the program for the evening was a film called *The Dancer of the Nile*, a decidedly non-pornographic historical drama starring Carmel Myers which had seen wide release the previous autumn, to no particular fanfare—"a good Egyptian picture which took place in the days of King Tut," as Pfeiffer described it. The night seemed to have been a success. "As they passed out, the men remarked that this was a very good idea, to get all the men together to spend an enjoyable evening, and they asked to have more of them. Of course, as I said before, many were disappointed, especially some of the younger element."[73]

[73] "'Film Smoker' Is Success," *Exhibitors Herald*, February 9, 1924, 45–6.

The next week's issue featured a letter from Mr. Len Brown of the New Astor Theatre in St. Paul, who was not amused.

> Mr. Pfeiffer's method of advertising this particular show immediately conveys to the mind of the least susceptible that it is to be a smut show, an exhibition for men only, a show in which an appeal to the baser instincts will be made ... Pfeiffer himself admits in his letter, if one be credited with sense enough to read between the lines, that he knew they would come expecting to see something which could not lawfully be shown. To my way of thinking, he must have made more enemies than friends from his smoker.[74]

The editors of the journal chimed in as well, though they were somewhat more forgiving. While conceding that the strategy was "out of the beaten path" and that "various methods of handling the stunt may be devised, since there is always a chance of misunderstanding in such matters," ultimately the "idea in all probability will continue as the working basis."[75] Mr. Pfeiffer's experiment revealed an ascendant exhibition industry concerned about its image (about which more will be said in the next chapter), but also, perhaps, a public familiar with private screenings, and the special attractions to be found there. For all of the howling this elicited from Pfeiffer's peers, exhibitors, and the producers which supplied them with films, would not entirely shy away from his strategy, though they might employ a lighter touch. Conscious of the appeal of "indecency," they knew they could count on the general awareness of this forbidden kind of entertainment in order to seem to promise that which it has no intention of delivering. In the meantime, stags were left to the underground, who would make good on their promises to their audiences.

---

[74] "Protests against Film Smoker," *Exhibitors Herald*, February 23, 1924, 59.
[75] "'Film Smoker' Is Success," 45.

2

The Stag Scene and the Debut of 16mm Film: 1923 to the Second World War

This chapter will cover the time when stag movies, propped up as they were in the United States by various renegade professionals in the entertainment industry, became established in something resembling a stable ecosystem of production, distribution, and exhibition. The catalyst for this was the invention and debut on the market of 16mm safety film. The impact of this has been widely, if superficially, acknowledged by most of the previous historical writings about pornographic films. I will not only describe some of the immediate effects of this technological shift—demonstrating some ways that it changed the business of production and distribution—but also suggest some ways in which pornographers may have operated against the background of a growing amateur film movement. I will also follow the progress of stag exhibition, and point out some of the characteristics of the various audiences for these films.

This section will be addressing a relatively long span of time, from 1923 to 1941; as there's a lot of material to cover, I will not always progress in a strictly linear fashion, and will at times proceed from one broad topic to the next. I do this in the hopes that my narrative can be followed with less difficulty, but it seems only fair to advise the reader to keep this in mind in order to keep potential confusion at bay.

By the 1920s, the commercial film business had begun to consolidate into a proper industry. If any single incident from around this time could stand in as a harbinger of what the studios would become in the ensuing decades, one could do worse than pick the 1925 merger of the exhibitors Balaban & Katz with the studios Famous Players-Lasky; at the stroke of a pen, "the most powerful movie company in the world was formed, and the United States film industry entered

the age of big business."[1] The scale at which the new studios were beginning
to operate meant greater integration with the world of finance capital, which
had long been wary of the movie business up to this point "based on observed
industry instability and the lack of any business methods that Wall Street analysts
might understand as rational."[2] Regularizing the basic practices of production
and distribution, then, became a top priority for the studios; finding themselves
now having to service loans and interest payments, they sought to make their
industry as predictable as possible. Famous Players-Lasky made the transition
fairly quickly, and could claim, not long after its founding, that it had "adopted
uniform bankers' forms, ironed out the seasonal spurts of production that had
[up to that point] made it impossible to predict cash flow, and eliminated most
production waste."[3] With large profits at stake, the studios—specifically the
aforementioned Paramount Publix, but also including their vertically integrated
competitors—sought to appeal to as wide a customer base as possible. To that
end, they began a concerted campaign to convince the public at large, but
especially women and families, that the exhibition spaces under their control
were safe, clean, and respectable, and that the films shown there never broached
the outer limits of middle-class propriety.

The film industry had been trying to solicit approval from middle-class
audiences for some time; in the very early part of the twentieth century, there
were sporadic efforts to align, at least rhetorically, with some of that era's reform
movements (there were some opportunistic attempts to suggest cinemas as an
alternative to taverns as leisure destinations for working-class men, for example,
as a means of currying favoring with temperance advocates).[4] The reason for
attempting to attract a different breed of audience was a dual one. By producing
films reminiscent of the plays and novels which were the barometer of middle-
class taste, they could both attract an audience willing to pay slightly higher
ticket prices and fend off the censors and regulators. A similar motivation was
behind the construction of new, opulent movie palaces, which were meant to
strike a contrast with the more humble nickelodeons that had been the mainstay
of earlier working-class audiences. "Film producers and exhibitors responded to
their critics by attempting to transform movies from a cheap amusement for the

---

[1]   Douglas Gomery, *Shared Pleasures: A History of Movie Presentation in the United States* (Madison:
     University of Wisconsin Press, 1992), 34.
[2]   Richard Koszarski, *An Evening's Entertainment: The Age of the Silent Feature Picture 1915–1928*
     (Berkeley: University of California Press, 1990), 91–2.
[3]   Ibid., 92.
[4]   Tom Gunning, *D.W. Griffith and the Origins of Narrative Film: The Early Years at Biograph* (Urbana:
     University of Illinois Press, 1994), 180.

masses into a respectable entertainment for all classes ... Farsighted showmen ... believed they could keep censors at bay and attract a more prosperous clientele (and thereby charge higher admission) by producing longer films of more artistic merit."[5] As is so often the case in film history, formal considerations were downstream from industrial ones.

Thus, appeals to a taste for bawdiness would be significantly curtailed; no more incidents of the type which occurred at the Princess Theater, in which advertising heavily implied that a stag film would be shown, would happen. Though the nature of the specific films shown was an essential part of the success of the exhibition sector, it was by no means the only part; a line, quoted by Gomery, from Balaban and Katz's how-to book about business management— "We cannot afford to build up a patronage depending entirely upon the drawing power of our feature films as we display them"—seems to confirm this. However, the very next sentence of their guidebook (also quoted by Gomery) is the essential second half of this sentiment: "We must build in the minds of our audience the feeling that we represent an institution taking a vital part in the formation of the character of the community."[6] This appeal to the middle-class character of their audience, echoes of which were seen in their general approach to presentation, would preclude the screening of movies which appealed too narrowly to the bachelor crowd. It would be some time before an established, mainstream movie theater would dare to show any sort of pornographic footage, or at least do so publicly.

As the business of movie exhibition was coming into its own, the live entertainment industry, specifically vaudeville and burlesque theater, began a period of irreversible decline. As attendance continued to plummet, panicking promoters and club owners turned toward raunchier acts in order to try to win back some of the audience, triggering something of a race to the bottom in the burlesque scene. "By 1928 there was no longer any pretense at 'refined' burlesque ... In those cities where the police could be properly added to the expense account, managers bid desperately for the male trade with shows that went the limit. 'And the limit in burly,' *Variety* grimaced, 'is about the most disgusting stage show ever publicly presented.'"[7] While this initially attracted enough spectators to keep the scene alive, audiences eventually burned out. In

---

[5] Steven J. Ross, *Working Class Hollywood: Silent Film and the Shaping of Class in America* (Princeton, NJ: Princeton University Press, 1988), 30.

[6] Gomery, *Shared Pleasures*, 43.

[7] Abel Green and Joe Laurie, Jr. *Showbiz: From Vaude to Video* (New York: Henry Holt and Company, 1951), 306.

1929, *Variety* put the fork in: "This year ... proved that burly is shot. Even the morons are getting fed up with the dirt."[8]

These had been the two main styles of pornographic film exhibition up to this point. The demise, or at least severe diminution, of these types was a consequence of the development of the larger commercial film industry; namely, the standardization of most film exhibition to appeal to (what were assumed to be) prevailing codes of decency, and the cannibalization of the audience for live amusements, hastening the decline of that sector of the entertainment industry. Given the difficulty and expense involved in producing stag films on 35mm film, the disappearance of these two outlets might have spelled doom for the genre altogether.

There occurred around this same time, however, a development which would prove to be of great significance to small-scale filmmaking of all kinds, but particularly to the production and exhibition of pornographic films. This was the entry into the market of 16mm safety reversal film in 1923. Invented for the domestic market as a safe, economical, and (relatively) simple alternative to either previous small-gauge stocks or 35mm nitrate film, this new product made film available to nonprofessionals to a degree that was heretofore unprecedented. Hobby cameramen and home projectionists alike took to 16mm film en masse; the consequences of this were both a renewed interest in amateur filmmaking and the creation of a booming consumer market for 16mm films.[9] Both of these would of course be significant for the trade in stag films, and are therefore worthy of being explored in full.

---

8 Ibid., 307.

9 It may be argued that the later arrival of 8mm film (and the much later arrival of Super 8 film) also deserves dedicated attention from my narrative, as this was a format widely adopted by amateur filmmakers and projectionists alike, possibly even to a wider degree than 16mm at the height of consumer film's commercial reign. Debuting in 1932, 8mm became especially popular after the end of the war, where both the unprecedented boom in the consumer economy and the relatively more simple operation of its cameras and projectors made it a particularly attractive choice for those interested in documenting their domestic life but who may have been otherwise discouraged by a perceived lack of technical aptitude. While it is likely that pornographers did not hesitate to adapt the smaller gauge for their own purposes—and they certainly did for the production of cheaper, lighter prints, as my own collection of stag films can attest—a sustained examination of 8mm here does not seem necessary to me. My research leads me to believe that, with regard to practices of production and exhibition, the 8mm format simply followed the paths dug out by 16mm; though it was certainly successful, it did not alter the landscape in the way that its predecessor had. The release of 16mm safety film created the market for consumer film; once this occurred, I'm broadly convinced that the historical development of stag films would have proceeded along more or less the same lines had 8mm never been invented. The smaller gauge, then, represents little more than an innovation in a purely technical sense—interesting enough on its own terms to be sure, but not worthy of an extended detour in a work already crammed with several of them.

Before 1923, the amateur filmmaking hobby was only available to people of some means—motion picture cameras and film were expensive, as was the laboratory processing necessary to create a positive print from an original camera negative, to say nothing of any editing equipment. One typical early enthusiast for amateur film production was inventor Hiram Percy Maxim, who had the money (much of which was inherited from his father, who had invented an early model of machine gun), leisure time, and social position to pursue what was then an eccentric, expensive hobby.[10] In addition to the short 35mm reels used by the likes of Maxim, many other types of home cinema systems were manufactured and sold in the United States. Film companies had long been experimenting with various kinds of substandard (i.e., smaller than 35mm) gauges, such as 9.5mm and 17.5mm films, hoping that the resulting smaller, lighter cameras would appeal to the small amateur community.[11]

It had long been the dream of film and camera manufacturers to establish filmmaking as more than a niche hobby. Kodak, unsurprisingly, was in the forefront here; their technicians performed some of the earliest research into a nonflammable film base, actually inventing a working model of acetate film in 1909 which nevertheless proved to be too structurally weak to withstand the multiple runs through the projector that exhibition required.[12] But they were undaunted in pursuit of an economically viable safety film. Not only did they have the most to gain, potentially, from making this available to the average consumer, but their earlier success and status as one of America's great companies allowed them the type of resources that could be devoted to the problem; their dominance over the whole of the photography industry was such that it had established a laboratory devoted to pure research, with little concern for the ultimate utility of the results to the bottom line.

Which is not to say that their eventual success in this endeavor wasn't very profitable indeed. Kodak was able to perfect the technical requirements for not only safety film, but the cameras and projectors which could handle the new, narrow gauge of 16mm, adopted so as to discourage the amateur from handling nitrate-based 35mm film in their home cameras. Aside from its relative safety, this new standard was the first commercially available reversal film. Unlike most previous kinds of motion picture film, which required at least two generations

---

[10] Alan Kattelle, *Home Movies: The History of the American Industry, 1897–1979* (Nashua: Transition Publishing, 2000), 375.

[11] Ibid., 65–8 *passim*.

[12] Ibid., 61.

for a projectable print (beginning with the original camera negative, from which a positive print was struck), the film in the camera could be developed into its own positive image, effectively halving the amount of money the amateur would spend on film.

Despite competition from the other substandard gauges, the new 16mm safety film was an immediate hit.[13] The result was not only a significant increase in Kodak's business, but a concomitant expansion of the amateur film production. The ease of use, efficiency, and economy of the new film proved to be irresistible to those interested in this newly viable hobby. As historian Charles Tepperman put it, the "invention of 16mm reversal film in 1923 provided the crucial precondition for the emergence of an amateur filmmaking culture in North America, reducing the cost of amateur filmmaking to less than a quarter of professional 35mm production."[14] Once this barrier had been overcome, participation in this kind of production grew exponentially. The most active of these small-time producers were not simply driven individualists, but eager partners with other similarly movie-mad people from across the country—film production after all being a naturally collaborative venture.

This spirit of cooperation came to its fullest flowering in the formation of the Amateur Cinema League, an organization dedicated to the promotion of nonprofessional filmmaking everywhere. In the words of amateur film expert Alan Kattelle, "No better evidence of the emergence of this new market can there be than the founding in 1926 of the Amateur Cinema League—the first national organization with a monthly magazine devoted entirely to amateur filmmakers."[15] That magazine, *Movie Makers*, continued to publish for decades, taking as its editorial mission the explication of the finer technical points of what, even in its stripped-down, hobbyist's iteration, was still a highly technical enterprise. That it could be sustained for as long as it was is a testament to the tenacity of the amateur film community.

I have taken some trouble to establish the sudden growth of amateur cinema because I believe it has serious, and undertheorized, implications for the historical understanding of stag film production, distribution, and exhibition. Amateur and home cinema of all types has been a subject of interest of film scholars for many years, with interest picking up in earnest during the

[13] Ibid., 83.
[14] Charles Tepperman, *Amateur Cinema: The Rise of North American Moviemaking, 1923–1960* (Oakland: University of California Press, 2015) 22.
[15] Katelle, *Home Movies*, 83.

mid-1990s (with the publication of Patricia Zimmerman's *Reel Families* as an early milestone in the scholarship) and with researchers continuing to find ever-more obscure objects of study—individual titles, regional auteurs, collective efforts from every conceivable type of organization—ever since. The work which resulted from these inquiries, archeological as well as theoretical, has broadened the scope of our understanding of the wide variety of uses to which the moving image has been put, and brought to light a surprising range of production practices and exhibition cultures.

The term "amateur" seems precise enough, simply denoting "nonprofessional" in its strictest sense; in the case of cinema, it can also be said to connote the presence of substandard gauges and non-theatrical exhibition. But even within the bounds of this simple designation, several different types of amateur films were produced. Reporting on the proceedings of a 1997 FIAF symposium on amateur cinema in Colombia, Jan-Christopher Horak hinted at the implied diversity contained within the term, as well as the difficulty of nailing down precise subgenres.

> The symposium's most important revelation was that amateur films, far from being just home movies, define a cinema almost as rich in form as professional cinema, and certainly as sophisticated, even if the gauges in question are sub-standard. At least four general directions in amateurism were visible in Cartagena: ethnographic/travel films, documentary, familial "home movies", and avant-garde films. After a few days' proceedings, it also became clear that these genres are not mutually exclusive, but rather intertwined: familial narratives become documents of history, documentary images are fictionalized, all of them inscribed by the subjectivity of their makers, by the desire of the audience.[16]

Kattelle, writing in 2003, lamented that the richness of amateur cinema was hidden behind the homogenizing term "home movie," which, to his mind, consigned all nonprofessional production to the level of a filmed record of a birthday party. Criticizing an earlier study of amateur works that had appeared in *The Journal of Film and Video*, he pointed out that the publication had betrayed amateur cinema's heterogeneity when it asserted a simple classification system for all of non-narrative cinema. There were eleven types of films [according to this view]: documentary, avant-garde, cartoon, newsreel, ethnographic, travelogues, medical, scientific, industrial, instruction, and the home movie.

---

[16] Jan-Christopher Horak, "Out of the Attic: Archiving Amateur Film," *Journal of Film Preservation*, Vol. 56 (June 1998), 50–1.

It is apparent from the rich and diverse body of films from the ACL that there are amateur productions that deserve placement in all of those categories, not just the last one.[17]

Amateur cinema contains multitudes. It makes no more sense to place any two (or more) individual films under that umbrella term without further clarification than it would to simply regard (say) *Rio Bravo*, *Reflections in a Golden Eye*, and *Abbott and Costello Meet Frankenstein* as essentially interchangeable examples of postwar classical Hollywood cinema.

The overall neglect of stag films in the scholarship of amateur cinema[18] is probably due not to any conscious antipathy against the genre, but to the fact that the study of stag films has long been regarded as the province of scholars of pornography. I have already discussed some of the relevant works in the preceding pages, but it is useful to say again that the most articles or book-length studies of stags which have been written in English are squarely within the field of pornography or sexuality studies. This should not strike us as particularly unusual; obviously, this field of study has many useful things to say about stags, and my own knowledge and understanding has been broadened considerably by its canonical texts. But while stags were indeed shot and shown within the historical context of, for example, certain broad notions of gender roles, or a particular legal climate, or traditions of other types of pornographic works (such a photography or literature), they also existed against the background of a robust culture of amateur moviemaking, one which provided inspiration, advice, and concrete resources for those who, for whatever motives, wished to express themselves with the moving image. This is a background that pornography studies often ignores, to its ultimate detriment; amateur film scholarship, meanwhile, takes this as the very object of its study, although it has only rarely considered pornography from this angle. Despite this, many of the insights of amateur film scholarship can be easily addressed to stag films.

Tepperman has built his history of amateur production in the twentieth century from a deep dive into the papers of various figures associated with

---

[17] Alan Katelle, "The Amateur Cinema League and Its Films," *Film History*, Vol. 15, No. 2 (2003), 243. Ironically, the Camper article that drew Katelle's ire actually attempted a taxonomy of the home movie which, though somewhat arbitrarily constructed, is at least an honest effort towards recognizing the variety of generic and formal differences between these supposedly homogeneous works. See Fred Camper, "Some Notes on the Home Movie," *Journal of Film and Video*, Vol. 38, No. 3/4 (Summer-Fall 1986), 9–14, especially page 10.

[18] A notable exception is Dwight Swanson's "Home Viewing: Pornography and Amateur Film Collections, a Case Study," *The Moving Image*, Vol. 5 (2005), 136–40, which is preoccupied with archival questions rather than (strictly) historical ones.

Figure 2.1 Frame from *Untitled Stag Film,* year unknown. (Film from personal collection of the author.)

amateur clubs and also the periodical literature produced for those hobbyists, such as *Movie Makers* and *Educational Screen.* These and other magazines kept track of new technological developments, trends in production and presentation, and documented the way in which amateur filmmakers interacted with forces in the wider world. The pornographers of the early twentieth century might not have even considered themselves to be amateur filmmakers—in the sense of one devoted to an activity out of love for the medium or the process or one's fellow hobbyists—and, in their subsequent neglect, the twenty-first-century scholars of nonprofessional cinema may have followed their lead. But, certainly from 1923 on, amateur filmmakers are exactly what they were. The research tradition which has taught us so much about figures such as Hiram Percy Maxim, Marion

Norris Gleason, and Ephraim Horowitz can certainly be used to tell us about their less reputable cohort. "Examining the emergence and expansion of amateur filmmaking as an organized activity," writes Tepperman, "permits us to see the cultural role of motion pictures in North America in a new light, compared with traditional film histories."[19] By bringing the study of stags into the mainstream of amateur film scholarship, I am attempting nothing less than that.

To begin with, I think it is useful to consider stags as a variety of what Tepperman calls "advanced amateur" films. "Advanced" here doesn't refer necessarily to any particularly lofty standard of technical competence or narrative complexity per se—by that measure, many stags fail, and fail badly. Though Tepperman argues for the aesthetic sophistication of many amateur films, his use of the term here, taken in its strictest sense, simply differentiates films which employ technique of any sort, in contrast to the home movie's more visually spare and utilitarian record of daily life.

> Advanced amateur films differ from home movies in ways that require further attention: though both are produced outside professional filmmaking contexts using mass-marketed small-gauge film formats ... films by advanced amateurs employ more polished filming and editing techniques and feature elements of narrative or thematic continuity. And while home movies are generally produced as private records of family and friends, more advanced amateurs have had a wider group of potential viewers and viewing contexts in mind.[20]

Again, "advanced" is not necessarily a judgement of the success of a particular film's construction, only an acknowledgment that, unlike other kinds of nonprofessional films, it *has been deliberately constructed*, via editing, lighting, directed performance, etc., and that it has been created for viewers other than (or in addition to) the subjects, the filmmaker, or their immediate social circle; that is to say, for an audience of strangers.

It seems to me undeniable that the simultaneous growth of (non-pornographic) amateur filmmaking as a hobby and the expansion of stag film production point to a common origin. Unfortunately, the practices that went into the making of these latter films—how they were cast, where they were shot, where the film was developed, how prints were made, what kind of equipment was used—were not documented to the same degree as were the typical Amateur Cinema League

---

[19] Ibid., 45.
[20] Tepperman, *Amateur Cinema*, 6.

fare, for obvious and understandable reasons. Where we can refer to *Movie Makers* and other journals for one kind of film, we are forced to rely on the mass market press and police reports for the other.

One prominent element of stag films which might have kept them from being considered true amateur films, even more than their *outre* content, is the commercial nature of their production. We have already learned that most stag shows charged an admission fee, and a relatively exorbitant one at that, compared with the price of a ticket to a Hollywood movie. Albert Vogelstein and Charles Kessler, two Baltimore men arrested for setting up a screening of stag films in 1928, were able to charge $10 per head (or $159.65 in 2021 currency) for an evening's program, an offer enticing enough to attract 200 patrons.[21] Stag films were, for the most part, intended to be a money-making operation, and were probably the most profitable amateur films ever made, relative to initial investment. This mercenary character was in opposition to many of the myths that the purest-hearted amateurs told themselves. Tepperman quotes an essay by an Amateur Cinema League member, in which the D.I.Y. auteur is praised for possessing "the understanding of the artists without the artist's urge of bread-winning," and for his willingness to explore "esthetic possibilities that the amateur will exploit for their beauty and not for their profits."[22]

In truth, amateur films and filmmaking often flirted with commerce, if not usually quite so crassly as stags. Dan Streible and Melinda Stone, introducing a collection of essays on the topic, admit as much: "The utopian and independent impulses of amateurism have been complicated by professional, commercial and official interests from the beginning." Examples of this are easy to find:

> From 1936 to 1947 commercial productions by established professionals were allowed in annual "amateur" contests. In 1942, Lowell Thomas narrated not only Movietone's piece about the OSS, but also the industrially sponsored *Railroads Speed the Freights*, which was named to the [Amateur Cinema League's] Ten Best list, as was *Listen—It's FM!*, produced by the General Electric Company. Dwight Swanson's account of the first community of amateur 16mm film producers shows the degree to which they were tied to the Eastman Kodak company and its promotional efforts.[23]

---

[21] "2 Accused of Possessing Obscene Films Give Bail," *Baltimore Sun*, February 10, 1928, 3.

[22] Tepperman, *Amateur Cinema*, 26–7 *passim*.

[23] Melinda Stone and Dan Streible, "Introduction: Small-Gauge and Amateur Film," *Film History*, Vol. 15, No. 2 (2003), 123–4.

Seen against this background, stag producers' pursuit of a modest profit should not bar them from consideration as amateur films; if sponsorship by some of the twentieth century's gargantuan industrial firms doesn't disqualify the films mentioned by Streible and Stone, nor should an inflated ticket price keep out the much less pretentious smoker. Some sense of proportion must be maintained here as well: despite the insistence of some of the more breathless newspaper reports of pornographers captured by police—which would routinely make the evidence-free assertion that these filmmakers were making millions—even the savviest of this era's stag exhibitors and distributors couldn't dream of anything like riches from their labors. Still, the stag trade was a trade, and it was one that was growing noticeably in the immediate years after the introduction of 16mm film.

The earliest acknowledgments of the very existence of stags that I could find in the post-1923 press came, not from articles about any specific screenings or films, but rather from pieces on pornographic film as a general phenomenon. Although the mainstream press was nominally curious about the way in which these films were produced, sold, transported, and shown, very few journalists made a concerted effort to investigate these questions in any rigorous way. Despite the great number of news reports on specific incidents of arrests and prosecutions that this era would produce, the speculations on the work of the pornographer almost never mentions any specifics—the who/what/why/where/how that is supposedly the very stuff of journalism (and which, incidentally, would have been no small help to future researchers). A 1938 *Muncie Star Press* article fits the type all too well; though promising to provide a quick sketch of the life cycle of pornographic films, no source or authority is quoted. It may be assumed that the alleged facts here are a mix of information from both Post Office inspectors and the general store of rumor.

> Operating on the fringes of Hollywood, this racket corrals the hopeful young women who can't quite make the big pictures and offers them a fancy price for appearing in indecent films.
>
> The pictures are taken on 16-millimeter film and offered to owners of private projectors, particularly to men's clubs and "smokers." A 400-foot film which runs about 10 minutes sells for $25 to $50 ....
>
> Most distributors advertise their goods through the mail, then ship by express. Both are an offense against the law, so the Postoffice has them coming and going.[24]

---

[24] "Obscene Films," *The Star Press*, July 24, 1938, 8 *sic*.

Some of these details recur in other news stories—a distributor in another story was said to have "obtained models for pictures by visiting drug stores and cafeterias where unemployed actresses congregated."[25] The congruence of these kinds of details seems true, but is essentially unverifiable, even at the time.

But other items cast serious doubt on the credibility of the press. In 1936, the *Minneapolis Star* reported on an attempted extortion plot, planned by a federal prison inmate by the name of Frank Fowler in concert with some associates in the Twin Cities. The men had apparently contrived a scheme to blackmail several opera stars (including Rosa and Carmela Ponselle, Lucrezia Bori, and Lily Pons, according to a wire-service story quoted in several newspapers[26]) with faked obscene photos purporting to show them in compromising positions. These were to be constructed from what, by the *Star*'s telling, amounted to fairly crude cut-and-paste techniques. The ambitious Fowler had allegedly intended to produce motion picture images to accompany these stills, though the *Star*'s explanation of how these were to be made is frankly bizarre.

> Usually they are filmed by first-rate Hollywood camera men who have been outlawed from work in the picture city. Scouts are sent out to discover girls who are doubles of reigning queens.
>
> When one is found, she is trained to mimic the gestures and facial expressions of the actress whose part she is to play in the obscene movie. The result, when filmed, is often so perfect that intimate friends of the star are fooled into believing she actually is the girl in the picture ....
>
> The racketeers saw and made good on the possibilities of sound films as well, according to investigators. They recruited voice imitators from radio amateur hours and "dubbed in" fake voices for the fake stars.
>
> Profits from the obscene movie racket come from selling the films to "stag" parties and from the frantic attempts of the defamed stars to buy the prints.[27]

Obviously, this would require much more effort and coordination than most pornographers would have been willing to put into their work, if for no other reason than such a baroque arrangement would be difficult to keep secret. In particular, the process of, in 1936, substituting an imposter's voice for that of an on-screen performer with any accuracy—let alone verisimilitude—would be well beyond the means of this scale of production, no matter how "first-rate" the

---

[25] "Site of Suicide Leap also Scene of Triple Slaying," *Minneapolis Star*, August 2, 1940, 31.
[26] "In Extortion Plot?" *Mason City Globe-Gazette*, November 23, 1936, 10.
[27] "First Instance of Faked Photo Racket in City," *Minneapolis Star*, November 25, 1936, 5.

crew members. Whatever it was that Powell and his co-conspirators had actually planned to do, it is unlikely that they were willing to incidentally break new ground in the craft of sound recording and editing to accomplish it, or that such an approach was as common as the article implies.

What stories like these represent is not so much a look at the real activities of producers but rather a sign of the general confusion on behalf of the press— and, by extension, American society at large—over how to think about these films. Confronted with the by-then undeniable reality of pornographic films, some found it more credible to imagine them as the product of a vast, highly centralized conspiracy of technically adept criminals rather than the much more prosaic, ad-hoc operation that it probably was. With no accurate information readily available on just how these films were produced, these fantasies became even more elaborate, as shall be seen in the next chapters.

No hard figures (or even reliable estimates) exist which can account for the number of stag films produced before 1923, so it is impossible to say with absolute certainty at this remove whether production increased with the introduction of small-gauge safety film. However, there is a strong circumstantial case to be made that a greater availability of stag films should have followed on the heels of a sudden availability of cheap, light, easy-to-use film equipment. For one thing, the 1920s saw newspapers begin to write about pornographic movies not only as isolated incidents, but as a general phenomenon. This was in response to the new awareness of the trade in these kinds of films by various institutions, primarily law enforcement agencies. Late in 1923, New York Deputy Attorney General Maurice Gottlieb warned his constituents that his office had learned of a plot to sell "indecent German and Austrian films" in the United States. "The films, he said, were manufactured after the [first world] war to satisfy a jaded public. Later they became a drug on the European market, and their producers began efforts to unload them here, despite censorship laws."[28] At least initially, there was reluctance on behalf of law enforcement to assign responsibility for this to American citizens; as noted in my first chapter, the certainty that the taste for pornography was a European vice ran deep.

The volume of stags in circulation continued to grow, to the point where representatives of the Post Office finally announced a crackdown in 1925, declaring new resolve in the fight against obscenity in the mail. Although this

---

[28] "'Indecent' Film Plot Is Exposed," *Detroit Free Press*, December 8, 1923, 22.

effort was directed at all manner of obscene material—the story mentions still pictures, magazines, and books in addition to movies—the official in charge of the push admitted that motion picture film had been a particular problem, due in large part to the increase in films of all types in the mail. As a Post Office official admitted, "'More and more bona fide motion picture films are being shipped through the mails and it will be a hard job for our men to ferret out the indecent films from the others,' he said."[29] "Bona fide motion picture films" can here be taken to refer to any kind of film intended for home viewing, whether produced by professionals or amateurs, which would not have run afoul of obscenity regulations; it is likely here that the vast bulk of films shipped via the mails would fall into this category. This comment would appear to at least anecdotally support the idea that the proliferation of consumer production and exhibition equipment generally led to an expansion of the stag film market—the rising tide, so to speak, lifted all boats, "bona fide" and otherwise.

Even at this fairly late date, the Post Office continued to propagate the notion that this activity originated outside of the United States, saying that "distributors make their headquarters in New York city and rent alleged immoral pictures said to be imported from Europe to clubs and other organizations for private showings." The Post Office was not alone in its reluctance to admit the possibility that stag films could be produced by Americans within America. Whether out of sincere conviction or unwillingness to admit the obvious, this remained a shocking idea even to many journalists. When a stag screening for a 500-strong audience was broken up by police in Rochester, New York, in 1925, the *Democrat and Chronicle* made a special point to write that the man who arranged the festivities had admitted to stealing the projector and the film and "posed the obscene pictures" himself.[30] That this would be surprising to journalists in the very world capital of amateur filmmaking speaks to the degree to which such an idea was still unbelievable to American society generally.

Eventually the domestic origin of the new films could no longer be denied. By 1927, the New York state legislature was forced to amend its obscenity statute, which had, up to that point, explicitly forbade any manner of transportation of obscene material within state borders. This, as it happened, had placed Kodak in an awkward position, since the amount of undeveloped motion picture film they

[29] "Drive On to Rid Mails of Obscene Films," *Mount Carmel Item*, April 29, 1925, 4.
[30] "Alleged Exhibitor Fights Charge of Showing Obscene Films in Raided Garage," *Democrat and Chronicle*, June 27, 1925, 19.

received depicting allegedly indecent acts had grown sharply in recent years, leaving them with a growing stash of reels they could not legally possess, mail, or even so much as throw in the trash. An exception was hurriedly added to the law which allowed the lab to transport the films to city dump for purposes of disposal only.[31] The acknowledgment of domestic stag production had been written into a state's legal code, and the notion that such films could only have come from abroad was now stripped of whatever credibility it may have previously enjoyed.

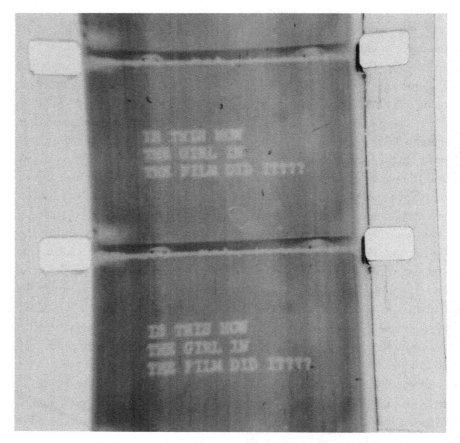

Figure 2.2 Intertitle frame from *Untitled Stag Film,* year unknown. The phenomenon of stag films became undeniable, to the point where the genre itself acknowledged its own existence. (Film from personal collection of the author.)

---

[31] "Obscene Matter Measure Passed," *Democrat and Chronicle,* March 25, 1927, 37.

The relationship between availability of amateur equipment and the proliferation of stags soon found popular expression, as it soon became widely understood that the substandard amateur gauges were the preferred format for pornographic movies. A number of anecdotal statements attest to this popular association. Looking back at his arrest of Sam Efrus, Charles Bamberger would later ruefully comment that, for all his success in the early twentieth century, "since the perfection of 16mm moving films and camera, a new type of pornography has come into existence."[32] By 1945, the situation had gotten to the point where a syndicated movie news column could report on the consternation some independent small-gauge producers felt at being identified with the stag trade; in an (inadvertent, surely) echo of the Post Office statement from two decades earlier, the columnist noted that "bona fide 16-millimeter producers are organizing a Hays office of their own to counteract the unfavorable publicity handed out in the recent Los Angeles police raid on naughty movies."[33] Though the link between amateur cinema and stag films has not been acknowledged by scholars of the twenty-first century, observers from nearly a hundred years before considered it to be common sense.

Much more direct evidence for the expansion of the stag trade can be found in the massive uptick in reports of such events being disrupted by the police. In contrast to the handful of verified incidents from before 1923, I was able to find over 200 newspaper stories involving stag film screenings in one capacity or another during the span of years between 1923 and 1941. The connection between more news reports and more screenings might seem too obvious to belabor, but it is worth exercising some caution here; incidents such as these could sometimes lead to public embarrassment for prominent citizens caught in the net of the law, and one cannot always assume that every interrupted screening made the evening final. Furthermore, it is almost certainly true that, for every show stopped by the police, several more went on unmolested, and thus beneath the notice of the press. The point is to regard these news reports as a (somewhat) random sample, not a perfect census.

Increased coverage of stag-related raids is likely related in some way to an expansion of production and exhibition; greater attention to this matter from the press also revealed quite a bit more, however, about the active, if primitive,

---

[32] Charles J. Bamberger, "E-V-I-C R-O-T-A-C-I-D-A-R-S," July 1943, John Saxon Sumner Papers, 1904–61, Box 2, Folder 2 (Wisconsin State Historical Society, Madison, Wisconsin), 31.
[33] *Bakersfield Californian*, April 26, 1945, 20.

distribution network that supported both of these activities. More and more often, distributors themselves were being raided, with significant collections of films, cameras, and projectors captured alongside them. By the beginning of the 1930s, these arrests would turn up greater and greater quantities of material, leading to speculation that a centralized distribution system of some type had begun to form and was reaching a state of maturity. Unfortunately, the details reported to the public gloss over the specifics of these operations, opting instead for tantalizing hints about the size and nature of a distributor's collection. A simple lack of data condemns to fragmentary status many intriguing cases reported on at the time, such as that of Charles Rossi of Hoboken, New Jersey. Caught with a staggering 800 reels of obscene film in a warehouse, the judge in his case wished aloud that a capital sentence could be imposed; he had to settle for three years in the penitentiary.[34] Also lost to speculation are the precise machinations behind Sidney Pilie's operation. It's not clear exactly what volume of material he had—the paper claims that, in commission of the raid on his premises, "detectives were carrying part of 1000 indecent pictures and obscene movie film out of his flat for evidence"—but it must have been extensive indeed. Rather than give up his secrets, the Brooklyn man leapt out of his kitchen window to his death as the police ransacked his apartment.[35]

Although the Post Office first voiced concern about the pornographic film trade in 1925, it was not until 1928 that a large-scale mail-order stag operation was reported to have been broken up, with the arrests of William Larivee, H. W. Smith, and Harry Winter, all of Hollywood. Accused of operating a stag film distribution "ring," the three were "alleged to have taken obscene pictures in the hills back of Hollywood and broadcast them over the country through the mails …. Federal agents said the three indicted men had realized several hundred thousand dollars profit on the illegal venture, and that the investigation now under way may involve a dozen Hollywood business men and camera operators."[36] Though some editors and "a cameraman who formerly worked on the staff of one of the poverty row studios" were investigated,[37] no Hollywood figures of any standing were ever credibly accused of involvement with this case.

---

[34] "800 Reels of Indecent Films Bring Three-Year Sentence," *Asbury Park Press*, April 25, 1931, 1.
[35] "Site of Suicide Leap," *Minneapolis Star*, 31.
[36] "Love Scenes too Filthy for Jury; Picture Halted," *News-Review*, November 23, 1928, 1 *sic*.
[37] "Government Quizzes Two Film Cutters for Indecent Film," *Exhibitors Herald and Moving Picture World*, December 1, 1928, 42.

Post Office inspection records no longer exist for this case, so there's nothing to back up the claim made in these news articles that the men were raking in "several hundred thousand dollars" from producing and mailing pornographic movies. Also lost to history are the names and details of the twenty-three films, which were evidently strong enough to compel the Federal grand jury, charged with viewing them in order to determine the precise nature of the violation, to quit their screening midway through. "Part of one film was flashed on an improvised screen in the jury room yesterday but the performance was halted by the foreman, and today other members said that they 'didn't want to see such pictures.' The assistant U. S. attorney confessed that his conscience would hurt him if he witnessed any more of the 'private show.'"[38]

(It is useful to pause here over the jury's specific complaint at being subjected to such stuff, which seems to amount to an intolerable assault on their sensibilities. The sense of violation at viewing these images, even if only in the course of his professional and civic duty, provokes the very conscience of the presiding attorney, providing for the historian a visceral illustration of what exactly it was that was objectionable about pornographic films in that era. The grand jury, as well as presumably all other crusaders against the proliferation of stag films from this age, saw theirs as a moral campaign, protecting citizens of all types from exactly this kind of trauma, considered to be the natural result of exposure to sexually explicit imagery. While this justification would never entirely disappear, other ones, rooted in entirely different assumptions about the nature of the moving image and its relationship to the audience, would become more prominent in the decades to come, and provide both a moral and legal basis for resistance to dirty movies.)

We shall see that, by the 1960s, strategies for effectively marketing pornographic material by mail had been honed into, if not quite a science, at least a set of stable, rationalized practices; it is not apparent, however, that the same situation prevailed in the 1930s. No contemporary literature convincingly explains the precise methods by which films were distributed by mail; nor do the various ephemeral texts associated with such sales, such as catalogs, flyers, ads, or correspondence (most of the surviving examples of which have been dated to later decades). The way in which stags were able to be sold or rented by mail without openly advertising their wares in journals and magazines—something

---

[38] "So-Called Obscene Films too Bad for Federal Grand Jury," *San Bernardino County Sun*, November 24, 1928, 2.

they certainly would not have been able to do at the time—will remain something of a mystery. While it is likely that many different types of arrangements prevailed from one organization to another, we are left to speculate on the typical chain of custody of a film from producer to consumer. Did distributors buy films directly from producers, or did they also make their own films? How often did distributors also screen their films locally?

While there may never be sufficient evidence to generalize with certainty about these broad questions, some provisional inferences may be made based on the little information that can be found. In at least a few cases, it seems that trade in stags grew out of a previously existing mail order (non-pornographic) film business. Direct distribution of films to private viewers in the home dates back to the earliest days of the consumer film market. Shortly after the launch of the Parlor company's Kinetoscope, the very first projector manufactured and sold to customers in the United States, that same company marketed "'picture belts' [which] were available in lengths from 15 to 60 feet, costing from three to six dollars per dozen. Among the titles listed in the Parlor catalog were *Dance of the Rustic, The Elephants,* and *General View of the Beach at Atlantic City.*"[39] By the late 1920s, "film libraries were multiplying and expanding their catalogs; rental of 16mm prints of Hollywood films was as popular then as video rentals are today … Presumably in response to customer demand, about 1930 Kodak began as a separate operation, making 'Kodak Cinegraphs,' films to purchase, available at Kodak dealerships."[40] Well into the era of television (and even some time after the first appearance of home video), distributors of home movies such as Castle and Blackhawk were able to stay in business through direct sales to consumers of vintage silent comedy shorts, cartoons, highlights of football games, cut-down versions of popular theatrical releases, and other types of material. Naturally, producers and distributors of sexually explicit material of various types, including but not limited to stag films, didn't want to be left out of this burgeoning mail-order market, and there is evidence that they tried to break in as early as the 1930s.

This would seem to fly in the face of an assertion common to most previous stag scholarship, which seems to agree that pornographic films were not sold to individual consumers until after the Second World War. Thompson, for example, writes that only the onset of the "1950's explosion in home-movie technology saw many [stag] dealers begin to retail reels direct to the public. Many homes

[39] Katelle, *Home Movies*, 54.
[40] Ibid., 84–5.

possessed a movie projector now and many had amassed sizable film collections
... *For the first time*, it was possible to view a movie without waiting for the
road show to come into town, and slowly a way of life began to die."[41] This is
of a piece with the claim by Di Lauro and Rabkin that the "decrease in the cost
of projection equipment and the development of eight-millimeter technology"
could be dated to the 1950s.[42] But these claims are contradicted by a glance at
the journalistic record, where we can find direct evidence of stag films being sold
through the mail.

In 1939, two different outfits based in Elmira, New York—Arthur C. Miller's
Miller Cine Films and the Harold F. Jenkins Import Film Company—were
accused of sending indecent films through the mail. Though separate businesses,
they were raided virtually simultaneously by agents of the postal inspector's
office, which also announced the confiscation of "a number of allegedly salacious
films" from each. "The companies had been sending films throughout the
eastern section of the country, according to [postal inspector Clarence] Ford.
He said they advertised in numerous magazines and newspapers and that he
had received several complaints about the films in Rochester."[43] A glance at these
print advertisements reveals something of the way in which each man attempted
to find customers for their specialized products in the larger home-film market.

Both had indeed marketed their films via print ads in periodicals, albeit at
a much different scale. Jenkins seemed to confine his activities to upstate New
York, taking out ads in the local Elmira papers. He had entered the film business
some years earlier as a distributor for Univex film stock, and the earliest ad from
that business that I could find was an offer to trade $8 worth of unused raw film
for footage of the recent Wellsville oil fire.[44] At this time, he was operating out
of 108 W. Church Street in Elmira, which he seems to have shared with a radio
sales and repair shop.

Miller Cine Films also makes its first appearance in 1938, in a notice in the
amateur film journal *Movie Makers*; around the same time, its first ads appear
in the *Elmira Star-Gazette*, imploring the reader to "GIVE MOVIE FILM FOR
CHRISTMAS" and offering footage of "Mickey Mouse ... Dionne Quintuplets,

[41] David Thompson, *Black and White and Blue: Adult Cinema from the Victorian Age to the VCR*
(Chicago, IL: ECW Press, 2007), 149, emphasis mine.

[42] Al Di Lauro and Gerald Rabkin, *Dirty Movies: An Illustrated History of the Stag Film, 1915–1970*
(New York: Chelsea House, 1976), 55.

[43] "Distribution of Obscene Films Charged in Arrest of Elmira Pair," *Democrat and Chronicle*, May 3,
1939, 16.

[44] *Elmira Star-Gazette*, July 23, 1938, 12.

Joan Bennett, Wallace Beery, Hoot Gibson ... comedies, travel, western."[45] Some months later, in February 1939, Miller's new advertising strategy was unveiled in the *Philadelphia Inquirer*, promising a "Snappy Art Film Sample 10¢—3 for 25¢" and illustrated with a graphic of a semi-nude woman with her back to the viewer, looking over her shoulder.[46] This risqué move may have worked a little too well, possibly attracting unwanted attention from the postal inspector's office.

Although their businesses were independent initiatives by each man, they appear to have coordinated their legal defense strategy, which largely rested on an appeal to a kind of elevated, middlebrow cultural sensibility in order to differentiate their material from base pornography. They insisted that "they advertised only in high class magazines and newspapers and not in the pulp magazines."[47] Rather than playing to prurient interest, they claimed, these films were meant to be used as figure studies for aspiring sketch artists, after the fashion of a nude model in an art class. "One series of films on their list was 'Hollywood art.' Some of the figures were nude, they explained, but were not obscene and not of the type sometimes shown at clandestine stag parties." Furthermore, they pointed out that they refused to sell their films to minors (returning purchase orders which arrived without a signed age statement), and had been promised by the films' producers that their wares could legally travel through the mail.[48]

The authorities were unmoved by this argument. The Post Office's solicitor ruled that the law applied to images of nudity of any sort, adding that "the fact that the photo studies are to be used by artists is immaterial."[49] The indictment by the Grand Jury some weeks later worded their rebuttal in even stronger terms, with the Rochester newspaper quoting the verdict that the films in question "'would defile the public records of this court,' if described in detail."[50]

(Jenkins was not to be discouraged by this, and continued to involve himself in the mail-order film business for some time, though I haven't found anything to suggest that he ever ran afoul of obscenity laws again. This may have been as much due to luck as any other circumstance: in 1942, his company, showing the same address but now simply doing business under Jenkins's own name, was

[45] *Elmira Star-Gazette*, December 12, 1938, 16.
[46] *Philadelphia Inquirer*, February 19, 1939, 14W.
[47] "Two Charged with Mailing Art Films," *Elmira Star-Gazette*, May 3, 1939, 8.
[48] Ibid.
[49] Ibid.
[50] "Jury Finds True Bills on 16 Cases," *Democrat and Chronicle*, May 19, 1939, 23.

advertising a reel called "Waikiki Hula Girls;" undaunted, the ad insists on proof of age with each order.)[51]

Most other mail order services linked to obscene films were far more circumspect. Even the notion of a separate list of pornographic films available to repeat customers would seem to be a risky venture, considering that such a document could be used as material evidence of intent in a possible future prosecution. Yet even these more cautious businesses were not safe from would-be Comstocks.

For example, the following ad may be found in the respective classified sections of the April, May, and June 1940 issues of *Popular Mechanics*:

> 8-16mm Films: cartoons, comedies, travel, sport, war in Europe, world's fair. Silent and sound. Tremendous assortment. Bargain prices! Films rented everywhere. Trades accepted. Free catalogue (with sample film 10¢). Garden Film Service, 317 West 50th. New York.[52]

Despite this discretion, six months later, in January of 1941, the New York Society for the Suppression of Vice noted in its monthly report that same Garden Film Service (with the same address—317 West 50th Street in New York—noted in the report) had come under investigation by that organization for involvement in obscene films.[53] No other details of this case could be found in any other source, so the precise nature of the offense is not entirely clear. Nevertheless, this seems to be proof that even in these fairly early days, mailorder film retailers were trying to devise a way to find customers interested in risque material without announcing this upfront.

Other means existed by which to distribute stags, though many of these would develop further after the close of the war. Photographic supply stores (many of which, incidentally, served the amateur filmmaking community) have long been rumored to be a source of pornographic films. Knight and Alpert contend:

> Many camera stores began stocking a few reels of stag films for rental to special customers, since the films not only paid for themselves in two or three rentals but also served as a catalyst for the rental and purchase of movie projectors. The

---

[51] *Home Movies*, November 1942, 238.

[52] *Popular Mechanics*, April 1940, 42; *Popular Mechanics*, May 1940, 39; *Popular Mechanics*, June 1940, 43.

[53] "Report of the Secretary for the Month of January, 1941," John Saxon Sumner Papers, 1901–1961, Box 3, Folder 3 (Wisconsin State Historical Society, Madison, Wisconsin), 1.

rental of a 400-foot, 16mm stag reel averaged from $5 to $10; the purchase price of a reel, from $25 up.[54]

This scenario has passed into the folklore of mid-century pornography, apparently having enough credibility, or at least familiarity as an urban legend, to appear in Michael Powell's infamous *Peeping Tom* in 1960 (albeit in a British context).

Though Knight and Alpert put the earliest incidence of this form of exchange in the post-war era, there is reason to believe that this practice began even earlier. Recall that many of the businesses which distributed stags by mailorder were also brick-and-mortar camera equipment outlets as well; such was apparently the case with Jenkins above. It doesn't stretch credibility to assume that they had as few qualms about offering forbidden films under the counter in person as they had about mailing them across the country—probably fewer, since there would be no paper trail positively connecting them to a particular reel sold person-to-person. This may be the reason why there are relatively few arrests connected to storefront operations during this time, though not for lack of effort on the part of law enforcement and others. The Society, for example, began investigating photo equipment stores as early as the late 1930s; the January 1938 report registers a complaint against "Joe Fink [of] Garden Camera."[55] In late 1940, another investigation was launched into the activities of the Haber & Fink camera store "re obscene films. Secured information re east side exhibition."[56] This turned up very little of substance, however, with the agent in charge admitting that he had "tried to secure evidence re obscene films. Unsuccessful."[57]

The most storied method of stag distribution at this time comes in the figure of the itinerant projectionist. Again, the consensus of pornographic film historians suggests that most of these films were seen by American audiences from the 1920s through the 1950s thanks to these traveling operators, who crisscrossed the country staging "roadshow" screenings. As the story goes, these were typically shown to all-male civic organizations—the local chapter of the Elks Lodge, say—officially surreptitiously, but really occurring as something of

---

[54] Arthur Knight and Hollis Alpert, "The History of Sex in Cinema, Part Seventeen: The Stag Film," *Playboy*, November 1967, 172.

[55] "Report to the Secretary for the Month of January, 1938," John Saxon Sumner Papers, Box 3, Folder 2 (Madison, Wisconsin: Wisconsin State Historical Society), 1.

[56] "Report of the Secretary for the Month of December, 1940," John Saxon Sumner Papers, Box 3, Folder 2 (Madison, Wisconsin: Wisconsin State Historical Society), 1, *sic*.

[57] Ibid., 2.

an open secret. A typical summary of the essential features of this basic story can be found in the opening pages of Jack Stevenson's book *Fleshpot*: stag films "were brought to town by a traveling operator who might conceal his wares in a doctor's bag or tool chest, for example …. He ran the show, the images invariably flickering through a pall of cigar smoke, got paid in cash and was gone the next day."[58] Slade, in the first volume of his oft-cited *Pornography and Sexual Representation: A Reference Guide*, tells a similar story. "By and large [the films] were exhibited by their makers, who hired themselves, their projectors, and their reels out to fraternities, men's clubs, and American Legion posts." Slade also concludes that due to the films' "illegality and the fact that they were distributed by hand … the producers made little money from them."[59]

Despite the confidence with which these pronouncements are delivered, neither Stevenson nor Slade offers any examples of actual itinerant projectionists to illustrate this supposedly common practice. But there does seem to be some evidence that some men did engage in limited travel to project pornographic films to audiences within a broad regional footprint. The case of Frank Smith hews so closely to the story proffered by Stevenson and Slade that it is tempting to regard him as typical: raided as he waited in his car at a ferry dock in San Francisco, police found not only "a projection apparatus and five reels of film" but also "Miss Florence Jackson, 22, a dancer."[60] He had been on his way to Reno, where, as the *Reno Gazette Journal* was careful to note, "several films have been shown … to a select few at various places and it was reported that the pictures were anything but proper."[61] Smith would be charged with possession and exhibition of obscene films.

The phenomenon of traveling stag exhibitors is of course a by-product of the 16mm revolution, but this misses the bigger point, which is the sudden explosion of itinerant projection of all types after 1923. Just as the general expansion of stag production after 1923 was occurring in the context of a boom in home and amateur cinema in general, itinerant stag projectionists were not leading a new trend, but merely taking advantage of the same opportunities available to the "bona fide" world. Far from innovating uses of new technology, they simply adapted these practices to their own needs. Though nomadic film exhibition

---

[58] Jack Stevenson, "Blue Movie Notes: Ode to an Attic Cinema," in *Fleshpot: Cinema's Sexual Myth Makers & Taboo Breakers*, ed. Jack Stevenson (Manchester: Headpress/ Critical Vision, 2002), 9.

[59] Joseph Slade, *Pornography and Sexual Repression: A Reference Guide, Volume I* (Westport, CT: Greenwood Press, 2001), 80.

[60] "Man Arrested for Having Obscene Film," *Oakland Tribune*, September 13, 1928, 48.

[61] "'Indecent' Films Reno Bound Seized," *Reno Gazette-Journal*, September 13, 1928, 8.

occurred as far back as the late nineteenth century,[62] the new, lighter, more easily portable equipment seemed to lend itself to roadshow screenings, at least on the small scale on which most itinerants operated. Traveling projectionists were a viable form of exhibition then, reaching something of a high point during the Depression.[63] One example of such a projectionist was a man named Gene Fernett, who at this time ran his own circuit through Michigan showing (non-pornographic) serials and features, and who, in an article in the film-collector newspaper *Classic Images*, testified that itinerants were able to keep several 16mm film libraries in the black up to the advent of television; he pointed out that the legendary distributor Blackhawk Films began life as Eastin 16mm Pictures Company, and used to specialize in renting to roadshowmen.[64]

Like their "legitimate" counterparts, stag itinerants also seemed to operate on a dependable circuit, encompassing a particular region. Details on these exact routes will remain lost, but we can infer the general credibility of this model; hints can be found in tantalizing details in some news articles, such as the assertion by an investigating officer that David Vogt, arrested in Philadelphia as he was about to leave to project stags in Washington DC, "had been supplying improper films for so-called 'smokers' in this area for about 18 months."[65] The officer never defines Vogt's regional footprint in any more specific terms than that, but, like Fernett and others before him, probably catered to regular customers and audiences in a circuit of some kind.

That the occurrence of these kinds of exhibitions owed something to the increased mobility of projection equipment was not lost on contemporary observers. The connection between the new, commercially dominant film gauge and portability was seized upon by the detectives who arrested Robert Meyers in 1930 after he projected an "obscene motion picture show" for six couples in a Philadelphia apartment. "The raid was ordered after Superintendent of Police Mills obtained information from police chiefs in other large cities that portable projectors were being used to flood the country with objectionable motion picture shows."[66] The language here about "flooding the country" suggests a fairly rapid increase in the activity of these underground roadshows; whatever

---

[62] See Calvin Pryluck, "The Itinerant Movie Show and the Development of the Film industry," *Journal of University Film and Video Association*, Vol. 35, No. 4 (Fall 1983), 11–22.

[63] Gomery, *Shared Pleasures*, 12–13.

[64] Gene Fernett, "Itinerant Roadshowmen and the 'Free Movie' Craze," *Classic Images*, No. 88, 12.

[65] "Racy Books and Films Seized after Arrest," *Philadelphia Inquirer*, January 20, 1937, 4.

[66] "2 Held as Police Raid Obscene Film Exhibit," *Philadelphia Inquirer*, July 3, 1930, 2.

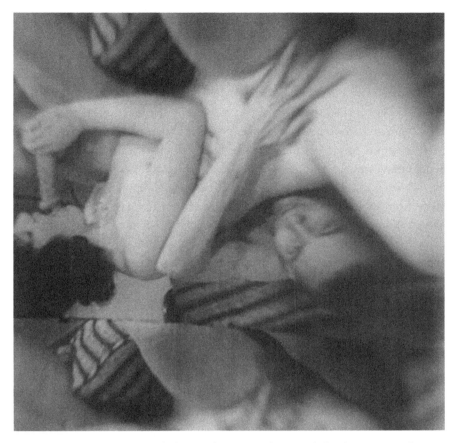

Figure 2.3 Frame from *Untitled Stag Film,* year unknown. (Film from personal collection of the author.)

their absolute number, it would seem that they appeared quickly enough after 1923 to still be found remarkable even seven years later.

Despite these general parallels in their operations, there is nothing to indicate that there was any widespread overlap between those itinerants who dealt in "legitimate" films and those who traveled with stags; the similarities between these two were, by and large, superficial, while the differences were crucial. Stag shows were, by their nature, designed for secrecy and for a select audience, whereas a traveling projectionist such as Fernett sought the widest possible audience. Itinerant distribution of pornography was at best an improvised means of transporting films beneath the notice of law enforcement, not necessarily an outgrowth of mainstream roadshows. The latter by necessity lived a very visible existence, requiring advertising and networking, conforming to certain presentation practices, all of it conducted aboveground and in public.

In contrast with mainstream roadshowmen, it is extremely unlikely that stag itinerants made their main living in this way. Vogt seems to have been an at-large dealer in pornographic material of all types—a post-arrest search of his apartment turned up "a truckload of books, pictures, and obscene movie films, valued at thousands of dollars."[67] Clearly, personally traveling to and from locations to project film was, for him, just one means among many to peddle his wares. I encountered no similar case from mainstream itinerants; the plausible explanation for this is that there was simply more money to be made from showing mainstream fare. The audience for stag films was, almost by definition, restricted to adult men, and, given the surreptitious nature of the whole enterprise, only men with certain social connections would even be apprised of the screening in the first place (although, as we have seen, this could sometimes amount to hundreds of people at one showing). The films shown by non-stag itinerants were the typical fare found in most commercial cinemas: short cartoons, newsreels, followed by one or two features. They tended to be a few years out of date, often projected from 16mm rather than 35mm, and probably from prints with significant wear, but even these would be more likely to attract an audience pulled from all available demographics, including women and children, and thus likely to sell a greater number of tickets. These kinds of calculations paralleled those of the exhibition arm of the film industry generally, resulting in a similar kind of appeal to middle-class moral standards. For someone like Fernett, who had sunk a considerable investment into prints, projection equipment, a vehicle, and sometimes even seats, a makeshift stage, a tent, or other kinds of presentation gear, to transport and exhibit forbidden films was a proposition that carried a great deal of risk for a negligible reward. Stag film screenings, hanging resolutely onto the continuing traditions of bachelor culture from which it emerged, evolved as an exhibition culture completely outside of these considerations. Itinerant projection was a by-product of various technological developments which were taken advantage of by both "bona fide" and pornographic film exhibitors, but any real similarity between the two ends there.

[67] Ibid.

If what is known about the exhibitors of stag films remains patchy, what of those in the audience? Other scholars have attempted this, tending to focus on either the psychological state of what is assumed to be a typical member of that audience, or on the social dynamics of the group during the show. Thomas Waugh, in his essay "Homosociality in the Classical American Stag Film" addresses the communal ritual of collective stag viewing, finding a homoerotic dimension that seems to him to have been underplayed in previous studies. Characterizing the spectatorial experience as "men getting hard pretending not to watch men getting hard watching images of men getting hard watching or fucking women," Waugh connects this undercurrent of libidinal overflow to the very nature of the screening as a communal ritual while also bemoaning the fact that this quality was not taken into account during the pioneering days of sexology. He finds it a particular missed opportunity that Dr. Kinsey, in his survey of American sexual attitudes and experiences, had only "asked respondents about the use of the stag film as an object of arousal, but apparently did not think to ask them about the *context* of erotic stimulation, about the same-sex public sharing of these cine-heteroerotic stimuli."[68]

Waugh recognizes that any arguments about the particulars of these screenings must remain speculative due to the paucity of verifiable information about them, lamenting the dismal state of the historical record and reminding the reader that, when it comes to historical studies of stag exhibition, "no direct quotes are available from any continent, and, to my knowledge, no oral histories. The fragmentary evidence of both milieus remains frustratingly nonspecific, unreliable, moralistic, and condescending."[69] Though he eventually relents to Di Lauro and Rabkin's version of events, in which films were screened exclusively for civic organizations or frat houses, he does so with some detachment, noting that the experience of homosocial bonding that is assumed to be the central point of such gatherings only has explanatory power in a "monolithically uniform masculinity," and does not account for variations among and within the audience (such variations include the experience of Waugh himself: "None allows for the traumatized silence I felt when I saw *Smart Alec* with my dormitory peers in 1968 and the queer difference I and others must have felt. Extrapolating

---

[68] Thomas Waugh, "Homosociality in the Classical American Stag Film: Off-Screen, On-Screen," in *Porn Studies*, ed. Linda Williams (Durham, NC: Duke University Press, 2004), 132.
[69] Ibid., 130–1.

back through the decades, it is impossible not to imagine that difference was not present in all of those classic all-male audiences.").[70]

While nothing that I encountered in my research could quite account for this either—individual reminiscences such as Waugh's are welcome additions to the store of information about stag exhibition, but notoriously difficult to come by—I have discovered a great deal of variation in the types of stag screenings that existed during this time. As Waugh suspected, exhibitions in civic lodges and fraternities were not the only type to occur during the twentieth century, and pornographic films were screened in a variety of different ways.

In spite of the secretive nature of stag shows, and the necessary restrictions this placed on advertising and promotion, a surprising detail about this era is the apparent frequency of very large-scale screenings. This age is rife with gatherings of several hundred men at a time; on two separate occasions (that I could find), police boasted of breaking up showings with over 1000 men in the crowd.[71] No previously existing association among any of the audience members is mentioned in any of the newspaper reports, and it would seem to strain credibility to imagine that hundreds of people could all be connected via the sort of thick social bond that united members of a club; therefore it seems reasonable to assume that these screenings were organized for paying customers, and not for a lodge or civic organization, with word spread among potential attendees via some manner of whisper campaign. Again, the exact mechanism by which this many men were brought together may never be known.

Let us recall here that stag parties often involved quite a bit more than simply a few reels of dirty movies. If we cannot, in any systematic way, determine what an average show might have entailed, we can make assumptions based on the records of the showings we do know of—those broken up by the police—and these tended to have a relatively consistent shape in this era. Here, I have found that the form that emerged in the teens was continued into the 1920s and 1930s, featuring a multitude of attractions, large numbers of customers, and, very often, dancing women in, it is implied, various states of undress. After the passage of the Volstead Act, gambling and liquor were often added to the mix; these last two vices were common enough that stag films often appear as an incidental point in a news article chiefly devoted to the latest adventure in prohibition enforcement.

---

[70] Ibid., 133–4.

[71] "1,000 Taken in Raid on Obscene Movie," *Baltimore Sun*, September 24, 1931, 7; "1000 Fight to Flee Raid on Lewd Show," *Oakland Tribune*, November 8, 1938, 3.

Though these gargantuan screenings are the most frequent single category that I found, other, smaller, showings occurred often as well. Even some of these gatherings, curiously enough, consisted of audiences in which none of the individual members had any previous association with each other; there seems to have been a much greater incidence of these than occurred in the pre-1923 era. Here I must set aside some space for Lloyd V. Hutton, probably the most enterprising stag exhibitor of this era, who constructed what amounts to a "little cinema" in the basement of his house for the purposes of showing pornography.[72] His luck eventually ran out, of course—police had received a tip "from a patron who said he had seen 'disgusting' movies there"—but the subsequent investigation revealed his surprisingly ambitious and well-developed approximation of the theatrical viewing experience, albeit at a much smaller scale.

> In a basement room, 15 by 30 feet, they found 30 seats, a small bar, a projection booth, sound movie machine and the films, stored in metal containers. Hutton was quoted by the officers as admitting the films were his and that he had shown them to groups and individuals. If the show was for a group he charged from $10 to $15 for five to seven reels, if for individuals the price was from 25 cents to $1 a person, he said.[73]

His entrepreneurial spirit and devotion to proper standards of exhibition would bring him six months in jail.

In most other cases, however, audiences made up of random strangers were the exception, and screenings tended to be somewhat improvised affairs in which viewers had at least some previous connection with each other. It is this scenario, much more than the mass gatherings alluded to above, that has survived as the main urban myth of the stag film. As the authors of the *Report of the President's Commission on Obscenity* would write some decades later, "Operators usually had well-established customers, such as respectable lodges, veterans' organizations and college fraternities."[74] The *Report* also points out that this scenario "became an integral part of the folklore of this country."

This last assertion is true enough; whatever its relationship to historical fact, lodges, halls, meeting-houses of various civic groups and other private, all-male

---

[72] Hutton's activities here are reminiscent of the exhibition strategies of the "bona fide" amateur film community of the 1930s; Tepperman's precis of these in *Amateur Cinema*, pp. 74–8 is worth considering in this light.

[73] "Obscene Films Seized in Home Movie Raid," *St. Louis Post-Dispatch*, September 27, 1940, 29.

[74] *Technical Report of the Commission on Obscenity and Pornography, Volume III* (Washington, DC: U.S. Government Printing Office, 1971), 190.

gathering spaces proved to have surprising staying power as a regular setting for the urban myth of the stag film. Even in the late 1990s, Something Weird, a video label specializing in lost and forgotten films, could build this into their sales pitch for a series of tapes compiling old stags. In their 1997 seasonal catalog, a section devoted to these collections ("Grandpa Bucky's Stags, Loops & Peeps") is introduced with the following text:

> Bucky was up in the attic of the family beaver dam and found grandpappy's stash of dirty movies from the good old days of forbidden porn! While [1960s-era director Alex] de Renzy was still in diapers, amateur filmmakers were shooting illegal sex flicks that often showed up in the backrooms and basements of men's lodges and stag parties (much to Grandpa Bucky's delight, he *always* paid his membership dues on time!)[75]

As with the figure of the itinerant projectionist, this rumor has been taken seriously by porn historians for many decades. Mentions of this can be found in many of the scholars I've cited; Thompson, for example, claims that a crucial factor in the spread of stags in the 1920s was the attempts by "many of America's historical fraternal orders [to] launch aggressive recruitment drives ... in a bid to combat a fall in membership that had been threatening their existence since the turn of the century, as younger men turned to such less-strictured recreational clubs such as the Rotary and Kiwanis."[76] The lack of both citation and qualification here (which "historical fraternal orders" are he referring to? And in what ways were the Rotary and Kiwanis clubs "less-strictured?") makes it difficult to take this at face value, though probably the precise extent to which this or that club dealt with stag films is impossible to determine without a thorough dig into the paper archive of any one organization.

Incidents of civic groups in this era attracting police attention for this reason are actually somewhat light on the ground, and surprisingly so, given its place in urban legend. The only confirmed raid on an actual space belonging to a lodge that I could find occurred in 1933, when Cincinnati police went after the Knights of Maccabee's Temple. Having received "a tip that immoral motion pictures were to be shown," police "surrounded the Temple and trapped the occupants. Immoral pictures, a quantity of beer and a chuck-a-luck game were

---

[75] "Grandpa Bucky's Naughty Stags, Loops & Peeps," *Something Weird Video Blue Book* (Seattle, WA: Something Weird Video, 1997), 92.
[76] Thompson, *Black and White and Blue*, 76.

Figure 2.4 Frame from *Untitled Stag Film,* year unknown. (Film from personal collection of the author.)

found in the hall."[77] Of the forty-four people arrested, five men, all members of the lodge, were given serious charges, including "exhibiting a picture without a state permit."[78] The only other reference to screenings from civic organizations I was able to turn up involves a simultaneous pair of raids on the "Officers of the Grand Lafayette Lodge," who were gathered in the National Winter Garden in New York, and the "Free Sons of Israel" at another location elsewhere in town.[79]

Documentation is even slimmer for the case of fraternities. In one sense this is not unexpected, as the percentage of the population of the United States

[77] "Fifty Persons Arrested," *Cincinnati Enquirer*, March 4, 1933, 14.
[78] "Prejudice Is Charged," *Cincinnati Enquirer*, March 9, 1933, 18.
[79] "Court Releases 292 Seized at a Show," *New York Times*, April 29, 1934, 16.

enrolled in colleges or universities at this time ranged from only 6.1 percent to 9.1 percent of the 18–24-year-old population,[80] with a smaller proportion of even those participating in the Greek system. I was able to turn up evidence of just one campus showing during this period: in 1932, a pair of University of Oklahoma police forced their way into a fraternity house—"packed with student spectators"—where a screening was then in progress. Nothing was written about the film itself, other than the telling detail that it "was reported to have been imported from Paris."[81] Two students were charged with "the showing of an allegedly licentious motion picture film in several fraternity houses."[82] (The fairly bland character of the original charges is thrown into relief by the wild incidents which followed as a result. Several days after the arrest, a student named Bill Stephens was kidnapped from his quarters, taken to a remote location and "flogged with a rope" by what the Associated Press referred to as an "outlawed hooded secret order" known only as the DDMC. Stephens was at the time moonlighting as a journalist for some local papers, and was told by his captors that "the punishment was given because of a newspaper story he had written about fraternities." There was speculation that the arrest [and eventual expulsion] of the fraternity members for the stag screening, and their exposure in the press, might have precipitated the incident. While these villains were still at large, the "militant girl editor of the Oklahoma Daily," the University's student paper, "issued an editorial challenge for the masked abductors to meet in the union building on the campus this afternoon. None appeared. The student editor compared the position of the college hoodlums to 'hit-and-run drivers.'")[83]

It is probably true that civic organizations and fraternities did actually host such activities, probably in greater numbers than were reported in the press. However, one should still exercise caution in generalizing too hastily based on the small number of overall incidents. Part of the problem here is that the degree to which these have entered the stag film mythology as the primary screening spaces for pornography significantly exceeds the amount and proportion of busts of such places during the 1920s, 1930s, and 1940s; put simply, if these were used so frequently as exhibition spaces, why are they not represented in greater numbers in the litany of arrests? That this is not the case would either indicate

---

[80] *120 Years of American Education: A Statistical Portrait*, Thomas D. Snyder, ed. (Washington, DC: Center for Education Statistics 1993), 65, 76.

[81] "Students Held after 'Obscene' Film Show," *Des Moines Register*, December 4, 1932, 2.

[82] *Courier-Journal*, December 5, 1932, 2.

[83] "Bizzell Wars on D.D.M.C.," *Miami Daily News Record*, December 11, 1932, 1.

that the significance of such spaces to stag exhibition is overstated, or that there is some other factor in play. I tend to assume the latter. The great advantage that these places had over almost any other spot was their privacy. Frats and clubs almost by definition operate within a privately held space, and, while, as a general principle, they always hoped to increase their membership, they tended to draw even their prospective recruits from specific communities within society as a whole. As closed, private societies consisting of relatively few members, these groups could keep stag shows from the prying eyes of the public. Not only would this secrecy sharply decrease the likelihood of police interruption, but in many states, exhibiting pornographic material to a social grouping of adults in a private setting might not even have been illegal.

Somewhat less secure than fraternity or civic group screenings, but surely not any less frequent, were those shows for an audience drawn from a common professional environment. It would seem credible that workplace association was a regular source of connection for an audience, moreso than civic organizations or college fraternities, as the number of people who simply had to work for a living certainly dwarfed those belonging to exclusive clubs. These types of gatherings also varied greatly in scale, from an audience of forty house painters celebrating a colleague's birthday in Brooklyn (at an address listed as "200 Stagg Walk," no less[84]) to a raucous party of 300 volunteer firemen at the Pittsburgh-area Slovak Hall.

The latter case is reported with the sort of journalistic panache that justifies a lengthy quote. Not quite rising to the level of a criminal case, the Slovak Hall incident made the papers due to the hackles it raised with the state liquor board, which reconsidered the hall's fitness for a license to sell alcohol based on this.

> The talk about the scenes in movies they showed at Natrona's Slovak hall got so dirty yesterday that the State Liquor Control Board decided its stomach was upset.
>
> A liquor control board agent had got into Reel No. 2 in his description of the film dealing with the man who was trying to sell the girl a rowing machine when both sides agreed they had heard enough to convince them it was somewhat immoral. Everyone in the room, in fact, looked a little red in the face, even though they were of the male persuasion ....
>
> President John Achkio vowed in his testimony that it was no fault of the Slovak Hall Association that its quarters were used to show obscene films at

---

[84] "House Painter Accused of Having Indecent Film," *Brooklyn Daily Eagle*, November 9, 1940, 2.

a party held by 300 volunteer firemen. He said he didn't know what town the firemen were from, but they were the ones who put on the show.

Bruce Sciotto, deputy attorney general prosecuting the case, accused the organization of being "notorious" for promoting such shows—a charge that Achkio denied.

As Achkio related it, the show that was specifically mentioned was one in which four or five reels of obscene pictures were shown, and Achkio himself had no intimation that such an exhibit was to be staged until he delivered a speech of welcome to the firemen.

Then arose the chairman, he said.

"Boys," said the chairman, "we're going to have some pictures that'll be hotter than the ones you seen last week."[85]

But again, one must consider that screenings associated with a professional gathering were in greater danger of police disruption than those based on membership in a private club. At a workplace, whether office, shop, or factory, the likelihood of invitations to stag shows drifting beyond the circle of men in the know was much greater, and the attention of various busybodies and snitches harder to avoid. There is even some indication of real-life tension between the working-men's groups and the more self-consciously middle-class civic organizations; a defense attorney representing audience members arrested at a screening organized by the UAW-CIO "asserted that 'police can crash that [working class] kind of a party, but they never crash the Elks Clubs because there would be too much backfire.'"[86] However, even professional-class workplaces were not entirely free from unwanted scrutiny.

Just such an arrest at a workplace gathering occurred in 1940, and carried with it a whiff of the greatest pornographic myth—the decadence of one's social betters. In February of that year, approximately 300 employees of the Social Security Board were arrested outside of Baltimore at a classic stag show involving "indecent dances by women performers" as well as "a movie projector and several reels of obscene films."[87] As if to demonstrate the impossibility of keeping a secret in the office, the head of the vice squad said that the raid was brought on by the discovery of "a mimeograph notice that had been distributed in the board's office to employees who bought tickets to the show. It warned that

---

[85] "Slovak Hall Movies Held too Snappy," *Pittsburgh Post Gazette*, April 27, 1939, 15.
[86] "Union Stag Party's Movies Not Obscene, Jury Decides," *Detroit Free Press*, July 18, 1939, 4.
[87] "'Stag' Party," *Kingsport Times*, February 12, 1940, 8.

'headquarters are trying to find out where we are giving these affairs, so please be very careful.'"[88]

Headquarters found out, and were not pleased. Joseph Fey, chairman of the local Social Security Board, said he was "at a loss for words … I don't know what to say. We've tried to pick the best employes [*sic*] we could get—they're from all parts of the country, you know. I don't know whether the civil service regulations cover this thing or not, but you can be sure I'm going to find out. We're going to get to the bottom of it—quickly."[89]

As a taxpayer-funded agency, the Social Security Office would become the target of a very specific brand of ire for this incident.

The public resentment normally reserved for those of superior social position began, in this period, to attach itself as well to those whose connections to public and state agencies were seen to afford them an escape from the consequences of immoral or antisocial behavior. Reports of such sentiments would become more frequent as the bureaucratization of American society continued apace. One early example is the 1929 meeting of Wisconsin state highway officials in Madison, which was widely reported to have degenerated into debauchery after hours, with attendees indulging, by at least one account, in "booze parties, noise and hilarity, an obscene motion picture film and other disgraceful features."[90] Transportation fees and a daily stipend had been paid to each member to attend this conference; the *Oshkosh Daily Northwestern* bristled at this, suggesting that, since so many attended only for an opportunity for "'cutting loose' and 'making whoopee' after school hours are over," the state "make attendance optional and require the delegates to pay their own expense."[91] Rhetorically, however, the Social Security Board incident seems to be a decisive shift. As far away as Helena, Montana, there could be found editors inveighing against the loose morals of these allegedly privileged bureaucrats.

> All involved were employes [*sic*] of the Social Security service. Of the affair itself, it may be said that lewd dancing by naked women probably was the least offensive feature. Forbidden movies were seized. These things are bad enough when indulged in by ordinary citizens; when employees of the nation, especially employees in an agency that would not exist were it not for this crisis, are

---

[88] Ibid., *sic*.
[89] Ibid., 1 *sic*.
[90] "Having a Good Time at Road School," *Oshkosh Daily Northwestern*, February 2, 1929, 10.
[91] Ibid.

involved, it is time to use a broom. The average taxpayer will not get much of a glow at the thought of his money going to naked dancers from the underworld and in rent of obscene films.[92]

Fascination with the scandalous behavior of the decadent elites is of course a perennial of mass-market journalism, though the 1920s and 1930s may even be something of a golden age in this regard. These kinds of stories often concentrated on adultery, divorce, drunkenness, drug abuse, or some manner of criminal activity occurring amongst the smart set, who, it is implied, ought to know better. Stag films of course make an occasional appearance in many of these stories; in fact, it is possible that many more readers were introduced to the very concept of pornographic cinema by the shenanigans of the well-heeled than through the much more numerous raids of union-hall screenings. In 1931, for example, actor Pat O'Brien (who had just found success in the original cinematic adaptation of *The Front Page*) was arrested at a party that had gotten out of hand at a fellow actor's house. The Associated Press account of the evening contrasts the rough-housing of the actors in attendance—who immediately attacked the police as soon as they knocked at the front door—with the somewhat more refined quality of the decadence inside, where were found "a score of fashionably gowned women and men in evening dress drinking and gathered around gambling tables. Roulette wheels, dice and a gallon of liquor were seized. A motion picture projection machine containing a film, which police said depicted nude subjects, also was taken."[93] This incident did not include the civic dimension of some of the bureaucratic scandals mentioned above, but was able to generate interest all the same.

Probably the most interesting blue-blood-adjacent scandal from this era involving stag films, even if only tangentially, was the ongoing Sallade divorce case. This was a long, court-mediated split between Edith June Sallade and her husband Willey Ulysses Sallade, the latter of whom had been a chauffeur to Pierre Dupont and, on leaving his service, had received a generous compensation package. Edith had sued for divorce on the grounds of neglect—her husband had apparently taken an early, solo retirement on their honeymoon and continued this pattern for years afterward; or, as an early lede had put it, Ms. Sallade had suffered "too few kisses and too many locked bedroom doors."[94] Mr. Sallade

---

[92] "Baltimore Scandal," *Independent Record*, February 15, 1940, 6 *sic*.
[93] "Hollywood Party Is Ended in Court," *Palm Beach Post*, March 1, 1931, 1.
[94] "Wife Asks Divorce from Du Pont Aide," *Philadelphia Inquirer*, October 17, 1935, 3.

countersued, charging that his wife was ultimately after his fortune only, and had spent most of her married days entertaining male guests in an improper fashion, including with pornographic movies. The accusations he lobbed at his spouse were several, but the most colorful involved his walking in on one such screening.

> Then he told how on one occasion he visited a police conference in Washington— police work being his hobby—and returned home unexpectedly, to find his wife, two neighbors and a stranger, giggling over what he described as "obscene" films shown in the basement. He said he stood in his socks upstairs and listened while his wife joked with the neighbors.[95]

That they would warrant a mention in these stories (and other similar ones) seems to indicate that the stag had, so to speak, arrived as a type of vice, similar to liquor and gambling. As has been amply demonstrated, they were often found together in raids; this is probably an effect of Prohibition enforcement, which created an environment in which the vices would tend to attract each other and flourish.

This new awareness of the existence of stag films came about during a bout of great popular agitation for movie censorship, which would reach a fever pitch by the early 1930s due to lax enforcement of the Hays-administered Production Code. The pressure for some sort of regulation of the content of commercial films can probably be understood as a separate phenomenon from concern over actual pornographic films, both in this era and later. Concerned citizens often referred to Hollywood films they found particularly egregious as "obscene films," echoing the language of police and prosecutors (and journalists) who came in contact with hard-core stags.[96] Some of this vagueness was probably intentional on the part of reformers, meant to blur the genuine distinctions between pornography and the ribaldry of (say) *Trouble in Paradise*, and thus to mobilize some of the public consternation over the former against the latter. But not only were pornographic films not in the public mind in the early 1930s in a way that they would be later on, these critiques were probably rooted in an unease, if not outright anxiety, over the wide reach of the American film industry, which, in the course of fewer than two decades had installed theaters in all but the smallest and most remote towns. Though the evidence does suggest

---

[95] "Denounces Wife as 'Gold Digger,'" *Philadelphia Inquirer*, October 18, 1935, 5.

[96] See Amy H. Croughton, "Some Say," *Courier-News*, April 25, 1933, 6, or "The Screen," *The Houston Herald*, May 11, 1933, 4 for examples of this.

that the distribution of stag films became more sophisticated and widespread during this period, they were not anywhere near as accessible to the average American, and, furthermore, required that the viewer either owned a projector or was connected to some social group which did. In any case, regulating stag films in the same way as mainstream films would have been pointless, as no producers would have even bothered to submit their films either to the scrutiny of Joseph Breen or the various municipal or state censorship councils.

If the drive for reform in various aspects of American life was ascendant in some ways, it's important to remember that though these forces were politically and socially powerful, they by no means held complete sway over public opinion. As early as 1925, an editorial in an Arizona newspaper could dissect the recent objections of some reformers to "immorality" in movies.

> "Immoral" in America has come to mean anything that has anything to do with sex. Show a picture in which sex is treated in any way but the simpering manner of a maiden lady of 40 holding her hands in front of her eyes while she peeps eagerly through her fingers at the most sacred fact of life, and you're condemned as being "immoral."[97]

This is not necessarily a full-throated defense of unbridled free-speech libertarianism—the anonymous editorial writer might indeed have blanched at genuine hard-core pornography—but it certainly indicates that reformers' ideas about sexual propriety did not enjoy anything like complete hegemony over society.

This strain of worldly toleration never quite disappeared during this era, even in the face of the more anguished displays of public prudishness. Regular expression of this attitude can be found in journalists' accounts of the many obscene film raids that occurred in the years immediately preceding the Second World War. If anything, stag films would often be treated in the press with a sort of jocular irreverence. Some examples of this have already been seen, but there was no shortage of reporters who, assigned to cover a recent local stag bust, took the opportunity to channel their inner Ring Lardner. Note, for example, that the *Milwaukee Journal*'s coverage of an interrupted screening attended by 200 members of the Master Builders Association—in town to attend the organization's national convention—is completely free of any hint of indignation at the audience's low morals; instead, several column inches are devoted to a

---

[97] "Truth Is Beauty, Beauty, Truth," *Arizona Daily Star*, May 27, 1925, 10 *sic*.

description of the hapless, anarchic nature of the incident, which quickly spread out from the makeshift screening room and into the surrounding neighborhood.

> With Broadway a milling crowd, the police shouting directions and orders, and the visiting builders trying to hide their identity and voice their indignation at the same time, a group of newspaper photographers arrived and the booming of flashlight guns added to the gaiety of the scene.
>
> The club is next door to the quarters of Engine Company 1 and one door removed from the county jail and less than half a block from police headquarters. Sleeping firemen threw up the sash and begged the crowd to be quiet and let them sleep, but they couldn't command attention. Then an alarm came in and the rush of fire apparatus and the sound of bells and sirens added to the din.
>
> The noise woke up Sheriff [Charles] Schallitz and dressing hurriedly he came out and took up his station in front of the county jail where he made audible remarks about what a shame it was to break up a business men's convention that way and stop them from having a little fun. The tired business men heard him and his remarks prompted a cheer and a hurrah for Schallitz. Charley bowed and smiled.[98]

Though pornography was certainly frowned upon in general, it was often the case that no particular stigma appears to have been attached to those who distributed or exhibited it (though this charity might not have been extended to on-camera performers). Many times throughout the course of my research I have come across stories of men who had mailed or projected an obscene film, were caught, fulfilled some service to void his debt to the community, and then re-entered polite society without any lasting concern over their crimes thereafter. The example of Harry Heskett can stand for many other similar cases. Arrested in 1929 along with an audience of about 100 men at the Willow Brook Grove club, he was officially charged with "possessing obscene and contraband films" and arranging for "dances by seven Cleveland women." The news article in the *Akron Beacon-Journal* covering this particular event did not neglect to mention that "Heskett has been arrested once previously on a charge

---

[98] "Builders' Stag Party Raided," *Milwaukee Journal*, February 4, 1928, 2. A few weeks later, the Chief of Police, stung from criticism of the raid, had arranged for a screening of the confiscated films to "an audience of business, civic and church leaders" in order to demonstrate the nature of the offense, only to be told shortly before the scheduled date by the district attorney that such a show would be a violation of the law. In typically dry *Milwaukee Journal* fashion, the paper made sure to mention that "a considerable audience had planned to accept the invitation to attend the showings, not more than three or four sending regrets." See "Action Would Not Be Legal, Wengert Says," *Milwaukee Journal*, February 8, 1928, 1.

of exhibiting indecent movies." Confiscated in this raid was "a $350 projecting machine and three obscene films from Heskett. Heskett valued the films at $300 each."[99] After receiving a $50 fine (subsequently lowered to $25 after some bureaucratic maneuvering). Heskett seems, by all subsequent accounts, to have returned to the normal life of a solid citizen, with his name appearing many times in the *Beacon Journal* in notices about various civic functions and social events. He shows up most frequently in updates on the Barberton East High School golf team, of which he was the coach; he died in 1942, and his obituary makes no mention of his earlier legal troubles. His previous association with ribald entertainment didn't seem to have inspired any special concern among the community over his capacity to control himself in public, or that he was too contaminated with moral turpitude to claim the right to participate in local politics, business, or society.

Nevertheless, as reports of stag screenings became more commonplace, the social pushback began to stir. Pornography was not only supposedly becoming more prevalent, but the very case against it, and the particular reasons for why it was a uniquely malign force, were evolving. One common objection that was beginning to gain purchase was the fear that pornographic films could inspire sex crimes. Casting the movies as a spur for antisocial behavior was not a new phenomenon. The Motion Picture Production Code itself banned any depiction of criminal activity (such as burglary) specific enough that it might function as advice to the criminally inclined. Here, under a similar kind of logic, stag films were supposed to have driven men to commit sexual assault; this despite the fact that relatively few surviving stags depict clearly nonconsensual encounters (in any case, it was the sexual explicitness of stags per se, rather than any single depiction of sexual assault or rape, that had been the substance of moralistic criticism). The commissioner of Pennsylvania's State Police, announcing in 1940 a renewed effort to stop the flow of "obscene literature and films," linked the prevalence of such material to a "31 per cent increase in rape over the nation in the past five years."[100] In a similar vein, a district judge presiding over the sentencing of several men indicted for trafficking in various types of obscene material, including film, harangued the defendants after hearing their pleas for leniency. "What about the harm this business is doing to young people of the

[99] "County Squad Raids Obscene Film Show," *Akron Beacon Journal*, July 20, 1929, 5.
[100] "Sex Crimes Draw Activity," *Indiana Gazette*, April 22, 1940, 2.

country—what about the criminals it makes? When you read of the horrible attacks around the country you begin to realize where the offenders get their ideas."[101] This was, at the time, a fairly novel theory for the harms of pornography; compare with the grand jury in the 1928 Larivee case, mentioned above, who stopped midway through their screening of the forbidden films not out of concern for their power to control their own behavior, but out of a more general fear that "witnessing the score of alleged obscene motion pictures confiscated here by the postoffice department would corrupt them."[102] The danger of sexually explicit films in that case was purely moral; fewer than fifteen years later, they were held to have a quasi-hypnotic, subliminal power.

These anxieties would not disappear during the war, and nor would the trade in pornographic films. Both would in fact continue to evolve, responding to each other in what would prove to be a pivotal if tumultuous time for each.

The technological advance of the substandard gauges was probably the single biggest boost to the spread of pornographic films in the United States and responsible for the most dramatic change in its status until the *Stanley* decision of 1969. From the wide press coverage that came about as a result we can learn much about the way in which these films were shown, and about who exactly went to see them. But I also hope that I have made a case here for the consideration of other sources of information besides those which directly mention stag films. Although the practices of itinerant projectionists or amateur cinema clubs may, strictly speaking, be tangential to the activity of underground pornographers, I think that considering the wider context of film culture can only enrich our understanding of the stag scene. This works in the other direction as well: to truly understand the scope of amateur cinema, it's important to consider it in even its most disreputable form, one which simultaneously broke the law in many states by its very existence, but which also attracted audiences that the boosters in the Amateur Cinema League could only have dreamed of.

---

[101] "Sentences," *Cincinnati Enquirer*, February 15, 1941, 22.
[102] "So-Called Obscene Films too Bad for Federal Grand Jury," *San Bernardino County Sun*, November 24, 1928, 2.

3

Stag Films during the War Years: 1941 to 1945

The war's most obvious effect on the trade in pornography was not a direct intervention in the practices of producers, distributors, or exhibitors, but on the (potential) audience, which was effectively split in two after the attack on Pearl Harbor. Mass conscription and largely successful efforts to encourage volunteers meant that a significant portion of the male population of the United States were sent from their home communities and into the regimented, bureaucratic world of the military (whether or not they were stationed in an actual theater of war, they were still removed from the structure of their old life—family, work, religious observance, region, ethnic community, etc.). This would seem to be the most dramatic possible upturning of their old lives and habits, severing any connection to their previous social world, including the typical rituals of initiation into proper masculine habits—in which stag parties often played a part. Though it would by no means rank among the worst of these disruptions for the men affected by this situation, it would seem logical to imagine that this movement of men would have had serious consequences for the stag film market; Eric Schaefer ventures that "we might also assume that at least some of the customer base for adult films went into military service where their hobby would have been curtailed."[1] And yet, it is worth recalling that "stag," once again, means "men only," and that the military in this era was far more segregated by gender than was any part of civilian life. In this chapter I will investigate the extent to which it is possible or likely that stag films were shown to men in the active duty military. Rumors to this effect have been aired in the past, though, as per usual with these kinds of stories, no evidence has been presented. I will try to get as

---

[1] Eric Schaefer, "Plain Brown Wrapper: Adult Films for the Home Market, 1930–1969," in *Looking Past the Screen: Case Studies in American Film History and Method*, ed. John Lewis and Eric Smoodin (Durham, NC: Duke University Press, 2007), 209.

close to the bottom of this question as possible, while suggesting avenues for further research.

The other audience for stags was, of course, the remaining civilian men, who for one reason or another managed to avoid (or were rejected by) the service. Though obviously not as directly affected by the war as were those in active service, they still found themselves in a drastically different world from the one they had inhabited before, with both a greater degree of freedom in some regards and greater deprivation in others. As this remaining rump of the (potential) stag audience weathered the storm of the war, the active producers, distributors, and exhibitors found themselves in new working conditions also. Previous scholarship has conjectured on the nature of these changes, though, as before, their conclusions have always suffered for being overly speculative and thinly sourced. I will attempt here to see exactly what can be learned about how the producers and sellers of these movies coped with their new conditions, and how—or if—they were able to put their films before what remained of their audience. Suffice to say for now that the stag business did change significantly during this time, but largely in ways that have not been noted by many other historians of pornography.

Paul Fussell has characterized the life of the serviceman as one of "drinking far too much, copulating too little," though he did admit that the dismal erotic opportunities available to him during his time in the military were "what front-line troops would stigmatize as a rear-echelon problem." Faced with more proximate concerns, soldiers in combat tended not to fret over this—Fussell assured his readers that "the front was the one wartime place that was sexless."[2]

But this may not have been entirely true. There is reason to believe that military life could, under particular circumstances, distill the sexually charged homosociality that was an undercurrent of American society at that time down to its essence, creating a subculture much more finely receptive to such tensions than was its civilian counterpart. Though writing specifically of the measures taken by gay male soldiers to fit into an environment at once both aggressively masculine and physically intimate, Allan Berube's observations on the bonding functions of sexualized rhetoric common to that setting describe something essential about all of military life.

---

[2] Paul Fussell, *Wartime: The Experience of War, 1939–1945* (New York: Oxford University Press, 1989), 108.

To cope with sexual anxieties during basic training, male recruits pieced together their own sexual culture. They posted pinups of women, told sex stories, and used sexual slang to adapt to what Menninger called "a very abnormal life and living arrangement." Sex jokes heterosexualized everyday activities and brought into the open the recruit's private discomfort with the homosexual milieu of military life.[3]

Even mild displays of eroticized homosociality such as those served to reinforce the masculine atmosphere of military life (as well as displacing whatever homosexual anxiety might have accompanied the sudden physical closeness new recruits found themselves in). This echoes nothing so much as Williams's conception of the stag audience, which, aroused by but also pointedly denied satisfaction from the spectacle before their very eyes, "must seek satisfaction outside the purely visual terms of the film—whether in masturbation, in actual sexual relations, or by channeling sexual arousal into communal wisecracking or verbal ejaculation of the 'homosocial' variety."[4] If that dynamic were to be found in a military setting, then such an environment, already receptive to the way in which erotica could instill a sense of communal male bonding, would seem to be the ideal place for stag films.

However, the rigidity, discipline, surveillance, and geographical remoteness of military life meant that procuring such material was no simple thing. Fussell confirms that proper pornography was not easy to get ahold of, driving desperate Marines to resort to compulsively re-reading a communal copy of Kathleen Winsor's novel *Forever Amber*, "the dirtiest available on their ship."[5] Pornographic films do receive an off-handed mention in Fussell's memoir, but as something "viewable only at stag parties"—that is, in civilian life.[6] If even decent literary smut was so hard to come by, the odds of stag films somehow sneaking into a combat zone seem to have been slim indeed.

Nevertheless, the possibility is an intriguing one to consider. No system of prohibition is perfect, and the labyrinthine bureaucracy of the military may have inadvertently presented opportunities for restricted items to be smuggled in. An office known as the Overseas Motion Picture Service, in collaboration

[3]   Allan Berube, *Coming Out under Fire: The History of Gay Men and Women in World War II* (Chapel Hill: University of North Carolina Press, 2010), 37.

[4]   Linda Williams, *Hard Core: Power, Pleasure, and the Frenzy of the Visible* (Berkeley: University of California Press, 1989), 74.

[5]   Fussell, *Wartime*, 107.

[6]   Ibid., 105.

with the Hollywood film industry, distributed prints of current releases to every
part of the theater of war, from every supply depot to very near to the front. The
otherwise fairly stolid official history of the Signal Corps describes the breadth
of this operation with uncharacteristic flourish:

> Unquestionably the greatest source of comfort and relaxation for soldiers
> everywhere was the nightly movie. All theater commanders unhesitatingly
> granted air priority for shipment of films. On the grassy hillsides of Italy, in
> the mud of Germany, in the steamy heat of Pacific jungle outposts, wherever
> soldiers rested for the night the Army shows went on. Sometimes the screen
> went up in a half-ruined building, and quite often on the side of the mobile
> motion picture service van. Okinawa, Iwo Jima, Manila, and Saipan all had their
> own film exchanges within days after the beachheads were taken.[7]

Most crucially for the topic at hand, the wide reach of these exhibition
services ensured that projection equipment was readily available—the Army
had purchased 22,000 "standard commercial 16mm sound projectors, which
possessed the essential characteristics of light weight, portability, and simplicity
of operation."[8] As crucially, the equipment was accompanied by a projectionist
who had been specifically trained and outfitted for the job by the Signal Corps
(each had been issued a toolkit replete with, among other items, "a Technical
Manual, Lubrication Chart, camel hair brush, oil can, and a supply of light
lubricating oil").[9]

Exhibition resources for small-gauge film were as readily available in the
military as they were in civilian life, if not moreso; the same, however, could
hardly be said for pornographic films. But even if these could, hypothetically, be
screened, acquiring hard-core stag films in such remote locations would not be
a simple thing. Certainly, sending a reel through the military's own mail service,
which inspected every package and censored each letter, would be out of the
question, and the OMPS film distribution service was, in true martial fashion,
exceedingly baroque, requiring every transaction to be logged,[10] seeming to
leave little room for any sort of unauthorized transaction. Then again, the sheer
numbers of films moving through the various libraries—43,306 features and

[7]   George Raynor Thompson and Dixie R. Harris, *The Signal Corps: The Outcome (Mid-1943 through 1945)* (Washington, DC: Office of the Chief of Military History, US Army, 1966), 561.

[8]   Ibid., 562.

[9]   Capt. Edwin B. Levinson, "Operation and Maintenance of Projectors in the Field," *Business Screen*, Vol. VII, No. 1 (December 1945), 64.

[10] See Thompson and Harris, *The Signal Corps: The Outcome*, 558–62.

33,236 shorts, by the Signal Corps's own count[11]—would appear to present a favorable environment for sneaking a forbidden film into the herd. After all, military supply chains were notoriously subject to theft and fraud during the war, so it is not inconceivable to imagine that an ambitious GI could circumvent the regulations.

The conditions for such films being shown, then, clearly did exist, even if that in itself is not proof that that occurred. Definitive documentation of any particular screening is, obviously, difficult to come by. In James J. Fahey's *Pacific War Diary 1942–1945*, during a lull in the action in May 1943, Fahey, a seaman in the Pacific, observes that "we have movies at night now on the ship. Some of the fellows went to a smoker on one of the carriers."[12] The point made in an earlier chapter about the term "stag"—which refers only, in a literal sense, to an all-male gathering, and doesn't necessarily denote the presence of pornographic films in and of itself—also stands for Fahey's use of "smoker" here. Two things about these seemingly tossed-off lines suggest to me the possibility that such films might have been present, however. First, using the word "smoker" as a way to refer simply to a gathering of men would be redundant in this particular case, as Fahey wrote those words while on a light carrier in the western Pacific Ocean—everyone on board was a man. Second, the sequence of sentences which puts the report of the smoker directly after the mention of film exhibition—his first of that topic in the diary—suggests that perhaps the two observations are linked, not simply coincidentally side-by-side.

Any other evidence which exists for screenings of stag films in a military setting will likely be found in oral histories, diaries, and other direct testimony of the soldiers themselves; the sources I have relied on to this point, mainly newspapers and magazines, will certainly have nothing to say on this topic. It is probable that this question belongs to the realm of micro-history, as any incidents that might have occurred were probably isolated, and of little value as a means of generalizing about the behavior and habits of the military as a whole.

If there is only so much that can be said about stag film screenings in areas under direct military control, the situation improves somewhat when we return our attention to civilian life. Whatever trouble they may or may not have had procuring pornographic films in under military society, soldiers could find them at home just as easily as could civilians. In fact, producers and distributors of

---

[11] Ibid., 559.
[12] James J. Fahey, *Pacific War Diary, 1942–1945* (Boston, MA: Houghton Mifflin, 2003), 33.

stags seem to have sought G.I.'s out as a special audience. In James Jones's novel *Whistle*, the events of which were based in part on his own war experiences, the injured soldier Strange, recuperating in a Tennessee hospital, broods on having "stared heatedly and hungrily at all the photographs and drawings of wide-open vaginas that were available just about everywhere across America in his youth. He had sat and watched the stag films that always, somehow or other, found their way to all the NCO clubs across the country."[13] Jones's sentences here are ostensibly fictional, but both the rest of the novel and the rest of his work carefully cultivate a self-consciously blunt realism, especially as regards the conditions of the war. If this passage doesn't refer to a particular incident (as in Fahey's account), it may be provisionally accepted as a reliable description of a general situation.

Other, real-life events give some weight to Jones's literary embellishments. It so happens that the enlisted man's appetite for lewd entertainment, including but not limited to stag films, was such that the Army itself took notice, and made efforts to clamp down on the new vogue for obscenity, often working in concert with cities designated as "war centers." In 1942, *Variety* reported that the Michigan Liquor Control Commission was collaborating with the Army to this end, releasing a joint statement promising that "in war centers shows with rough stuff, even spots that permit 'gossiping,' will be prosecuted."[14] Chairman of the Commission Ralph Thomas, intriguingly, linked the sudden popularity of vulgar shows to the booming war economy. "'Because people have more money there seems to be a tendency to think that the best way to get it is with off-color shows … Well, the night club boys have to learn we're in a war and that public morality as well as morale is an essential in winning it.'"[15] In Thomas's own rhetoric we can see a recognition that social dislocation, general anxiety, and economic prosperity could disrupt the sexual mores that, to that point, had seemed to be unshakeable.

Aside from their usual habitats, stags in this period appear more often in areas catering to soldiers, or at least to those workers involved in the broader war effort. Both the mobilization of the military and the rapid expansion of industries related to the war caused the population of cities across the United States to balloon, as people poured in to follow work or marching orders. The

---

[13] James Jones, *Whistle* (New York: Delta Trade Paperbacks, 1999), 191.
[14] "509 Club Det., Fined for 'Obscene' Shows," *Variety*, October 14, 1942, 45.
[15] Ibid.

new arrivals, flush with disposable income and free of the social supervision of home, may have been soldiers or may have been laborers, but in either case, stag exhibitors saw an audience. These were the men on hand at a screening for shipyard workers in Philadelphia,[16] for a party of war workers in Los Angeles (who were charged $1.50 admission),[17] and in at least eight separate establishments in Pittsburgh, which were subject to a mass raid in 1943. As in the Michigan incident above, this last event was the result of coordination between the municipal Liquor Control Board and military police; a spokesman for the latter "promised to continue to aid the drive [against obscenity] with military police assistance in the raids as a protection to service men."[18] Throughout the war, the homeland authorities appeared to be as committed to defending the serviceman from threats to his moral integrity as his commanding officers were to protecting him from bullets and bombs; both were seen as essential to victory.

All over the United States, the occasion of the war inspired new vigor in the struggle against lewd entertainment. Along with Detroit, Los Angeles also made a public commitment to fighting vice,[19] and Milwaukee passed a new municipal ordinance against "the showing of vulgar, obscene or indecent reproductions or films," which was additionally justified with a prediction that fines issued in the course of enforcing this measure would net the city an extra $75,000 annually.[20] Assuming that this forecast was made in good faith, it seems to indicate that the scale of the obscene film trade had grown recently, and that previous efforts had done nothing to mitigate it. There may have been an element of simple moral panic to these new measures, but it was one which appears to have been addressing a real state of affairs.

These cities' anxiety over the proliferation of pornography found an echo in Washington DC, where the FBI, under the auspices of Director Hoover, established a unit specifically to investigate interstate transportation of obscene material. Though federal law enforcement had pursued pornographers before—most notably the postal inspector's office, which was mentioned in the last chapter—not until the war years did any agency devote regular resources to the matter, creating a specific department for this particular violation. This is

[16] "Four Held after Raid on Lewd Show," *Philadelphia Inquirer*, November 21, 1942, 19.
[17] "Immoral Film Causes Arrest," *Los Angeles Times*, July 20, 1943, 6.
[18] "70 Arrested in Liquor Raids," *Pittsburgh Press*, February 5, 1944, 1 *sic*.
[19] "Drive against Obscenity Started in Los Angeles," *Motion Picture Herald*, July 18, 1942, 39.
[20] "Seeking Licenses for Sound Machines," *Motion Picture Herald*, June 27, 1942, 54.

important for two reasons. First, from this point forward, the FBI will be an active force in the nexus of pornography in the United States; that is, in the relationship between producers, consumers, distributors, and exhibitors which made up the trade in pornography. Legal prohibition and, consequently, law enforcement was always a part of this structure, but this mostly consisted of either local police efforts, or isolated campaigns from national bodies in response to particular events (see again the PO's work). The entry of the FBI is significant because it is the beginning of a centralized strategy to combat the spread of porn in a systematic way. This involved not only chasing individual violators, though they certainly did that, but also studying, understanding, and chronicling the ecosystem of the trade, in order to fashion a more effective strategy against it. This would lead to a nationalization and centralization not only in basic enforcement, but also in the social and legal arguments for the continued suppression of this kind of material; compare this with the largely local efforts which occurred within states and municipalities up to this point— authorities prosecuting pornographers in Milwaukee and New York didn't need to have been operating from a consistent legal logic. Beginning in this period, the FBI, and federal prosecutors, did; the ultimate result of this, however, was that, once it became clear what their arguments were, those accused of violating obscenity statutes could respond with legal strategies of their own. Secondly, and of more immediate concern here, the creation of the Obscene Unit also resulted in the founding of a rich source of documentation.

The full story of this initiative can be found in Douglas Charles's *The FBI's Obscene File: J. Edgar Hoover and the Bureau's Crusade against Smut*, which is highly recommended as a case study of the Bureau's efforts to not only suppress sexual deviance of any kind, with no distinctions drawn between, say, production of pornographic films and the work of the Mattachine Society. This file's primary interest for my purposes is as a document of an early attempt by law enforcement to both study the ways in which obscene items made their way across the United States and then to try to walk them back to a recognizable source. The information obtained by the Bureau, and the ways they obtained it, is of some significance to my project as a whole, and so will require a bit of a digression.

The papers of the so-called Obscene File document the Bureau's campaign to collect and analyze samples of pornographic material from police agencies across the United States, as a means of determining the ultimate sources and parties responsible. The basic strategy of their investigations was to exploit the agency's cross-continental reach, as well as its bureaucratic centralization, to allow it to draw disparate pieces of evidence into comparative relationships.

A memo from 1944 explains the methods behind this activity.

> As specimens were received in the Laboratory from different geographical areas and various jurisdictional sources, they were compared with each other with the idea of securing leads as to the number and location of manufacturers and distribution centers .... Specimens sent in from one jurisdiction were identified with those sent in from other jurisdictions in entirely different cases by means of the printing. In other words, in unrelated cases under investigation, evidence was found that the crimes were part of the same conspiracy to distribute the products of the same printer.[21]

In contrast to the more haphazard pursuits of local law enforcement, this was the first effort from an organization which had both the broad geographical reach necessary to find samples of forbidden material wherever they appeared and sufficient internal centralization to catalog, describe, and make accessible (to investigating agents within the Bureau) a collection which would quickly grow to a point which would have overwhelmed any smaller institution (and would very nearly become too much for even the FBI to handle).

As one might expect, a concerted effort by the highest law enforcement agency in the United States to document the production of pornographic material has left behind evidence which is of matchless historical value. Sadly, some gaps are still present. What remains extant is the administrative portion of the file, which, as Charles explains in his own work, "provides information about FBI officials' policy decisions regarding obscenity and pornography targeting and about creating and maintaining the sensitive and centralized Obscene File itself."[22] The other part of the Obscene File consisted of the actual materials collected—films, books, cartoons, etc.—as well as the lab reports associated directly with those objects, which would have likely contained the greatest amount of information on a particular item. By the early 1990s, these parts of the collection were known as the Pornographic Materials Reference File [PMRF]; a memo from that late era admits that, while "the file was used to help establish Interstate Transportation of Obscene Materials (ITOM) violations," by then it had "been reduced to a library of obscene materials since ITOM matters are now

---

[21] Memo, E.P. Coffey to E.A. Tamm, August 26, 1944, FBI 80-662, 1.
[22] Douglas Charles, *The FBI's Obscene File: J. Edgar Hoover and the Bureau's Crusade against Smut* (Lawrence: University Press of Kansas, 2012), 4.

all but nonexistent except for child pornography cases; however, the material submitted does not require comparison to the PMRF."[23] Since the vast majority of the accumulated physical holdings of the file were of no further investigative use (as the material being held no longer violated any obscenity laws), all such items were incinerated—a memo dated from March 4, 1993, distributed to the Bureau as a whole, announced the collection's imminent destruction and advised that any part of it which an agent wished to save was to be requested "NO LATER THAN APRIL 30, 1993."[24] Despite the loss of what would have been a great historical resource, important primary information can still be recovered from the remaining administrative file.

The records of the Bureau seem to confirm that the increase in police efforts against pornographic films during the war was based at least in part on the fairly robust activity of the stag trade during that time. As their records only go back to 1942, it's impossible to make an exact comparison to how many films they may have seized before the war; however, a 1944 memo assessing the state of the Bureau's collection notes that 400 films had been submitted, 200 of which were unique items. The memo also mentions the presence of thousands of other items retained in the file, including cartoon books and photographs; the then-recent (1944) arrest of Joseph Bennett Harris alone, who ran a significant printing operation in New York, had led to the seizure of "8 million lewd pictures and cartoons," 10,391 of which were forwarded to the FBI's lab for comparison with other items.[25] Numbers such as these would seem to indicate that the market for smut of all sorts was still a very strong one, and that the war did not seriously inhibit the trade in general.

This sharp increase in police activity against pornographers came about at a time when, according to some historians' accounts, the stag film trade was actually in a state of decline. Whatever effect the combined efforts of local law enforcement and the FBI might have had, the war is assumed to have been the major culprit here; both Knight and Alpert and also Thompson have observed that, like all Americans, stag filmmakers were operating in an environment of sudden deprivation, with supplies of both film and projection equipment drying up quickly at the onset of hostilities. Just as shortages of rubber and gasoline led to consumer rationing, which in turn led to decreased automobile use, so, the

---

[23] Airtel, Director Louis Freeh to All SACS, March 5, 1993, FBI 80-662.
[24] Ibid.
[25] Memo, F.L. Price to Mr. Rosen, August 25, 1944, 1.

hypothesis goes, did the production of lewd films decline as these producers found themselves hemmed in by similar shortages.

As with most historical claims about pornographic cinema in this era, very little can be verified by any definitive evidence. Paucity of information on this era of stag production is an unavoidable challenge of the investigation; the scholars of the twenty-first century must pick their way among the stray facts, urban legends, and archival scraps and, from these, build something we hope to be of lasting value. Working in this tradition, the previous historians have, of necessity, come to their picture of the wartime stag scene by judicious review of more circumstantial evidence.

Thus, Knight and Alpert, and Thompson, assume that the sacrifices made by American consumers during the war extended to amateur filmmakers, who felt the sting in their own ways. This seems to have been largely true. Photographic equipment, and specifically motion picture equipment, became quite scarce indeed after the beginning of the conflict between the United States and the Axis powers, for all of the reasons one might expect. Most of the industrial capacity used to produce the necessary cinematic machinery was diverted to more immediate, military concerns, thus depressing supply. The Signal Corps historian writes:

> Eastman stopped making cameras in 1941–1942, and began again only in a limited way in 1943. Ansco stopped soon after Pearl Harbor and throughout the better part of the war produced no photographic material except paper and film .... Lens-making facilities were particularly small, and late in 1942 the Army-Navy Lens Board was set up to effect a fair distribution of the small supply.[26]

Not only was the motion picture equipment itself valuable to the military for surveillance and intelligence (as well as to screen films for men in uniform), but the kind of light industry required for their manufacture was badly needed in other areas.

Even outfits which continued to make motion picture equipment for the amateur market found that much of their stock was going to the Signal Corps, which had recently expanded to take on extensive new responsibilities such as shooting footage for news, propaganda, and intelligence purposes. That department's lack of prewar planning, followed by its rapid, fevered expansion

---

[26] George Raynor Thompson, Dixie R. Harris, Pauline M. Oakes, and Dulany Terrett, *The Signal Corps: The Test (December 1941 to July 1943)* (Washington, DC: Center of Military History, US Army, 1957), 410.

after 1941 led to something of a scramble for machinery wherever it could be found. The Corps' historian explains:

> Although standard commercial products were used almost exclusively, there was seldom an adequate supply of even these on dealers' shelves. For many months private owners were being urged to sell appropriate items to the Signal Corps. Persons from forty-four states made offers and more than 1,000 purchase orders were placed early in the war for privately owned cameras, such as Mitchell, Bell and Howell, Akeley, and Eyemo 35mm. motion picture cameras; Cine-Kodak Special and Filmo 16mm. cameras; and still picture cameras such as Speed Graphic; also for tripods, exposure meters, range finders, pack adapters, and so on.[27]

Though mechanical hardware was the main resource sought after by the army, film itself was also needed, and control of its production fell under the sway of the authorities. "Film was officially classified as a scarce commodity and as such it was controlled and allocated by the War Production Board."[28] The Board meant business; though its mandate was simply to regulate the production and use of certain essential materials, its power could be used for purely punitive purposes as well. A group of stag producers arrested in California in 1945—who will be re-appearing later on in this chapter—found themselves facing more than just the usual obscenity charges, as "War Production Board officials and agents of the Federal Bureau of Investigation were reported interested in the arrests to determine whether rationed film is being used for illegal purposes."[29]

This seems to confirm the basics of the deprivation hypothesis, but it is one thing to note the changing circumstances throughout the country, and quite another to prove that these particular factors influenced stag filmmakers. Is there anything to indicate that the pornographers of the homefront changed their practices? In the face of circumstances that had very suddenly become very modest indeed, how did stag filmmakers react?

I have made the point several times during this book that the activities of stag filmmakers were, by design, undocumented, or at least were intended to be so. To discover broader trends among them at a certain time, then, we must turn to other sources that might illuminate the conditions of similar groups. Here it may be useful to remember, again, that stag films were amateur films,

---

[27]   Ibid., 408.
[28]   Ibid., 410.
[29]   "Complaints Pouring in on Lewd Photo Charges," *Los Angeles Times*, April 5, 1945, 7 *sic.*

and that the activities of (bona fide) amateur filmmakers of this period were extensively documented. It must always be kept in mind that the makers of stags were operating under material conditions—in terms of access to cameras, projectors, film, and other equipment—identical to those amateurs competing for the Hiram Percy Maxim Award. It would seem, therefore, that, if production was affected by the war for the latter group, we might assume that the same state of affairs prevailed for the former.

Some broad sense of the effect of wartime circumstances might be gleaned from a survey of film-themed publications from the period. That a magazine like *Movie Makers* was able to stay in continuous publication through the war demonstrates that the amateur community was robust enough to sustain the challenge of the war's hardships; that journal's pronounced optimism in the face of these challenges was likely a boost to the hobbyists' morale. Though the journal did readily acknowledge the challenges faced by amateur filmmakers, whatever concern there might have been for the current state of affairs was shoved aside in favor of a general can-do spirit, and attendant zeal for making films useful to the war effort.

However, their enthusiasm was tempered somewhat as the conflict dragged on. The reality of the restrictions on consumer items began to be felt in everyday life, and this was acknowledged in the amateur press, most prominently in the advertisements. As mentioned above, projector manufacturers—such as Ampro, Bell & Howell, and Revere—found most of their industrial capacity redirected to war production, leaving them with nothing to market to the amateur filmmaker. Nevertheless, probably out of a desire to at least keep the company name in that community's mind, they continued to advertise in *Movie Makers*, selling nothing in particular but promising great things once victory had been achieved, all the while cloaking in patriotic grandiosity the somewhat sheepish nature of their appeal.

So Ampro, maker of various types of film production equipment, took out an ad in the June 1942 issue of *Movie Makers* consisting entirely of the following text: "Although the demands of the U. S. War program may make it impossible to fill your requirements immediately—every person interested in better 16mm projection should get full details of the Ampro story right now! Write today!"[30] Bell and Howell similarly spent the war making both increasingly flamboyant claims about its role in the conflict and about the wonders it would offer the

---

[30] *Movie Makers*, June 1942, 225.

Figure 3.1 Bell and Howell's Filmosound V model was produced exclusively for the armed forces during the war, but advertised to civilians via the amateur film press, promising that the new projector would be available to all upon victory. (Ad from *Movie Makers*, January 1943, page 3.)

consumer afterward. In an ad published in January 1943, they assured the reader that although "the new Filmosound 'V' Model is available only to our armed forces, it is indicative of the better 'things to come' from Bell & Howell craftsmen when peace is restored."[31]

Readers were constantly encouraged toward thriftiness, and enjoined to recycle what equipment they could for the war. As one 1942 editorial concerning the recycling of spools and reels put it:

> At a time when saving is important for war purposes, it is the duty of every user of these supplies to see that they are used many times and that they are not thrown away …. Admittedly, it is inconvenient to put forth this effort, because we have become accustomed to a land of plenty. However, conditions have changed in the United States since December 7, and we must all determine to do whatever we can do, each in his own personal fashion, to conserve necessary material for war use. Certainly, it is important to us all, as movie makers, to make certain, as far as we can do so, that any shortage in these minor—but vital—items does not result from our unwillingness to bother about saving them.[32]

Exhortations of this sort occurred frequently during the next three years' worth of issues; the flip side of these noble sentiments can be found in the equally plentiful articles dispensing advice to amateur filmmakers on how to improvise clever work-arounds in the face of shortages. While the amateur cinema community wasn't about to give up shooting film, they had begun to realize that it would be necessary to take some creative measures if they wished to continue.

Interestingly enough, many of these articles focused on issues that were somewhat ancillary to the process of exposing celluloid. Difficulty in properly lighting shots ("Although flood bulbs are rationed, it is still possible to light interior movie scenes in the home and school, for there are many other sources of illumination which we usually neglect only because of the convenience and economy of flood bulbs.")[33] and especially the declining potentials for production of travelogues (due to rationing of gasoline and rubber) are addressed far more frequently than scarcity of film itself. Editorials did occasionally mention film shortages and quotas, but only did so to assure the reader that their sacrifice was for the sake of the collective struggle. One 1943 editorial made the general case for conservation of one's resources, attempting

---

[31] *Movie Makers*, January 1943, 3.
[32] *Movie Makers*, March 1942, 99.
[33] *Movie Makers*, February 1943, 53.

to address but neither over- nor undersell the genuine crisis of supply that existed at the time.

> Buyers of film should cooperate with cine and photographic dealers by refusing to ask for more than their fair share. If each film user will depend upon a carefully chosen dealer for his film supply and will refrain from buying a little here and a little there, conservation can be affected fairly. We all believe in fair play. Let us work with our manufacturers and dealers in self imposed film conservation![34]

That the press should have devoted so many column inches over the course of several issues to the problem of scarce equipment might lead one to conclude that the situation was grim indeed.

The most compelling evidence for the wartime restrictions' tempering of new production comes from a phenomenon that both Knight and Alpert and also Thompson seem to have independently discovered, which is that of the recycling of old stag films by thrifty distributors and exhibitors. According to them, this curious innovation was born of the era's unique privations. As Thompson puts it:

> Many enterprising producers attempted to circumvent this [lack of material] by recycling their existing collection of movies into compilation-style films, a practice popular since the 1920s (*Keyhole Portraits* and the French *Le Trou*—a 1928 hotel stag that should most certainly not be confused with Jacques Becker's 1960 prison drama!) but which now took off in a big way.
>
> Some spliced together scenes from a variety of different stags to create a new one, with only the vaguest suggestion of an interlinking device to explain how the blonde woman in one position suddenly became a brunette in another; others took to creating what we might call "specialist" compendiums, similar to the *40 Squirting MILFs Volume 73*-type compilations of today, with all the action focusing on one particular sexual act.
>
> Others still, assuming their audience would accept sexual rationing with the same stoicism as they accepted gas and food shortages, adapted other kinds of movies altogether. Old burlesque routines were a favorite, spiced up with the addition of a few moments of spliced-in sex, as though the dance or pose beforehand was simply the foreplay to the main attraction.[35]

Knight and Alpert's version of this claim is virtually identical. They contend that, due to the scarcity of raw stock during the war, "some stag entrepreneurs

---

[34] *Movie Makers*, November 1942, 443 *sic*.
[35] Dave Thompson, *Black and White and Blue: Adult Cinema from the Victorian Age to the VCR* (Chicago, IL: ECW Press, 2007), 128.

attempted to make up for this shortage by pasting together segments from existing films into what the [Kinsey] Sex Institute calls 'potpourri pictures.' Some producers also began combining nonpornographic 'girlie' films with actual pornography—using the former to establish the story line and the latter to introduce the sex activity."[36] These scenarios are so similar in their details that one is tempted to assume that the basic claim is credible. From all of this, a clearer picture of the stag trade during the Second World War seems to be emerging.

But perhaps not. A closer look at both these historians' claims and the evidence of the time reveals that the war might not have been as disruptive of a force as has been assumed. While it certainly had an impact, the assumption that it necessarily motivated such desperate measures as those outlined by Knight and Alpert, and Thompson, is probably not correct.

Moving from the particular to the general, what one notices at first about the "potpourri film" hypothesis—that they sprang up after Pearl Harbor as a stopgap means of recycling old images when the manufacture of new ones became materially prohibitive—is that both Thompson and Knight and Alpert simply assert that this was a common wartime practice rather than demonstrate that it was so. The lack of specificity in their contentions is particularly unhelpful here, since the very nature of their claim—that separate titles were cannibalized and eventually combined into a pornographic composite—depends on a stable sense of what the original titles were in the first place. Which movies were reappropriated to make these portmanteau films? What were some of the names of the new works? When were they shown? And, most pressingly, how could it be determined that they were actually cut and then re-assembled during the war, and not after (or before)? Thompson undermines the case for his argument right out of the gate by pointing out that the renegade re-editing of stags was (supposedly) "a practice popular since the 1920s" (interestingly, he is able to provide specific examples of potpourri films from that decade). If this was already commonplace during a time of relative plenty, then there is no reason at all to assume that it was a tactic unique to the war years, deployed only as a means for coping with newly straitened circumstances.

Furthermore, to pull shots and scenes from several old titles as fodder for a single "new" one does not make much sense as a response to the problem of scarce

---

[36] Arthur Knight and Hollis Alpert, "The History of Sex in Cinema, Part Seventeen: The Stag Film," *Playboy*, November 1967, 178.

materials. If a stag producer was suddenly faced with radically reduced means to make another film, what would be the advantage to cutting up his existing stock? Perhaps this may have been done to give audiences the impression that new material was being shown, but since the raw material for this would have been the same shots and titles shown some weeks or months before, it would seem difficult to sustain that illusion.

Also, this hypothesis directly contradicts another claim that Knight and Alpert make elsewhere, which is that stag distributors and exhibitors had no qualms about showing titles which had been shot many years, even decades in the past. As of the time of their writing in 1967, the two had declared that "films often remained in circulation for 10, 20, 30 or more years. Some of the more popular titles originally produced in the Thirties and Forties ... are still to be found on the market today."[37] Unlike many of the other arguments made by the duo, this is confirmed in other sources, and can be given quite a bit more credence as a result. The Bureau, for example, would often receive a newly seized film from the provinces, only to discover, upon further examination, that it had in fact enjoyed a long career as something of a perennial on the stag market. Something like this may be seen in the arrival at the Bureau of a print, seized at a 1961 screening in Fredericksburg, Virginia, of *The Golden Shower*—a movie that had been made, by the estimation of the memo's author, "in Cleveland, Ohio, in 1931 or 1932."[38]

The FBI was not the only collecting agency to have noticed this phenomenon. The Kinsey Institute has in its archive of stag films multiple separate iterations of the same work; most of these individual copies seem to have arrived at the archive years apart. The records of their film collection note the range of dates when they were admitted to their holdings, generally shortly after seizure by a police department (thus the Institute's own copies of *The Golden Shower*, which they date to 1922, were turned over by both the Chicago Police Department in September of 1965 and someone else named "Wallick" in April of 1960).

It seems to me that these two phenomena—the practices of continuing to circulate and project old stag movies for as long as possible, and of cutting up existing prints to create a superficially "new" product—could not exist side-by-side. If these films could physically survive for such a great length of time, if the stag market really could subsist on a kind of "long tail" of movies, such that

---

[37] Ibid., 172 *sic*.
[38] Memo, Hoover to SAC, Richmond, June 16, 1961, FBI 80-662, 2.

audiences in the mid-1960s were happily consuming films then entering their fifth decade, then why would even a total interruption of new production move these creators to such desperate measures as chopping up their inventory— inventory that, by the logic of this argument, they would have had good reason to believe would be difficult to replace? "Potpourri" films obviously existed, and are held in significant numbers at least one of the major archives of pornography on film. But nothing about the case that has been put forward by either Knight and Alpert, or Thompson demonstrates that it was a response to the pressures of the war years, or that it occurred more often during that time than any other.

Finally, it is not certain that those years were quite as daunting as assumed. My earlier glance at the amateur press confirmed that wartime restrictions were onerous enough to be remarked upon, but a second look at that same source does not demonstrate that these, by themselves, would have necessarily curbed production of amateur films. Though the war had created inconveniences for the amateur, it's far from certain that it kept him from his hobby entirely. It should be pointed out that, as often as the rhetoric of service to the war effort was used to sell the notion of shared sacrifice, it was deployed far more often as a means to encourage further amateur production and exhibition, even in the face of constrained circumstances. An article from 1943, to pick one of many examples, urges filmmakers to push back against the new hardships:

> We may be absolutely positive that no more benefit will result to the country by giving up our movies than by giving up reading or visiting our friends. There is nothing unpatriotic about personal movies …. Therefore, let us do whatever filming we can manage to do, with a clear conscience and a knowledge that our hobby is both justifiable and constructive. Let us not forget that we want all the family records we can make, in these days that disrupt family ties so greatly. If we are fortunately able to make movies to help the war—such as those that aid the Red Cross or the Office of Civilian Defense—we can film with full confidence that we are doing something worth while.[39]

The author of this piece still felt the need to acknowledge the privations that the war had brought, even going so far as to justify the filmmaking hobby as an activity that might speed the day of victory; nevertheless, shooting, editing, and projecting new material is treated here (and elsewhere in the amateur press) as something that is still eminently achievable.

---

[39] *Movie Makers*, February 1943, 45 *sic*.

All of this is to demonstrate that, if these publications still encouraged amateur filmmaking, despite the difficulties imposed by war but also because of them, that would seem to suggest that the production situation was perhaps not nearly as desperate as Thompson and Knight and Alpert seemed to think it was, for both stag and "bona fide" communities alike. It is even possible that stag filmmakers in particular, having been used to operating clandestinely, would not be deterred by some extra obstacles in their path. Admittedly, there is no conclusive proof one way or the other as to whether or not stags were produced at the same volume as before the war (in part because it is difficult to estimate what that earlier volume would have been). But the certainty that this must have been so, repeated so often that it has become an accepted part of the history of pornographic films, clearly cannot stand in the face of this analysis.

Here, as in many other cases, scholars of pornographic film find themselves falling back on assumptions borrowed from the study of mainstream commercial cinema, assumptions which fail to consider that the practices of the larger film industry were themselves the results of historically contingent circumstances, not laws of physics. I suspect that the notion that stag film producers were hamstrung by the shortage of new equipment and general scarcity of new film stock was, at least to some degree, inherited from an acknowledgment of the circumstances which forced the Hollywood studios to thin out their production schedule for the duration of the war, and to cut the number of new release prints manufactured per year; this is basic film historical knowledge, and it is not unreasonable to imagine that a similar state of affairs would prevail for production at all levels. But the equipment shortages experienced by Hollywood were not due to the "natural" economic consequences of the war's disruption of business, but rather to a standing order from the War Production Board, which imposed upon the studios to reduce their film consumption by 25 percent.[40] Also, the comparison of the gargantuan production needs of the major studios with those of their vastly less ambitious counterparts in the stag world does not quite scale; it doesn't stretch credibility to imagine that the latter could very easily continue production on even 25 percent less film stock. Finally, unlike the Second World War-era Hollywood studios, then churning out new product on a weekly basis, those in the stag trade were not similarly compelled to entice an audience through the production of new works. None of their films needed

---

[40] Thomas Schatz, *Boom and Bust: American Cinema in the 1940s* (Berkeley: University of California Press, 1999), 143.

to have been sold by the usual means used to market mainstream cultural products—most notably the accentuation of a superficially "new" arrangement of familiar elements—because these patrons of stag screenings, seemingly, didn't assign the same (or, by the looks of things, any) value to novelty in this case. The prospect of watching the same smut film more than once during several evenings of revelry was probably no barrier to attracting an audience, hence the practice of continuing to circulate old titles for decades, which would have kept stag distributors and exhibitors in business even under a total interruption of production.

Whatever the effect on the production of new stag films, the war didn't seem to make much appreciable difference to the circulation and exhibition of pornographic movies generally. Given the removal of millions of men from their home communities, where they would otherwise have presumably been exposed to the same stag films watched by their fathers, uncles, and older brothers, and via the same institutions, one might expect a crucial interruption in viewing patterns. Nothing of the material I consulted from this era seemed to suggest that this was the case.

On the domestic front at least, the war years represent little more than an extension of the trends of the previous decade-and-a-half of distribution and exhibition. From 1942 to 1945, screenings were broken up and men were arrested at approximately the same rate as they had in decades past. Looking through the records of the period, we find films shown in the same spaces—clubs,[41] hotels,[42] private homes (displayed specifically for an audience[43]), and civic organizations.[44] From the evidence I could find, the first half of the 1940s demonstrates the resilience of the usual stag exhibition models; whatever changes the war brought to material and social conditions of American life, they did not seriously disrupt the practices that had prevailed since the 1920s.

---

[41] "2 Men Arrested in Gambling Raid," *Philadelphia Inquirer*, February 21, 1942, 6; "142 Are Arrested in Pictures Raid," *Pittsburgh Post-Gazette*, April 18, 1942, 4; "4 Held after Raid on Lewd Show," *Philadelphia Inquirer*, November 21, 1942, 19; "12 Convicted for Staging Lewd Show," *Philadelphia Inquirer*, July 29, 1943, 21; "City, County Stag Raids," *Pittsburgh Post-Gazette*, January 1, 1944, 9; "Films at Smoker Lead to Arrest," *Democrat and Chronicle*, January 17, 1944; "70 Arrested in Liquor Raids," *Pittsburgh Press*, February 5, 1944, 1; "Year in Prison Imposed," *Pittsburgh Post-Gazette*, May 5, 1944, 15; "Dance in Nude Charge Lands Nine in Court," *Detroit Free Press*, September 26, 1944, 7.

[42] "100 Seized By Raiders at Smoker," *Philadelphia Inquirer*, March 23, 1942, 19; *Morning Call*, May 18, 1943, 24.

[43] "Police Raid Naughty Film," *San Mateo Times*, March 28, 1942, 1.

[44] "Police Raid Movie, Arrest Exhibitor," *Herald Courant*, September 27, 1942, 7; "7 Are Fined in Film Case," *Baltimore Sun*, July 16, 1943, 5.

Careful attention can reveal the beginnings of trends that would prove to outlast the war, however; while the stag business continued on much as before, some of the developments which would have a significant effect in the ensuing decades were in their nascent state during this time. Despite the diversion of much of the United States' industrial capacity to the military, developments that would lead to new forms of exhibition were just coming to technological viability at this point; the most prominent of these is the coin-op viewing machine. These are, in some ways, echoes of some of the original experiences of moving image spectatorship, such as the Mutoscope or the Kinetoscope: as with those devices, the new machines would accept a coin, and a lone spectator enjoyed a short program, often sans narrative, or with only a very primitive one. These original machines from the 1890s had a reputation for showing all manner of risque content, though it is doubtful that they were ever stocked with hard-core stags.[45] The suspicion that these kinds of machines could act as a delivery system for explicit images may have had to do with the possibility that they could only be viewed by a single viewer at a time, in conditions at least somewhat approximating privacy. Also, they were often left unattended, with no attendant on hand to bar certain spectators, such as children, from access.

Montana Senator Burton K. Wheeler was certainly playing on these historical anxieties when, in 1941, he condemned slot-machine viewers as purveyors of "lewd and lascivious" films.[46] However, it is likely that there was not much more substance to this accusation than there had been to those against the Kinetoscopes, Mutoscopes, or other solo-viewing machines. The isolationist Senator was probably only cursorily concerned with the alleged smuttiness of films; at this time, he was mainly preoccupied with allegations that Hollywood films were propagandizing for entry into the European war, and was connected to a legislative inquiry into this very question. More saliently, the most prominent manufacturer of coin-op viewing machines at that time was the Mills-Globe Company, then enjoying great success with their Panoram machines and Soundies films; the production arm of that company was headed by James Roosevelt, son of the very President who Wheeler had come to regard as a rival, so it is likely that his condemnation of that part of the film industry owed as much to political calculation as sincere conviction. His statement brought quick rebukes from many of the other companies involved in these new

---

[45] See Dan Streible, "Children at the Mutoscope," *Cinemas* 141 (2003), 91–116.
[46] "Barry Asks Sen. Wheeler to Retract Lewd Charge," *Film Daily*, October 24, 1941, 1.

machines; the sentiments of John F. Barry, president of Minoco Productions (a studio specializing in short films specifically for machine viewing), were typical: "By contract every picture made by this company must conform in every detail to the code governing morality as applied to the regular motion picture industry. Also, every picture made, before it is publicly shown, has been presented to the state and county censorship boards for their approval."[47]

But while films produced specifically for these machines might have abided with local decency laws, their day-to-day operators and end users sometimes had other plans—unlike earlier stand-alone viewing machines from the turn of the century, these devices could accept regular 16mm film of any origin. This may have been what led to a 1942 incident, in which the manager of an Akron penny arcade was arrested for "displaying immoral pictures." It had been alleged that "juveniles" were watching the machines' offerings, including "such pictures as 'Lovable Lady,' 'Alluring Lips,' 'Balloon Girl' and 'Sweetie.'" (The viewing devices were identified in local press accounts only as "'peep show' machines,"[48] so their exact make and model is lost to history.) Charges were soon dropped, however, after the presiding judge, having "made a personal investigation [by] going to the arcade where he looked at the pictures," determined that they were not obscene. His final pronouncement confirms that such fare tended toward the risque-but-not-pornographic: "The pictures are probably not for juveniles but on the other hand they are not as bad as many others that are on display in magazines."[49] The source of the films was not revealed in any of the press on the incident, so it is unclear whether or not they had been supplied by the machine's manufacturer, or from a more dubious source.

Coin-op machines seem to have been turned to prurient purposes almost immediately upon their debut, with Mills-Globe's Panoram machine a special target for alteration. Peter Alilunas has demonstrated that more than one company offered add-on kits for purchasers of Panorams which would partially obscure the screen, ensuring that only one person could view the film at a time. The availability of these ready-made kits leads Alilunas to infer that "local Panoram operators surely had been modifying their own equipment prior to the introduction of mass-marketed conversions (thus suggesting a market), and there was plenty of adult material playing on the machines throughout the country

[47] Ibid., 8.
[48] "Raid 'Peep Show,' Arrest Operator," *Akron Beacon Journal*, November 20, 1942, 8.
[49] "Norwat Goes Free on Picture Count," *Akron Beacon Journal*, December 18, 1942, 35.

to justify the need for such conversions."[50] It's obviously unclear exactly how widespread these sorts of ad-hoc tinkerings were, but this appears to have been one of the rare instances in which stag films did inspire technological innovation of some sort, superficial as this one may have been. As I have demonstrated, the general pattern throughout this story has been for pornographic films to adapt themselves to already existing technologies and practices, whether in production (through the use of the same nonprofessional equipment and base of knowledge as officially recognized amateur filmmakers), distribution (via advertising in the likes of *Popular Photography* and other publications that catered to an audience of small-gauge film enthusiasts), and exhibition (integrating film with other live acts in the vaudeville era). The kits designed to augment the Panoram were designed to address a real problem with the display of salacious films in coin-op machines: a lack of privacy. Since these machines were designed for use in public space—bars, clubs, and other places open to anyone—there was no guarantee, absent the common social relationship which protected the audience at a secret stag show, that someone might not express their disapproval by calling the police. Though we shall see in a later chapter just how this problem was eventually solved, during the war years there was no effective way to play a stag film in a public setting while preserving the viewers' privacy.

Such films were played on coin-op machines on at least a few documented occasions, however, with neither the privacy of viewers nor the sensibilities of onlookers receiving a second thought. In 1943, Detroit police took into custody two reels of film from a pair of coin-operated viewing machines at the Olympic Recreation Room; the film was then declared obscene by the official police censor later that very night. The specific nature of the complaint is vague, with the films variously described as "nude hula dancers cavorting on a beach"[51] and "nude bathing beauties"[52] (curiously enough, the censor speculated that "some of the film seemed 'more than 20 years old with a sound tract dubbed in on it'";[53] unfortunately for the technologically curious, he offered no more explanation than this). The two machines, as it happens, were models from the Globe-Mills Company, though the films found within were obviously not Soundies. The viewers had been purchased by a man named Frank Healy, who

[50] Peter Alilunas, *Smutty Little Movies: The Creation and Regulation of Adult Video* (Berkeley: University of California Press, 2016), 45.
[51] "Police Confiscate Films as Indecent," *Detroit Free Press*, February 14, 1943, 10.
[52] "Dirty Jukepix Burns Det. Cops," *Variety*, February 17, 1943, 3.
[53] Ibid., *sic*.

then leased them to the Olympic. Apparently unbeknownst to them, he had cued up the offending films before delivery, believing that films featuring nudity would attract both eyeballs and coins in equal measure. Perhaps nervous over redoubled efforts against obscenity on behalf of Detroit law enforcement, the owners of the Olympic pulled the plug on the viewers on discovering the nature of the films, and called the police themselves. Other than the arrest of Healy, the major effect of this incident was a renewed crackdown, not on obscenity per se, but on all of the so-called "jukepix" machines in the area, which saw "police going out, hanging 'Out of Order' signs on other jukepix boxes and bringing the film for inspection."[54] My previous chapter demonstrated how small-gauge projectors became associated with sexually explicit films in the minds of some elements in law enforcement, but the coin-op, solo-viewer exhibition machines became the target of much more police action, probably due to the inherently public nature of their operation.

The fate of these devices was decided not by censors and police but by the war. As early as late December of 1941, the same demand for materiel and manufactures that put a dent in the projector business essentially shuttered the coin-op trade. At that time, the Office of Production Management "ordered production of coin-operated music and film machines cut 75 per cent by February [1942]. It also banned making of slot machines, after the first of that month. And it ordered immediate elimination of aluminum, in production."[55] This was all to the delight of theater owners and operators, who claimed to have been losing millions of dollars to the coin-up viewing trade (though the Soundies Corporation did continue to distribute films to the remaining machines until 1946). Though a dormant force for the remainder of the 1940s similar machines would reappear after the end of the war, eventually becoming an important means of exhibiting pornographic films in semi-public settings. The temporary demise of the Panoram and its counterparts in the coin-op viewing industry appears to have been the one way in which wartime industrial quotas actually did hamper the activities of the stag trade; this seems to have gone unremarked upon by most other pornography scholars (Knight and Alpert, and Thompson evidently did not find it worthy of note), with Alilunas seeming to be the exception.

No other technological development seems to have had any significant impact on the way in which stag films were shown during this period; as they

---

[54]   Ibid.
[55]   "War Knocks Out the 'Juke-Box' Movie Line," *Motion Picture Herald*, December 27, 1941, 67 *sic*.

had since the mid-1920s, most exhibitors were content to show films to secret gatherings on 16mm (or, occasionally, 8mm) projectors. The innovation that had the biggest impact during the war years occurred not in the realm of exhibition, but distribution, which had become far more streamlined and rationalized since the 1930s. Though these years saw a comparable number of per-capita arrests compared to the period in the previous chapter—and many of these, like before, were of small-time, or even lone operators—three big busts in particular, occurring sequentially in 1943, 1944, and 1945, revealed the extent to which the stag trade had developed. That these three incidents involve many common factors and occurred all at roughly the same time leads me to provisionally conclude that these groups were representative of at least some significant part the underground industry as it existed at this time. Of course, these kinds of operations existed at the same time as the rather more small-time exhibitors featured earlier in this chapter, and the elements present here are not constitutative of every type of pornography ring. However, so that I may tease out the broad similarities between these three, it will be necessary to tell the story of each bust sequentially.

In 1943, federal investigators uncovered and then broke up a film ring that was unique in that it was a genuinely interstate operation, with its reach spanning more than half of the continental United States. This particular enterprise seems to have divided up its various administrative tasks geographically, with the mail-order business headquartered in Philadelphia (according to the *Philadelphia Inquirer*, "the local headquarters, which traded under two corporate names, contacted prospective clients and accepted orders from at least four States for the films, as well as literature and postcards"[56]), while the films were produced in and mailed out from California.

John Shade and his wife Olga were accused of masterminding the business from Pennsylvania, but eventually acquitted. Far more interesting is the saga of the west coast end of the operation, where six men in total were named as conspirators. Nearly every one of them had been involved in the small-market film industry to some extent. For example, one of the accused, W. Merle Connell, was active in a company known as "Educationettes," which, according to a report in *The Film Daily*, "photographed subjects of well-known musical numbers" meant for domestic and educational use.[57] Connell was the only one of the gang

---

[56] "Arrests Bare Lewd Film Ring Here," *Philadelphia Inquirer*, July 28, 1943, 25.
[57] *The Film Daily*, February 27, 1940, 10.

who had worked exclusively in the "legitimate" industry (and would go on after the war to have a hand in many exploitation pictures); the others, meanwhile, while all involved with the technical end of "bona fide" film production, also had some direct link to sex films of some sort in the their recent past.

Arrested alongside Connell were Otto Hertzwig, Robert I. Lee, and T. H. Emmett, all of whom were reported (by the *Philadelphia Inquirer*) to have been "employed in a Hollywood technical film laboratory."[58] Hertzwig had already been arrested in 1938 for participating in a different, very much smaller stag film exchange. At that time, he had been captured with 5,000 feet of film and a large quantity of explicit photographs and drawings; on his arrest, the deputy district attorney in charge of the investigation claimed that the "entire collection is the most revolting imaginable … and of such a nature it is beyond description for the sake of decency."[59] Although newspaper reports called Hertzwig's enterprise as a "ring," these films seem to have only been sent to one other person, one Lecil Ross of Santa Ana, California, who was then working as an official reporter for the state Supreme Court. Hertzwig was able to avoid serious penalties in exchange for testifying for the prosecution against Ross, and was given a suspended sentence. (Ross, acting as his own attorney, admitted to the jury that his hobby of collecting pornographic films was perhaps "not an elevating one," but pleaded for lenience all the same, arguing that the proposed punishment was far in excess of his crime.[60] The jury agreed, acquitting him of all charges.)[61] As of the 1943 arrest, Hertzwig was said to have been involved in an outfit known as Candid Cinema Corp, which I could find no other information about.

Even more intriguing is the case of Robert I. Lee. Alongside his position at the lab with Hertzwig and Emmett, Lee was, according to the newspapers, also working as "the manager of a war plant."[62] Later reports revealed that neither of these claims were strictly true; Lee was, in fact, then in a position of some responsibility (no source spells out precisely what) at a mail-order film outfit known as Pacific Cine Films. According to Eric Schaefer, Lee began Pacific Cine "around 1935" after buying out two smaller film outlets. Pacific Cine began advertising its products almost immediately after that point, placing small notices in publications catering to amateur filmmakers such as *American*

[58] "3 Cameramen Fined for Obscene Films," *Philadelphia Inquirer*, September 28, 1943, 12.
[59] "Reedly Man Is Arrested, Lewd Pictures Seized," *Fresno Dee The Republican*, March 8, 1939, 9.
[60] "Ross Pleads Own Case before Jury," *Santa Ana Register*, March 17, 1938, 1.
[61] "Sentence in Mail Case Suspended," *Los Angeles Times*, March 22, 1938, 28.
[62] "Four Held for Obscene Films," *Indiana Gazette*, July 28, 1943, 12.

Cinematographer (which at that time had a special section for amateurs), *Movie Makers*, and *International Photographer*; the ads themselves seem superficially innocuous enough, offering, for ten to twenty-five cents, a list of the films they had available for sale, along with "three artistic End Titles."[63] These ads were in all appearances identical to any of the other similar services being hawked in the classified sections of these magazines.

But Pacific Cine had for some years been under suspicion, both official and otherwise, of participating directly in the production (and presumably also the sale) of films featuring some degree of nudity or sexual explicitness. Schaefer, for his part, is skeptical that any of their films would "have been suitable for a stag party if we consider that stag films featured unobstructed views of sexual activity. Stag films and their distributors would have been pursued aggressively by postal authorities or local law enforcement officials when, and if, they were identified."[64] However, pursuit is exactly what seems to have occurred—Pacific Cine attracted the notice of at least the postal authorities in 1935, and were forced to defend the mailing of what seems to have been an especially racy burlesque film. *Variety* devoted some lines to the incident:

> Federal grand jurors in Los Angeles got a good peep at a fan dancer in action when postoffice officials held up sending of a print made by Pacific Cine Films. Jurors, usually lax in attendance, turned out in force to see the questioned one-reeler three times. First it was run through backwards, then in slow motion and last the proper way.[65]

No follow-up article announcing the verdict ever materialized, though Pacific Cine was still in operation by 1943, which seems to indicate that they had beat the charge.

Though they were able to escape the clutches of the law, their reputation was tarnished. On at least two separate occasions, in two widely distributed published news articles, they were all but accused by name of producing and selling pornographic films. The first was from syndicated columnist Paul Harrison, a gossip reporter whose beat covered the goings-on of the Hollywood set. In September, he filed a story about the strange (if ultimately innocuous) behavior indulged in by fans of deceased actors at the Hollywood Cemetery, who would

[63] *Movie Makers*, June 1938, 310.
[64] Schaefer, "Wrapper," 207.
[65] *Variety*, July 31, 1935, 18 *sic*.

habitually litter their graves with various kinds of memorabilia. Tucked away at the end of the piece is this seemingly extraneous paragraph:

> The publicity man maintains a discreet silence about the indiscreet film enterprise which flourishes in the imposing stone building by the entrance. The organization is called Pacific Cine Film, and it manufactures "Hollywood Art Featurettes." The films are in 8 and 16 mm size only, and presumably are intended for private projection by earnest students of art.[66]

Nothing in the rest of his article has led up to this in any logical way, and he seems to have included it only due to the (apparent) proximity of Pacific Cine's offices to the cemetery. But already here can be seen the kinds of euphemisms that were beginning to become common descriptors of stag films: substandard gauges, private screenings, and even the term "art" had all become terms of art, connoting a type of film which is somehow not fit for public life. Perhaps Harrison's linking of Pacific Cine's stag studio with a cemetery filled with Hollywood's deceased was an attempt at a thematic echo: each location housing artifacts that the major movie studios would prefer not to associate with, and which only receive the attention of unhealthy obsessives.

Harrison may have been too subtle for some of his readers, but no similar mistake could have been made with Irving Wallace's "All This Is Hollywood, Too!" for the February 1941 issue of *Modern Screen*. This is a lengthy, impressionistic essay on the city, of the sort which will contain lines such as "Hollywood is many things. It's the crackpot's wonderland, the shopgirl's heaven, the incubator for genius. Hollywood is a small town in Sunday clothes, a constant first night, and endless County Fair—where lights are brighter, voices are louder, colors are more vivid than anything you've ever known or dreamed."[67] Devoted mostly to madcap descriptions of movie premieres and celebrity antics, Wallace shifts in the last part of the essay to an acknowledgment that "there is another Hollywood, too, and it's no use avoiding it. The Hollywood known throughout the wide world, as the wildest den of vice and the most prolific playground for wholesale sexual orgies on this mad mudball earth."[68] Cataloging the specific forms that Hollywood decadence was rumored to take, he shows some of them up as myths (happily reporting that "the day of the 'Casting Couch'—when a

---

[66] Paul Harrison, "Hollywood," *Wilkes-Barre Times Leader*, September 5, 1938, 1.
[67] Irving Wallace, "All This Is Hollywood, Too!" *Modern Screen*, February 1941, 34.
[68] Ibid., 89, *sic*.

girl had to exercise her libido instead of her talent for a job—is almost dead"),
but attempts a somber note for his final paragraphs, where he not only brings
up Pacific Cine's involvement in stag production but (probably coincidentally)
repeats the juxtaposition that Harrison found so evocative

> No matter. You need remember only one more thing about Hollywood. This—
> Within three blocks of each other there are three places symbolic of the heart of
> Hollywood. There is the Paramount Studio, which recently took Better Brewer,
> a poor, unemployed fourteen-year-old, off the streets and made her rich and
> famous, made her life something glorious and of fiction. There is the Pacific
> Cine Arts Film Company, where other unemployed girls become employed
> by stripping off their clothes, and for $3 an hour, performing in the nude for
> two days at a time to help make suggestive movies for stag parties. There is the
> cemetery, green and white, where a well-known movie woman was recently
> buried. She had been living beyond her means, and had inhaled monoxide to
> pay her debts.[69]

That Pacific Cine's activities could be such common public knowledge speaks
to the variation in local law enforcement's attitude to these matters—recall that
the Los Angeles municipal authorities only made a resolution to combat the
spread of smut in July of 1942, more than a year after the appearance of Wallace's
article (yet barely a week before the bust of the California-Philadelphia ring
that Pacific Cine was affiliated with). It is also notable that Wallace refuses any
of Harrison's ironic euphemisms, instead substituting a leaden allusion to the
human misery that (along with $3) was the wage for the women participating
in stags. This is wrapped in a broader concern for human disposability in
Hollywood; in this essay, pornographic films stand as a kind of synecdoche for
all that is rotten in show business.

Along with Pacific Cine, another production and distribution company
catering to the home market was involved in this scandal. William H. Horsley,
and T. H. Emmett, both arrested along with Hertzwig and Lee, worked at a small
production company called Hollywood Film Enterprises. As far back as 1930,
Horsley had been recognized as a pioneer in early attempts at synchronized
sound images, and by the latter part of that same year he had begun his own
company, part of an ambitious plan to build "a combination sound radio and
record manufacturing establishment, the first so far as is known of its kind in

---

[69] Ibid.

the world."[70] This new studio was to utilize the latest advances in audio recording to produce industrial and instructional films. Hollywood Film Enterprises continued to make advances in the home cinema market throughout the decade, manufacturing a miniature projector to be marketed to children,[71] and even securing the rights to distribute 16mm iterations of Disney cartoons to the home market.[72]

With all of this success in the bona fide home market at their fingertips, the decision by Horsley and Emmett to cater to stag audiences would be a quite baffling one, a strategy offering nothing more than significant risk for very little reward.

An intriguing possibility, albeit one raised by evidence that is highly circumstantial, is that equipment from their lab had been used without the knowledge of the principal managers. Amateur filmmaker Ephraim Horowitz worked for a time for Hollywood Film Enterprises, beginning just at the close of the Second World War as a color film processor. He related the following tantalizing anecdote—explaining the company's reaction to his request for a raise from his starting salary of 75 cents an hour—in a 2011 interview:

> And the time came where I said, I can't support my family, no matter how [many] hours' work he gives me, I can't support my family on 75 cents an hour at that time. So I went to the boss and I told him that I couldn't do it. He said to me, "You're the best employee I ever had, please don't leave me." I said, I don't have a choice. He said, "I tell you what, I'll pay you as much as I pay my manager, but don't tell him." So I said, how much do you pay the manager. He said "85 cents an hour." So I said to him, and you're gonna pay me 85 cents an hour? So I went to the manager and I said, you know, you're the biggest schlemiel. I'm like, how can you run this factory for 85 cents [an] hour[?] Because he was duping pornography on the boss's time and film at night! He's come back to the place, make pornographic film, and then sell it for a monstrous price, and then made enough money so that he didn't care whether he got paid or he didn't get paid at the job. That's why he worked for 85 cents an hour.[73]

Whatever evidence the Post Office may have had which linked Hollywood Film Enterprises to the secret mail-order stag operation was not revealed in any of

---

[70] "Hollywood Film's Sound Studio Will Stamp Its Own Flexco Records," *International Photographer*, October 1930, 37.

[71] "Toy Projectors Big Holiday Factor," *International Photographer*, November 1930, 33–4.

[72] "Mickey Mouse Makes Bow to 16mm," *International Photographer*, June 1932, 25.

[73] Interview with Havant Townsend, November 2011.

the news stories, and it may not have been very strong to begin with: of the eight people charged in this case, only Emmett and Horsley elected to plead not guilty and stand trial. I have not been able to find any record of how this trial ended, or if it even occurred at all, but Hollywood Film Enterprises continues to appear in the trade press for decades afterward, and no mention is made of this incident in any subsequent articles I could unearth, which leads me to believe that they were either acquitted or the charges were dropped.

If the first of the three groups relied heavily on marginal figures from the film industry, then a much different type of organization characterizes the second large bust of the war era, this one occurring in the final months of 1944. The case of Hertzwig (and others) was announced suddenly, with the coordinated arrests of everyone involved, leaving the press to explain the charges and business model of the group retroactively. The next case has the (quite accidental) advantage of much greater narrative clarity, beginning with the arrest of a single person, and quickly spreading out to cast a net over a larger group of participants. The first published article on the incident, as if to deliberately mimic this chain of events in its narrative structure, only introduces the central players of the conspiracy in its final lines: "Their arrests came after a 15-year-old junior high school student was found in possession of such literature, which he said he got from Stanley. Stanley said he was supplied by the Arnolds."[74]

"Stanley" here refers to Mason Stanley, proprietor of a bookstore in Minneapolis; as per the excerpt above, he had taken to selling obscene literature of some sort in his shop, his source for which was the married couple Einer and Mary Arnild (their surname is misspelled "Arnold" in the earliest news articles). After Stanley's arrest, police were sent to search the Arnild residence to look for further material. There they found a large hidden stash of pornographic items, as well as evidence of the pains that the couple had taken to conceal their activities.

> Near the bottom of the staircase leading to the second floor of the house they found a section of the stairs had been converted to a hinged door. Under the stairs they discovered 16 large cardboard boxes, each containing an estimated 3,500 pieces of indecent literature. On the second floor, a room adjoining one used to keep chickens, had been converted into a photographic studio. Both still and movie cameras and projectors were found there, besides a large number of nude and indecent photographs.[75]

---

[74] "Shop Owner Held for District Court," *Minneapolis Star*, November 30, 1944, 13.
[75] "Raiders Find Lewd Photos, Books Cache," *Star Tribune*, December 2, 1944, 2.

Both the quantities found on the scene and the equipment stashed away led the police to conclude that the Arnilds were both producing and selling pornographic material in the area; as was typical in these kinds of stories, there was some suggestion of interstate distribution, or even hints that Minneapolis had become the center of a dreaded "ring." The local paper reported that "recognition of local characters in pornographic pictures discovered here and subsequent arrests today indicated Minneapolis may be production and distribution headquarters for a nationwide business in lewd photographs and literature"[76] (though how the presence of local models in locally produced photographs would have by itself necessarily suggested a nationwide trade was never made clear).

As soon as Stanley and the Arnilds were taken in, a cascade of other arrests affiliated with the production of their photos and movies followed. Three models were taken in in short order, as was a mysterious figure identified in all news accounts only as "The Professor," and who seems to have been the author of much of Arnild's pornographic literature.

> William C. Simms, investigator for the county attorney's office and Detective Eugene Bernath Thursday night broke into the room of "The Professor," and found it piled to the ceiling with volumes of erotica and copies of indecent pamphlets. Simms and Bernath said "The Professor's" room was equipped with a special lock which no passkey would open. They said material was stacked even on his bed, leaving him only a narrow edge on which to lie. The collection, Dillon said, included many rare volumes, some of them expensive limited editions, some dealing with the psychology of sex and others with "memoirs" of notorious lovers. Dillion said he believed "The Professor" used the library for research in authoring some of the pamphlets founds in the room.[77]

Besides several others who had been accused of modeling for Arnild's photos and films (among these were included Arnild himself), a printer and yet another bookstore owner were arrested for involvement in the production or distribution of obscene material.

At least fifteen reels were found in their home,[78] and the disruption of his own production efforts was enough for one of the local papers to suggest that "availability of naughty movies shown at innumerable stag parties may be greatly reduced" after the raid. This also led to the search for and eventual

---

[76] "Dillon Hints City May Be Lewd Photo Center," *Minneapolis Star*, December 6, 1944, 15.
[77] "'Professor' and Lewd Books Held," *Minneapolis Star*, December 8, 1944, 1.
[78] "Lewd Picture Sift Spreads," *Star Tribune*, December 10, 1944, 8.

arrest of Nathan "Speedy" Marcus, described as "a loop character ... who has acted as projectionist for showing of obscene films at many stag affairs."[79] Though eventually only convicted of possessing obscene photographs,[80] eight additional reels of film were taken from Marcus. The FBI examined them and determined that "they contained nothing that violated federal statutes."[81] The federal investigators and prosecutors having discovered nothing that fell under their jurisdiction, all charges filed and fines collected were all done on behalf of the state of Minnesota.

Although nothing seems to have come from early press speculation that the Arnild's operation was nationwide in scope, the amount of material seized was apparently vast—as many as 50,000 individual items, according to one report.[82] The attendant publicity led one anonymous wag to send to the prosecuting county attorney "a facetious offer for the mass of lewd photographs and literature his office has accumulated since starting the drive against such material. Offering [prosecutor] Dillon 30 percent commission on sale of the material, the writer said: 'You will find me a good guy to work with.' The letter was mailed in Eau Claire, Wis. Dillon doesn't plan to answer it."[83]

The last of the three busts shared elements common to the other two. As with the first, most of the action occurred in California, and involved many figures, however marginal, associated in some way with the movie industry; as with the raid in Minnesota, a huge number of local people were eventually revealed to have been a part of the conspiracy to produce and sell stag films, with consequences that proved to be disastrous for the man at the head of the operation.

On April 4, 1945, Gerald Stout, who owned and operated a photo studio in Los Angeles, was arrested. Press accounts at the time reported that this lab was the center of a "lewd-picture racket that has flooded Southern California with thousands of indecent photographs and films," and that it was here that the offending films had been processed and developed. Stout was the first to be taken into custody, but before the police investigation would finish, nearly two dozen people would be arrested, including the alleged ringleader, Frank Ries.[84]

---

[79] "Lewd Book Probe Hits Stag Films," *Minneapolis Star*, December 9, 1944, 1.
[80] *Minneapolis Star*, January 12, 1945, 13.
[81] *Star Tribune*, December 21, 1944, 8.
[82] "Pair Waive Hearing on 'Literature,'" *Minneapolis Star*, December 2, 1944, 1.
[83] *Star Tribune*, December 14, 1944, 12.
[84] "Lewd-Photo Raids Net 18 with Mass of Evidence," *Los Angeles Times*, April 4, 1945, 7.

Just like Connell, Lee, Emmett, and Hertzwig, who had had their own run-ins with law enforcement two years earlier, Ries was involved with the fringes of the film industry. He led something of a double life, working in both mainstream small-scale production and pornographic films with either no awareness or no concern about any contradiction between these two worlds. He seems to have been an accomplished still and motion picture photographer, shooting fashion spreads,[85] and keeping active in his local IATSE chapter. Whatever successes he achieved in the respectable side of the film and photography worlds, modest though they may have been, he could also later write, in a 1947 letter to the *Los Angeles Examiner* detailing his operation, that he was the "KING OF THE OBSCENE MOVIES," and insist that he had been responsible for "nearly 50 percent of all the 16 millimeter obscene movies in the United States."[86] While these statements may have been inspired as much by bravado as by verifiable numbers, remaining evidence indicates that his involvement in the lewd film scene was indeed significant.

Ries was no newcomer. He claimed to have shot his first stag film in 1928 at 1154 N. Western Avenue in Los Angeles (the 1929 edition of the *Film Daily Yearbook* lists this address as the home of Feature Studios, Inc.).[87] "I used a prostitute and a studio truck driver for my cast .... I had the 35-millimeter negative of this picture. From this I had a 16-millimeter reduction negative made. I started to sell prints to friends of mine." Shortly after this, he established his own photographic studio and laboratory. "This," he would write in his *Examiner* letter, "was merely a blind. I made contacts with girls who came to me to be models. I later used them in my movies."[88] In 1932, he was arrested by postal inspectors; the next day's issue of *Variety* simply noted that "Frank Ries, Hollywood photographer, was arraigned on charge of sending obscene matter for interstate transportation. Eston B. Juneau was arrested with Ries after a raid on what police said was the source of a big part of Los Angeles and Hollywood salacious literature."[89] Though this was an unenviable position to find himself in, Ries considered himself lucky that it had never occurred to the postal inspectors to search his studio. "I had all my records and negatives there. If [inspectors]

[85] *Los Angeles Times*, July 4, 1937, 8.
[86] "Blue Movies," *Los Angeles Times*, October 25, 2007, http://latimesblogs.latimes.com/thedailymirror/2007/10/blue-movies.html.
[87] *Film Daily Yearbook 1929*, 553.
[88] "Blue Movies," *Los Angeles Times*.
[89] *Variety*, July 5, 1932, 36.

would have found them [they] could have caught about 25 dealers in the U.S. alone." By that time, Ries was taking active steps to avoid the attention of the post office anyway. "I had a post office box in Beverly Hills to get my C.O.D. returns from my express shipments. All my business was done over the telephone or by Western Union. I never used the mails in my business."[90]

Ries claimed to have shot forty films (the only title that can be traced back to him is called *Casting Directory*, which I can find no other reference for) and distributed sixty additional titles from other producers; he would run these off in batches of 100 prints each. He cultivated a large customer base throughout the United States, and would regularly send a pair of men on long road trips to drum up interest. "They made connections and would telephone me the orders. I would send them by express or Greyhound bus. They would always collect in advance for orders. This is how I got my connections all over the country." Rather than offering the films for screenings that he himself would put on, as in the itinerant model, he seems to have sold most of them to middlemen, most often retail outlets. "Most of my agents were 16-millimeter camera stores, magic stories [*sic*] and bookstores."[91]

Ries's arrest in 1945 occurred in tandem with that of several others in his cohort, revealing the ambitious scale of the operation. Among those taken in were some with further connections in the film world (such as Thomas L. Cooper and George W. Richter, each of whom owned a film lab), as well as many others listed only as "models."

I hope that the reader will forgive the somewhat lengthy description I've given to each of these three incidents. Though I think they're interesting stories in their own right, I also believe they exemplify some of the essential features of the wartime stag trade, particularly the production and distribution wings, and that they can tell us something about the larger world of pornographic film as it existed at the time.

First, each of them demonstrated a fairly highly specialized division of labor. Recall that one of the earliest arrests after the debut of 16mm film was (as noted in a previous chapter) Walter Stewart of Rochester, who, in 1924, had procured his own film stock (through theft), shot his own films, and arranged the screenings—where he also acted as projectionist—all on his own.[92] By contrast,

---

[90] "Blue Movies," *Los Angeles Times*.

[91] Ibid.

[92] "Alleged Exhibitor Fights Charge of Showing Obscene Films in Raided Garage," *Democrat and Chronicle*, June 27, 1925, 19.

the war-era outfits seem to have delegated responsibilities in a way that almost reflected, in miniature, the quasi-Fordist organization of the classical Hollywood studio system, then in its fullest flowering. The Hertzwig group functioned as an interstate enterprise, splitting distribution and production arms up into offices in Pennsylvania and California, respectively. The Arnild's organization, meanwhile, while contained wholly within the state of Minnesota, still saw one party producing filmed material (Einer Arnild and his wife, with the help of some anonymous models), another written literature ("The Professor"), another (Speedy Marcus) exhibiting the films to stag parties in town, and yet another (Mason Stanley) selling everything, via the bookstore, to home consumers. Likewise, Frank Ries's operation was headquartered in one geographic region (though he served viewers throughout the United States, sending representatives on the road to personally solicit customers), and relied on the combined efforts of a network of photographers, models, and salesmen to keep the whole operation in motion. The full roster of participants in this latter scheme will never be known, but must have been considerable indeed given that the number of initial arrests topped out at nearly forty people (though several were let go for various reasons).

Obviously, any parallel with the studio system is more evocative than precise, meant to function more as an illustrative allegory than exact parallel. The wartime Hollywood studios were rigidly structured, byzantine, integrated, hierarchical systems, whereas the miscreants in this section came together probably on a highly provisional and contingent basis; one would never refer to the type of organization seen in these examples as an "industry" per se.

But the comparison is evocative in another way, in that, at least for the two California-based examples, several of the conspirators worked in the filmmaking business in one capacity or another. Granted, none of them had responsibilities in any of the major studios, but rather were involved in various small-time operations. Though pornographic filmmaking at this time was amateur in all but name, it did attract those with professional connections in its earliest days (as was demonstrated in an earlier chapter), and seems to have reverted to that during this period, at least in some cases. The reasons for why this might have occurred are obvious: a foot in the professional filmmaking world would allow for easier access to equipment, laboratories, actors, and sets, to say nothing of the expertise to properly use all of this. Once it had been determined that a market existed for these types of films—as occurred during the years covered in the last chapter, when stag production was going through its first boom period—it is only logical that some among the professional class would be willing to meet the demand.

It is notable as well that the smut peddlers in this chapter should utilize established forms of selling and marketing to find their customers. This includes not only mail-order sales to individual consumers, which has already been covered, but also more prosaic forms of retail, such as bookstores and camera shops. These two types of shops turn up with increased frequency as sources of pornographic films—sold surreptitiously—during this time, and it would stand to reason that proprietors of these kinds of small businesses would be found in these little conspiracies.

What these three groups represent, then, is a sort of culmination of trends that were glimpsed in the previous, prewar era, and which only seem to have come into their own at this fairly late stage. The same means of distribution— mail order, personal delivery, under-the-counter in legitimate retail outlets— and exhibition—both domestic projection for individuals and private screenings for previously acquainted groups—continued, and in fact did so at a higher level of organization. This is a very different picture from the one given by Di Lauro and Rabkin, Knight and Alpert, and Thompson, all of whom have claimed that the war was a lean time for pornographers. But the Second World War, rather than representing a slowdown in the business of hard-core films, saw at least some outfits reaching a point of comparatively high complexity and flexibility. While this might have been an effective means of putting forbidden films before customers, the size of these operations would eventually make them attractive targets for law enforcement; even under the conditions which prevailed during wartime, there were still hard limits on exactly how far these kinds of concerns could expand. For the time being, at least, the wartime stag scene seems here to have found a kind of stability in its operations.

But not stable enough for some; whatever the advantages might have been to this way of doing business, the benefits did not always trickle down to the fortunes of individuals involved. Though we have seen multiple examples of people who had participated in stag films returning to society free of any crippling stigma, not everyone was so lucky. Most of the specifics of the Ries case, like those of Herzwig and Arnild, have been culled from contemporary newspaper stories; however, we are fortunate to also have a first person account from Ries himself, via his letter to the *Examiner,* which frankly explained the details of his scheme, as well as the consequences of his arrest.

Officially, these amounted to only a year in jail, but the police, he claimed, had spread rumors that he'd shared the names of all of his contacts in the business; by the time of his release, he had been effectively blackballed from the pornography world.

> Through this, I lost all my distributors from San Francisco to New York. They all think I am a "stool pigeon" trying to save my own neck …. For the last year I have been traveling from San Francisco to New York trying to get outlets for my films, but no luck. No one will trust me. They think it is a frame-up, so that is why I am killing myself.[93]

Ries made good on this final promise; he and his wife Barbara were found dead in a Chicago hotel room a few days before the Los Angeles paper's receipt of the letter. The official police verdict was that a "murder and suicide or double suicide" had occurred.[94] Had he been able to hang on, Ries might have been well-placed to ride out the dramatic upheavals that would come after the war, and which would change the way in which pornography was produced and consumed thereafter. The kind of secretive operation he had built would soon be an anachronism, but his success in the clandestine trade might have found an echo in the mainstream in a few decades' time.

[93] "Blue Movies," *Los Angeles Times*.
[94] "Hollywood Man and Wife Found Dead in Chicago," *Los Angeles Times*, September 16, 1947, 2.

4

Postwar: 1945 to 1970

This final chapter covers what in many ways is the most tumultuous period of stag production, distribution, and exhibition. During the war, the circulation and exhibition of stag films had settled into a basic pattern, but the postwar era would see major changes in the way that filmed pornography found its audiences. In many cases, these changes were the result of the continuing development of previous trends—especially in those types of exhibition designed to appeal to solo viewers, most notably arcade machines and projectors intended for domestic use. After 1945, pornographic films would go from an underground phenomenon to, by 1970, not only being openly sold—and screened—in bookstores and small theaters across the United States, but the subject of a Supreme Court decision which specifically established the right to their private ownership and use. The end of this period would see the public promotion and exhibition of films which featured the kind of sexual explicitness that had been, to that point, unique to the stag film; these would be shown in theaters before an audience of ticket-holders, in just the same (or at least roughly similar) fashion as those who'd gone to see *Love Story*, that year's highest grossing movie. It would appear, superficially, that very little of substance had actually changed from the days when such material was strictly subterranean fare, now that its prohibition had been lifted—before, people had gone to see pornographic films clandestinely, now, they went to them openly. A closer look, however, will reveal that the basic situation had changed dramatically. The economic basis of the adult film business, the social attitudes toward sexually graphic material, and the type and behavior of the audience had, by 1970, become so different from what they had been even twenty years before that comparison now becomes difficult. By this point, everyone engaged with the enterprise in any way, whether as producer, consumer, facilitator, or commentator, was doing something new. This was a turning point, and provides a natural end to my narrative.

Up to this point, I have mainly relied on whatever disparate primary documentation I could find, both as a deliberate strategy for writing history and because very few reliable secondary accounts exist which are addressed to this niche of films. For the period covered in this chapter, and especially for the period immediately after, the situation is quite different, for both primary and secondary sources. Vastly more primary material from after 1970 exists than could be legibly assimilated into a single chapter of a work of narrative history, at least at the scale that I intend. A fortunate result of this is that we now find ourselves in the midst of a veritable renaissance of scholarship on this time, blessed with a surfeit of individual works addressing a great diversity of topics within the broader history of pornography. My excursions into this era will thus be limited. I will use this chapter to follow the trends that I have covered up to this point, some of which become exhausted by the end of the 1960s, a few of which continue on in much the same way as they had before, and some of which evolve into other kinds of phenomena entirely, giving shape and momentum to the way in which pornographic films would be produced and consumed in the coming decades.

For the first several years of the postwar period, very few substantial changes seem to have occurred in the stag underground. Films were shown in the usual spaces and to (and by) the usual people; films were circulated via mail order, or by personal automobile; they were developed in secret by men with access to photographic equipment, either after-hours at their workplace or in their home (as William E. Lawyer of Frisbie, Michigan did, "apparently making a commercial business of developing obscene films for customers who could not get such service at legitimate film-developing companies"[1]). Stories of stag raids seem to have occurred with greater frequency overall after the Second World War; the years from 1946 to 1969 averaged out to forty-nine news stories per year (that I could locate) that were in some way related to stag films, a sharp rise from the thirty-six such news reports annually during the war years (note, of course, that not every story was breaking news of a new raid; as often, it was a follow-up to an initial arrest from some days or weeks before, often reporting on the trial or sentencing of the main participants). Again, it can't be determined whether this means that such screenings occurred more often, that police were more zealous in enforcing prohibitions on obscenity, that newspapers had

---

[1] "Driver jailed, Fined on 2 Charges Here," *Battle Creek Enquirer*, May 20, 1950, 2.

become more willing to report on them, or that some combination of these and other factors were driving the postwar uptick.

In any case, the immediate effect was a continuation of the tendencies from before 1945. Such was the static nature of the stag film scene that, even after the war, some of the very same scenarios that arose in the 1930s and 1940s would repeat themselves in this era. Yet again, the question as to whether or not undeveloped—and thus unprojectable—footage of nudity or eroticism could be sent through the mails needed to be answered, on two separate occasions no less. In both cases, the films under review weren't even staged performances but merely documentary footage (respectively, tourist shots from G.I.'s in South America,[2] and film by the Bible Institute of Los Angeles of "a nude South American tribe" intended ultimately to be used as training for medical missionaries[3]). Even some of the same people return to our story; less than a year after V-E Day, George Richter—last seen in the previous chapter under arrest as part of Frank Ries's group—again found himself in trouble with the law, nabbed for shipping obscene movies through the mail from the film laboratory that he owned at this time.[4] Thomas L. Cooper—another Ries conspirator—made his return to the bar of judgment as well, first in 1953, and then again in 1958, having been caught with "80 100-foot rolls of pornograph films and a movie camera" in his studio. At his last hearing, the judge called him a "vulture."[5]

As before, the FBI continued to monitor these activities, though by this point it was becoming apparent that the scale of the situation was presenting a serious challenge to the agency. It is true that the Bureau continued to make arrests for obscenity violations throughout the postwar period; judged by that standard, therefore, the Obscene unit was effective in a brute sense. But only a relatively small number of offenders were being caught as a result of investigations into the archive. The initial purpose of the collection was to enable the Bureau to determine the extent of traffic in pornography *in toto*, and therefore to attack the broad network rather than just individual distributors; judged by that standard, it was something of a flop. Most of their victories came about by simply catching someone in the act, rather than tracing an item found in the field to its ultimate source. Very often, the initial break in the case would come from an arrest by

---

[2] "Court Orders Obscene Films to Be Destroyed," *Democrat and Chronicle*, December 11, 1945, 17.
[3] "U.S. Judge Rules Questioned Film Can Be Delivered," *Democrat and Chronicle*, December 20, 1953, 6B.
[4] "Jury Indicts Man for Obscene Films," *Los Angeles Times*, April 7, 1946, 15.
[5] "Lewd Movie Maker Called 'Vulture,'" *Pasadena Independent*, December 22, 1958, 25 *sic*.

local law enforcement, who would then contact the Bureau once it had been determined that federal laws may have been broken.

Fortunately for the FBI, many police departments took a dim view of the trade in pornography, and were more than willing to alert the agency on the slightest suspicion of interstate traffic. Additionally, there were several organizations of concerned citizens who were happy to do much of the legwork for the Bureau, turning the investigation over to them when sufficient evidence had been collected. A notable example of this sort of freelance crusading came about in 1948 in the person of A. F. Bond, an investigator for Chicago's Morals Protective Association (a sort of latter-day, Midwestern version of the New York Society for the Suppression of Vice). Bond had set his sights on J. H. Harlow, also of Chicago, who, it was claimed, both "maintained a film distribution center in his home" and "employed 60 girls as models, the majority of them strip-teasers from Loop entertainment spots." Bond ordered a package of films from Harlow, requesting that it be sent to a general delivery address in the suburb of Hammond, Indiana. Well aware that he was courting possible federal trouble if he was to send a package across state lines, Harlow balked, only to relent when Bond told him "I gave the general delivery address because I didn't want those films to get into my wife's hands."[6] His pity overcoming his caution, Harlow sent the films; federal charges were filed soon after.

Absent this kind of assistance, the Bureau's investigative efforts in the lab produced little in the way of results. Despite its failure to advance any of the ongoing research into the smut trade, the Bureau's collection of pornography continued to bloat with the influx of new acquisitions and submissions, resulting in significant logistical hassles. Management of the materials in such a way as to make a particular item discoverable to the agency's detectives would especially become a major and persistent problem. Furthermore, the unique challenges of celluloid film as a reference material frustrated many of the efforts of the agents put in charge of the collection. Reels of film are an inherently difficult medium to render easily accessible—unlike books or photographs, they cannot be simply picked up and leafed through by hand, and instead require either projection or manual review on a set of rewinds. Neither of these operations are especially laborious, but they can be time-consuming; the brief amount of time required to examine one reel could add up exponentially if an agent needed to investigate, say, thirty-five others.

[6] "Purveyor or Obscene Films Outwitted by Investigator [sic]," *Hammond Times*, July 1, 1948, 13.

The Obscene File's custodian's solution to this was to print up reference cards for each film, "filed alphabetically by title, [containing] in addition to the title the file number, size of the film, and any identifications which have been made. Recently a brief synopsis of what is on the film has been placed on all new cards which have been made."[7] This card-catalog system was supplemented by stills taken from each unique film, also intended to speed up the reference process. At the time of the quoted memo, the cards had not been arranged in any order, but the custodian recommended that they be divided into two subcategories—"1. Those movies with all white subjects. 2. Those movies which have negroes included as subjects."—and then further split into "1. Those films with all male subjects. 2. Those films with all female subjects. 3. Those films with both male and female subjects. 4. Those films in which some of the subjects use a form of disguise."[8] It is unlikely that this baroque system of classification was useful in any way, or that the access it provided to investigators was of any important aid to their probes into the stag film trade.

Stymied though they may have been by film, the forensic approach used by the Bureau to trace the origin and provenance of the other obscene artifacts they'd captured was occasionally effective with other types of media. They seem to have had some success with printed matter, such as comics and literature; for example, an annual report for 1952 states that "2,794 specimens were searched through the Obscene File, of which 1,815 were identified with material previously submitted. These identifications, particularly of printed matter, are of value to the field since such an examination points to a common printing source."[9] But the same memo contrasts this success with the rather dismal results of the efforts to trace photographic images, moving and otherwise, back to their source, admitting that "in the case of motion picture film and obscene photographs, it is not possible to identify the source of this material because of the practice of copying and recopying this type of evidence."[10]

Other film-specific problems arose. In 1949 the Obscene unit discovered the problem that Knight and Alpert would anatomize in their *Playboy* article some twenty years later (and to which I referred in my introduction): that of films sporting a number of different, inconsistent titles. In certain instances, a film

---

[7] Memo, G.F. Mesing to A.K. Bowles, January 12, 1951, FBI 80-662, 1 *sic*.
[8] Ibid., 3.
[9] Memo, A.K. Bowles to Mr. Marbo, January 14, 1952, FBI 80-662, 1.
[10] Ibid., 2.

would bear one title on its can, a different one on the leader, and yet a third in the projected credits. This generally wasn't a problem for distributors or audiences, but caused considerable confusion at the Bureau, which was then engaged in an attempt to build a systematically arranged, rationally administered, reference library of smut. A memo dated January 27, 1949, sought to clarify the rules for classifying films by title, a normally straightforward process which turned out to be unexpectedly tricky in this case.

> OBSCENE FILMS—INTERSTATE TRANSPORTATION OF OBSCENE MATTER—In order to avoid unnecessary confusion in the future it is requested that where obscene films are submitted to the Laboratory in metal cans or cardboard containers the titles which actually appear on the films should be checked by unreeling the first three or four feet of film. It has been found that titles on metal cans or cardboard containers are frequently different from the contents of these containers. Therefore, the actual title should be listed in the letter of transmittal rather than titles found on containers.[11]

That this memo should have been necessary is a sign of the degree to which confusion reigned in the Obscene unit's film collection. Whatever enforcement action the Bureau might have intended to make against those in the pornographic film business, it was thwarted by the difficulty inherent in making such a large amount of material useful. Furthermore, that so many reels were annually submitted to the FBI, even if a great number of them appeared to have been copied from still older titles, suggests that the postwar stag trade was as healthy as it had ever been, at least in terms of sheer output.

The continued productivity of the creators and distributors of obscene films was a source of consternation to the Bureau, in part because the organization seemed to really believe that such material was dangerous. In their internal correspondence can be found traces of the same broad cultural concerns about pornography which were circulating through the rest of society. Agents began to express concern about the effect of sexually explicit material not just as a generally corrupting influence, but as an important component in the psychological attitude of the criminal. The words of the agents in these papers anticipate Walter Kendrick's sketch of the type of figure that postwar American society feared would find access to pornography, a "sinister figure of a mentally defective adult—probably male, probably also of lower-class origin—who

---

[11] Memo, January 27, 1949, FBI 30-662.

wallowed in infantile idiocy and wished to make others do the same …. He had
to be restrained, therefore—and the best way to restrain him was still, as it had
always been, to control his access to representations."[12] In a memo outlining the
strategies of the Obscene unit as a whole, Agent F. L. Price made the case for the
uniquely pernicious nature of obscenity violations, likening them to violations
of "White Slave Traffic Act cases," and suggesting that "salacious material have
been found to be the working partner of the prostitute." Continuing, he put
forward an idea that had become increasingly common by the late war years,
suggesting that pornographic material could drive a person to engage in a kind
of generally antisocial behavior.

> Responsible police authorities have stated that the circulation of pornographic
> materials have contributed to racial agitation and juvenile delinquency. This is
> exemplified by a statement made by Chief of Police C. B. Horrall of the Los
> Angeles Police Department who advised the Los Angeles Field Division that he
> was personally interested in our pending investigation of the Culmer F. Dickson
> case … since in his opinion "the obscene motion picture film circulated no
> doubt has a direct bearing on the juvenile delinquency and the large number of
> sex crimes prevalent in this area."[13]

Pornography, in this view, was not simply a gross disregard for bourgeois
propriety, or evidence of a morbid fascination with the corporeal, but potentially
a threat to public safety itself.

The Bureau were certainly not the only ones who felt this way. Around 1950,
there emerged a newfound, intense concern among parents, police, public
officials, and legislators over the risk of exposure of obscene films to juveniles.
Certainly before this period there was, in a general sense, a prevailing notion that
pornography ought to be kept from children and teenagers. But this was taken
with varying degrees of seriousness among different sectors of society; outrage
over this danger was virtually an animating principle of the New York Society for
the Suppression of Vice, for example, but was often treated with a considerably
lighter attitude by many journalists. The interest of youths—particularly young
males—in racy images served, for example, as a bit of theatrical color to the
story of 1939 raid of a dance hall screening, where "it was reported a number of
young boys were attracted to the place and upon being denied admittance took

---

[12] Walter Kendrick, *The Secret Museum: Pornography in Modern Culture* (Berkeley: University of
California Press, 1997), 208.
[13] Memo, F.L. Price to Mr. Rosen, August 25, 1944, FBI 80-662, 1 *sic*.

up positions of advantage at the windows and peepholes in an effort to witness the show."[14] But from the closing years of the war on, the Society's view of the matter began to gain more credibility (even as the Society itself was dwindling into a rump organization at this time), and by the close of the 1940s, the prospect of children finding their way to obscene films had moved from ribald joke to social menace.

Maybe pornography truly had begun to fall into the hands of teenagers (and younger kids) more often than it had before; press reports of juveniles caught with stag films certainly begin to crop up more often in this era even before the new decade begins.[15] But it is likely that fear of juvenile exposure to adult material was a proxy for other, more diffuse cultural anxieties. Teenagers during and after the war were in the curious position of having somehow moved both closer to and further away from the world of young adulthood, with either move becoming a focal point of social angst. In the first place, they were working more (initially filling in for departed GI's at service jobs and then continuing to occupy an expanded number of such positions at the commencement of peace), and thus earning more money. Lucre in hand, they were able to support a new consumer culture marketed exclusively to them, including comics, clothes, records, and cars, all of which tended to antagonize some segments of their older cohort in some way. Also, there was a wider fear that they were becoming sexually active at an earlier age. It is not clear that this was actually the case—evidence is very patchy on this point—but the age of first marriage had dropped significantly immediately after the war, which not only tended to imply the first claim, but was also in and of itself a matter of some concern to their parents' generation as well.

And yet, this era's teenagers also remained in school longer, often as a response to intense social and economic pressure to earn a high school diploma, keeping more kids in classrooms past their eighteenth birthday. The submission to a large public institution also meant a greater mixing of kids from different racial and class positions, fanning fears that they could be drawn out of the social roles they—someday—would be expected to assume.[16]

---

[14] "Big 'Smoker' Is Raided," *Courier-News*, February 25, 1939, 12 *sic*.

[15] See, for example, "Obscene Movie Charge Holds 3," *Pittsburgh Press*, January 15, 1949, 15; "Boys See Obscene Films, Arrested," *Herald and News*, October 16, 1950, 12.

[16] James Gilbert, *A Cycle of Outrage: America's Reaction to the Juvenile Delinquent* (New York: Oxford University Press, 1988), 17–22 *passim*.

The contradiction within teenagers' status as both more dependent and more autonomous was expressed in a moral panic over their fitness for adult society as it had been conceived of up to that point; the specter of the juvenile delinquent—combining a mature young adult body, and all its capacity for action, with a child's mind and temperament—embodied this anxiety perfectly. It was thought at the time that teenage criminal activity had seen an increase after 1950, though later revisions of the relevant statistics have cast doubt on this. In any case, worry over the possibility was enough to inspire a cottage industry of studies, publications, and public initiatives to get at the root cause of this behavior. The new teenage popular culture was famously pilloried for this, most notably by Dr. Wertham's attack on comic books. Less prominent but worth noting was speculation on the effects of pornographic materials, including films.

By the 1950s, a change in tone and emphasis became evident in many news articles about stag exhibitions, with their potential danger to children addressed at least at the subtextual level. In reports of raids of in-progress screenings, it suddenly became more common than it had been for journalists to specifically emphasize the presence (and sometimes number) of juveniles in the crowd.[17] In articles which didn't directly involve kids, the certainty that obscene films might have fallen into their hands but for the heroic actions of the authorities would be dutifully mentioned. Constant vigilance was necessary, even if no threat was imminent; see the 1953 interview with a member of the Chicago Police Department's Crime Prevention Bureau who had been assigned specifically to monitor teenagers. Despite the headline touting a large drop in sexual assaults in the previous year, the officer persisted in raising alarm over the dangers to young people of "pornografic literature, vicious comic books, and indecent pictures and films"; all of these, she claimed, "continue to inflame some boys and men to assaults on women and children."[18]

This alleged catalytic effect of pornography was alluded to in an earlier chapter; what seems to be unique to the postwar moment is concern at the exposure of teenagers and children in particular to such material, and the worry that it would fatally retard their moral or psychological development. This was always an undercurrent of anti-smut campaigns, but it became especially pronounced during this period.

---

[17] For a salient example, see "10 Arrested Where 65 See Obscene Films," *Palladium-Item*, March 15, 1951, 17.

[18] James Doherty, "Reports Drop in Sex Crimes; 1,713 This Year," *Chicago Tribune*, December 31, 1953, 11 *sic.*

On New Year's Day 1947, the *Star Press* of Muncie, Indiana, reported on a screening held the night before at the Wysor Theater. Written not as a typical piece of reportage but as a more colloquial "open letter" (and appearing under the headline "Memo to the Boss: Teen-Agers Jam Theater for Lewd 'Strip' Films"), the story described a scene of debauchery playing out before a crowd of possibly already-corrupted youths.

> There was little that was subtle about the striptease pornography at the Wysor, Boss. It was raw with nature in the raw. And it had all the fury of any burlesque show, with shouts of "Shake it, Babe," and "Rip 'em all off" flung up from the crowd.
>
> Most of the 1,200 people who were there, Boss, were 'teen-agers [*sic*]. There were pimply-faced boys of 16 and 17, standing up straight, puffing on cigarets, stringing unprintable oats unendlingly as they waited in line for the doors to open at 11:30 o'clock. There were sweet-faced youngsters of 13 and 14, who undoubtedly had told their parents they were attending one of the other special theater attractions in the city. There were boys and there were many young girls.[19]

Confirming that this disapproving tone was not simply the lament of a lone obsessive, a letter to the paper published the very next day echoed the sentiment. "The showing of such obscene movies cannot be too strongly condemned. Shown as it was to mixed juveniles it seduces the morals of the very ones whose minds we taxpayers are trying to improve through our schools."[20] Expressions of concern for the moral health of teenagers in the face of smut could be found beyond Muncie, and had been a mainstay of much of the discourse on pornography, even back during the war. For example, it is hard to find anything from the postwar era to match the rhetorical heights reached by a concerned citizen named Mary Beyer, who wrote to Director Hoover in 1943 to share her dismay over the influence of obscenity on the youth:

> "God" and Nature takes care of us. If their was none of this obscene litature allowed their would be less sex sins and more Virtue. It is shocking to listen to the children's conversations these days. They have lost all their innocence and of them and when they lose their innocence they are no longer sweet like those pure little children they still believe in the stork.[21]

---

[19] Jack Hiner, "Memo to the Boss: Teen-Agers Jam Theater for Lewd 'Strip' Films," *The Star Press*, January 1, 1947, 1 *sic*.

[20] J.H. Mundy, "Obscene Film," *The Star Press*, January 2, 1946, 6.

[21] Letter, Mary A. Beyer to Director Hoover, September 20, 1943, FBI 80-662 *sic*.

Few put the case against pornography as forcefully, but a somewhat tempered version of this concern indeed became more prevalent in the immediate postwar years, becoming, as historian Whitney Strub writes, "critical in the emergence of pornography as an American crisis."[22]

Strub suggests that much of the language of the moral panic over pornography had been brought into the mainstream by Tennessee Senator Estes Kefauver, who chaired the Senate Special Committee to Investigate Crime in Interstate Commerce.[23] Originally begun as a means to explore the role of organized crime, the Kefauver Committee (as it became popularly known) eventually directed its attention to a variety of tangentially related social concerns, including the special dangers facing teenagers. From the allegedly corrosive effects of comic books, the committee drifted to the availability of pornographic items, including films, and their role in inspiring bouts of delinquency across the United States. In the report of the committee's proceedings, the assumptions about juveniles and pornographic material crystalize into their most lucid, consistent expression. Although little evidence was presented to substantiate such claims, the committee's work rested on the certainty that pornography was actively harmful to the moral sentiments, especially those of children, and sought to establish this as simple common sense. As Strub puts it, "Kefauver helped construct a new national menace against which he happened to stand as the nation's foremost opponent; though 'little attention has been given' to pornography, Kefauver planned to change that."[24]

Most of the hearings of the Committee on Obscene and Pornographic Literature and Juvenile Delinquency, as that version of the panel was then known, took place in 1955 (its interim report was issued in 1956). Increased concern over the social effects of pornography in general, and its availability to teenagers in particular, became more pronounced shortly thereafter. It may be in part due to the publicity generated by Kefauver's work that, for example, the FBI saw a significant increase in requests for identification of submitted material in the following year. A memo reviewing the state of the collection in 1956 stated that in "1955, 4609 specimens were searched through the Obscene File as compared to 1859 specimens during 1954. In 1955, 1904 specimens were identified in the

---

[22] Whitney Strub, *Perversion for Profit: The Politics of Pornography and the Rise of the New Right* (New York: Columbia University Press, 2011), 24.

[23] Ibid., 25–7.

[24] Ibid., 24.

Obscene File as compared with 823 specimens in 1954."[25] This was sufficient to put even further strain on the manpower allocated to the maintenance of the file. Incorporating newly acquired items into the collection was not simply a matter of placing it on the appropriate shelf or in the right box; each new book, film, drawing, photograph, or sound recording needed to be inspected, cataloged, and housed among the other items in such a way as to be easily retrievable. This was a greater drain on the Bureau's resources than had been anticipated. The 1956 assessment stated that "examination of evidence submitted in current cases and the addition of new material to the Obscene File take approximately 50 per cent of an examiner's time. This is a considerable increase over the time necessary for the maintenance of this file in previous years because of the large increase in submissions in this type of evidence."[26] The next year's evaluation of the collection would note that a second examiner had been added to the staff to manage the volume of requests. The point here is not simply to belabor the story of the Bureau's difficulties in maintaining their collection of evidence, but to emphasize that demands on this resource increased just as the Senate investigations, which had garnered no small amount of publicity, were concluding. The coincidence of the Kefauver committee's attention to smut and a growth in law enforcement resources devoted to it would seem to anecdotally confirm that concern over pornography had become a general social worry by this time.

This worry, when expressed, was often paired with various other cultural anxieties. Arriving as it did in the midst of the second red scare, there was suggestion from some quarters that the greater availability of obscene material was in fact a tactic of the international communist conspiracy, designed to weaken the moral fiber of the citizens of the free world, with youth in particular being a special target.[27] Schaefer has documented how the group Citizens for Decent Literature spread outrageously lurid rumors about Soviet use of pornography as a means to demoralize other Warsaw Pact countries, including one alleged incident in which "hundreds of sex criminals, perverts, and prostitutes had been shipped to a Polish town where they were 'turned loose in front of scores of Red movie photographers with thousands of feet of film.'"[28] Again, Ms. Beyer was

---

[25] Memo, A.K. Bowles to Mr. Parsons, January 13, 1956, FBI 80-662.
[26] Ibid.
[27] Strub, *Perversion for Profit*, 30–3.
[28] Eric Schaefer, "Plain Brown Wrapper: Adult Films for the Home Market, 1930–1969," in *Looking Past the Screen: Case Studies in American Film History and Method*, ed. Jon Lewis and Eric Smoodin (Durham, NC: Duke University Press, 2007), 215.

apparently alert to this danger as far back as 1943, warning Hoover that "such publications is nothing but Communism on the rampage and getting away with it. Communism is a way to destroy all morality and Christianity, then it will be able to bore in <u>their</u> and put over this kind of filth."[29] Anti-communist paranoia would enjoy a healthy resurgence after the war, and the sudden prevalence of smut was among the many ills for which the red menace would be blamed.

However, claims such as these never enjoyed more than fringe appeal. For all of the bloviating of the more Bircher-inclined types, the idea that pornography was a direct communist scheme to undermine society never completely captured the public imagination. If their internal documents are anything to go by, the Bureau didn't take this idea particularly seriously either.

Much more plausible, to a variety of official investigators, was the notion that the mob were the real forces behind the wave of pornographic films and literature. Investigation of this criminal underworld was the original mission of the Kefauver Committee, which perhaps predisposed its members to conclude that the production of smut was a syndicate operation, a deliberate gangster conspiracy rather than the diffuse work of many relatively independent actors. "The Kefauver Committee in effect institutionalized opposition to pornography, creating an image of it as a massive industry run by murky characters who, whether by design or lack of concern, targeted children and sexually corrupted them."[30] This seems to have been the prevailing wisdom in the Bureau as well; within that agency, this opinion actually predated the Kefauver hearings. A memo dating back to August 26, 1944, refers to "intensive efforts of Agents of the Bureau to reach behind the local distributor in order to investigate organized interstate distribution systems of increasing strength."[31]

If the organized crime angle seemed more plausible to them, perhaps it was because their general mandate was to combat large-scale activity from unlawful actors, whether subversives or mobsters. The FBI was correct that distributors of pornography were conspiring to send materials across state lines, and that their operations were becoming more sophisticated and efficient—the stories of the Hertzwig, Arnild, and Reis groups profiled in the last chapter prove as much—but this is not in the same league as that of the powerful organized crime families who were responsible for much of the racketeering and corruption in

---

[29] Letter, Mary A. Breyer to Director Hoover, September 20, 1943, FBI 80-662 *sic*.
[30] Strub, *Perversion for Profit*, 27.
[31] Memo, Mr. E.A. Tamm to Mr. E.P. Coffey, August 26, 1944, FBI 80-662.

the major cities of the United States at that time. The idea that a widespread, seemingly spontaneous phenomenon—such as the spread of stag films throughout most of the country simultaneously—could be the product of lone actors or independent small groups was simply anathema to the Bureau's native reasoning. But significant involvement from traditional organized crime outfits would not occur until the mid-1960s, which, not coincidentally, was exactly the period in which significant profits were beginning to be realized through the production and distribution of pornographic films. Up to that point, however, the disorganization of these usually isolated distributors, even within separate regions of the United States, let alone at a national level, is such that it made little sense to describe all of this dispersed activity as one kind of concerted effort; the word "industry" should only be used here if it appears between inverted commas.

The sudden attention given to this problem might suggest that a concerted effort to suppress pornographic material was on the horizon; in fact, it became much more widely available, and much more public, in the ensuing decade. Rather than suppressing sexually frank literature, films, or photographs, American society became comfortable with the idea of it existing in some kind of public arena, available to any adult who wished to watch, read, or listen to it.

But to put it that way is to rely too much on abstractions—"American society," for example, did not "become comfortable" with pornography, but rather the actions of various institutions and related changes to the way masses of people lived their lives worked in such a way as to nullify whatever moral, religious, or ideological objections remained that inhibited its availability. The emergence of pornography to the surface happened relatively quickly, but not overnight, and not without considerable ideological labor. In the last part of this last chapter, I would like to anatomize this process more precisely, and to demonstrate its effect on the way in which pornographic films were created, sold, and exhibited. This subject could fill a shelf, let alone a book, so I will try to maintain focus as much as is possible on how the circulation of films was affected. Just as in my chapter on the Second World War, I must admit there's something slightly perverse about considering broad social upheavals—of the sort that affected the fate of whole populations—only inasmuch as they influenced a relatively niche phenomenon such as pornographic movies, but whatever residual embarrassment this may cause is preferable to not recognizing the power of these larger forces at all.

It is something of a truism that the postwar era, roiled by the sexual revolution, saw a rapid change in the definition of obscenity, both in the legal and social realm. But it might be more accurate to say that it was only in this period that the first serious attempt to describe obscenity was made. As late as the mid-1950s, precise language on the part of those investigating the spread of pornographic materials did not rise to the level of any serious concern. This was not because of any confusion or ambivalence about the nature of any particular set of material; quite the opposite. Sexually improper works—films, but also photographs, cartoons, or written works—were so obvious in their transgressions that one term was as good as any other. For some, it was as though the severity of the breach of standards of taste and morality could only be properly accounted for in the great number of epithets available.

Roy Blick, the head of the vice unit at the Washington, DC police department, provides an ideal example during his testimony before the Kefauver Commission, as questioned by chief counsel James Bobo:

> Mr. Bobo. When I speak of pornographic material, would you describe what pornographic material comes within the jurisdiction of your squad?
> Mr. Blick. Filth.
> Mr. Bobo. Made up of books, pamphlets, film, phonograph records?
> Mr. Blick. Yes, sir.
> Mr. Bobo. Lewd and perverted character?
> Mr. Blick. Obscene, indecent, and lascivious.[32]

The vague and imprecise language here reflects an equally impoverished conceptual basis for what could be regarded as improper. Officer Blick and Mr. Bobo were then, in 1955, certain that all of those adjectives by themselves described a specific quality of an object, a quality which was conceptually coherent and could be objectively identified. No further elaboration was necessary, as they were confident that they were speaking of a shared standard of decency. That it could be otherwise seems not to have occurred to them.

A shorter version of this same sentiment (and a perennial reference in pornography studies) is Supreme Court Justice Stewart's declaration, in his 1964 *Jacobellis v. Ohio* decision, that, when it came to identifying a particular work as obscene or not, "I know it when I see it." Stewart seems here to implicitly agree with the same premise that motivates Blick and Bobo: obscenity exists as an independent value—he even claims it can be seen! Just as crucial as the

---

[32] *Hearings Before the Subcommittee to Investigate Juvenile Delinquency of the Committee on the Judiciary United States Senate, Eighty-Fourth Congress, First Session, Pursuant to S. Res. 62 Investigation of Juvenile Delinquency in the United States* (Washington, DC: Government Printing Office, 1955), 104.

seven oft-quoted words, however, are the six that immediately follow, usually omitted from the quote: "I know it when I see it, and this film is not it." That he could not articulate a positive value or concept of obscenity gave Stewart no choice—rather than fall back on an imagined, but unarticulated, notion of what made the film under review (Louis Malle's *Les amants*, which had landed an Ohio theater manager in jail for obscenity) illegal, he was forced to grant clemency.

This pattern would recur throughout the remainder of the 1960s: The court, asked to judge the merits of a lower obscenity prosecution, would reaffirm the general legal principle that some tangible quality existed which was common to all works deemed pornographic, but then would not only typically fail to find it embodied in the work before them, but, in attempting a more precise explanation of that quality, would simply confuse the issue even further. Stewart's sentence immediately preceding his famous one, in which he muses on what a workable definition of "hard-core pornography" would entail, perhaps ought to be the one on which his legacy rests, as it seems to acknowledge the futility of the whole enterprise: "I shall not today attempt further to define the kinds of material I understand to be embraced within that shorthand description, and perhaps I could never succeed in doing so."

The case that laid the intellectual foundation for this process was *Roth v. United States* (1956). The defendant, Samuel Roth—who had testified before the Kefauver Committee some years before—had been recently prosecuted for selling magazines containing mild eroticism and nude photography via the US mail. In this case, the conviction was upheld by the court but, in the text of the decision, authored by Justice Brennan, the judges ambitiously attempted to settle on a definition of obscenity that would both be intelligible to citizens and act as guidance for prosecutors. "Obscene material," wrote Brennan, "is material which deals with sex in a manner appealing to prurient interest, and the test of obscenity is whether to the average person, applying contemporary community standards, the dominant theme of the material appeals to prurient interest." Elsewhere in the ruling, he made the even more forceful declaration that the First Amendment did not cover such material, and that it implied "the rejection of obscenity as utterly without redeeming social importance."[33] The court likely thought that this was enough to settle the matter.

---

[33] Quoted in Kendrick, *Secret Museum*, 201.

But the gaps in this seemingly airtight rule have been pointed out ever since it was written. While this did establish that obscenity was not afforded First Amendment protection, and though its pronouncements were seemingly straightforward, the decision did not explicitly spell out what was and was not permissible. The criterion of social relevance in particular confounded contemporary commentators, and would prove to be a frustration to law enforcement. To demonstrate a total absence of social value would prove difficult for prosecutors, and finding some semblance of the same, in ever more subtle forms, became a specialty of defense counsel. As Walter Kendrick put it, "'Utterly' was the worst culprit, since it seemed to suggest that if the tiniest nugget of 'social importance' could be dug out of a book, it would neutralize a mountain of prurience."[34]

The court was attempting here to reconcile two principles which could not but come into conflict: the notion that some subjects simply ought not to be depicted, either pictorially or in written description, and that of individual freedom of expression. Their solution affirmed the existence of the obscene, but then relegated it to a purely conceptual sphere, never, or only rarely, to cross into the material world. Once some particle of redeeming social importance could be located in a particular work, the obscene was banished back to the spirit realm. Roth failed this challenge, but he was among the last to do so.

The court was prepared to dutifully follow the logic of its own precedent. An important follow-up trial which demonstrated this in action was 1967's *Redrup v. New York*. This was yet another case which treated a bundle of state and local prosecutions of print materials—magazines and novels—in one verdict. The decision reaffirmed that the court intended to follow a strict reading of *Roth*, even quoting each part of its three-part verdict to emphasize the point. *Redrup*, in many ways would prove to be as influential as any of the court's other obscenity rulings, as it was the cited basis of dozens of subsequent reversals of lower court decisions; this happened so often that the practice would become known, in the chambers of the court, as "redrupping."

These decisions did not clarify the situation as the court had hoped it would. The precise ingredients of both "obscenity" and of "social value" were so ill-defined that, in the later years of the 1960s, the justices were obliged to personally review each item brought in under an obscenity conviction, leading to periodic screenings

---

[34] Ibid., 201–2.

of films in a basement conference room (Justice Marshall cheekily dubbed these appointments "movie days"). Justices Black and Douglas would routinely skip these, believing that the plain language of the First Amendment did not allow for suppression of speech of any kind, obscene or otherwise. Other judges had their own idiosyncratic view of what might render a work impermissible. Justice White would overturn a conviction on any material so long as it contained "no erect penises, no intercourse, no oral or anal sodomy."[35] Justice Brennan, likewise, "was willing to accept penetration as long as the pictures passed on what his clerks referred to as the 'limp dick' standard. Oral sex was tolerable if there was no erection."[36] The diversity of private opinions could not, at this time, cohere into a legally sound principle that might have guided regulation among the states, counties, and municipalities. That the arbitration of obscenity law was guided by such disparate private opinions as we see here is a sign of the wider confusion that reigned over the regulation of pornography in this era.

If the lack of consensus demonstrated here by the court, in both its public proclamations and the personal convictions of its members behind closed doors, reads as faintly comical today, it should be recalled that their pronouncements had actual downstream effects, and these reverberated among law enforcement bodies throughout the United States. Without clear direction about what a prosecutor might legally go after, police were hesitant to take any action at all. This was a real institutional consequence of the court's confusion, and it would have a direct effect on the development of the nascent adult film industry, just now beginning to establish itself as a viable commercial entity.

The extent to which local law enforcement felt powerless to go after pornographic material in the 1960s can be illustrated in another comparison to the Kefauver Commission. The 1955 opening of their investigation into pornography was inaugurated by remarks from a man named Peter Chumbris, a lawyer working as a general counsel for the group. He gave a presentation which had intended to establish the case for the antisocial consequences of wide availability of sexually frank materials. A major piece of evidence marshaled in support was the findings of a recent, wide-ranging survey of local police departments, asking their opinion on how best to combat the problem. The respondents were in virtually universal agreement that the most useful

---

[35] Bob Woodward and Scott Armstrong, *The Brethren: Inside the Supreme Court* (New York: Simon and Schuster, 1979), 227.
[36] Ibid., 229.

measure would be stiffer penalties for violators. A statement from Los Angeles (Chumbris didn't specify whether it was from the police department or from a local prosecutor) summed up the consensus: "Under our present laws, it is sometimes difficult to obtain convictions that discourage further participation by the defendant, because the sentence imposed is quite often negligible. It is generally felt that if such a conviction would require registration as a sex offender, the frequency of repeaters would drop noticeably."[37] Chumbris pointed out by way of example that North Dakota, in response to the alleged crisis of inadequate penalties for obscenity violations, had proposed a law authorizing the confiscation of any mechanical equipment used to aid in the commission of the crime. He hinted that this might be a useful template for other states, quoting a complaint from an unnamed police department in support:

> We throw up our hands; we grab a man with $50,000 worth of pornography, and his equipment, his car, and they burn up the pictures and so forth; they give him back his car, they give him back his equipment, and right away he is setting up business again in another town after he gets out of the jurisdiction of that particular court.[38]

Fourteen years later, the President's Commission on Obscenity and Pornography, convened by President Johnson, returned to these same questions. Tasked with discovering, among other things, the extent to which obscenity violations had become a problem to law enforcement, the group sent out a survey of their own to hundreds of local prosecutors. After the fashion of Chumbris's work, they asked what would be the greatest aid in their battle against smut. As before, a near-uniform response emerged, but the need was not for increased penalties. Of those who regarded pornography as a serious problem within their districts (significantly, many did not), a striking number considered themselves hampered mainly by a vague and inconsistent legal conception of the crime itself, largely as a result of high court rulings. Where before there was a debate on how best to suppress a crime, now there was disagreement on whether or not it could be established that a crime had even occurred.

The imprecise language of the *Roth* decision in particular was regarded as pointlessly constraining, and many of the attacks on the ruling drilled down to its minutiae (those surveyed were attorneys, after all). One respondent wanted "the

---

[37] *Subcommittee to Investigate Juvenile Delinquency*, 54–5 sic.
[38] Ibid., 55.

courts to strike out the 'utterly' and emphasize the real dictionary definition of 'redeeming.' As the standard stands, it is a contradiction in terms, jabberwacky, strictly out of Alice in Wonderland."[39] Others were less verbose; asked to explain "any special difficulties in enforcing existing obscenity legislation," one Georgia prosecutor answered simply, "Without redeeming social value."[40]

These complaints were not merely academic, but, as far as those surveyed were concerned, a genuine response to a serious barrier to legal proscription of pornography. While these surveys were conducted in the final years of the 1960s, it must be kept in mind that the answers reflect not only the immediate situation of these prosecutors, but rather their experience under the *Roth* regime over the course of the previous fifteen years. One prosecutor explained that the precedents established by the Supreme Court, and adopted by lower courts, had, in his opinion, rendered investigations and prosecutions pointless. "Because of a past experience of acquittals and directed verdicts for the defendants in the cases that have been brought and the time, trouble and expense involved to establish the proof required by the decisions of the U.S. Supreme Court, police and prosecution officers are prompted not to get into this field of frustration and fruitless results."[41] The willingness of the courts to exempt material that would have surely qualified as actionable in years past led some to believe that they might never settle on a constitutionally approved definition of obscenity, rendering that formerly solid concept too much of a moving target to be of any use. One prosecutor despaired at what he saw as a lack of direction from above: "The selectivity for prosecution of that matter that apparently is hard-core [pornography] today tends to inhibit prosecution—for it may well not be so tomorrow—when it reaches the Appellate Court."[42] Yet another blamed "wholesale, indiscriminate reversal of convictions by appellate courts [which] blunts prosecution enthusiasm, ie, why waste time and money?" The same man sardonically advised that the best hope for overcoming this state of affairs was "jamming Justice Douglas' pacemaker and putting Justice Fortas on sabbatical";[43]

[39] Survey 83, 7 *sic*. Folder "Prosecuting Attorneys Working File," Box 116. Commission on Obscenity and Pornography Records, Lyndon Baines Johnson Library, Austin, Texas.

[40] Survey 16, 7. Folder "Prosecuting Attorneys Working File," Box 116. Commission on Obscenity and Pornography Records, Lyndon Baines Johnson Library, Austin, Texas.

[41] Survey 83, 3. Folder "Prosecuting Attorneys Working File," Box 116. Commission on Obscenity and Pornography Records, Lyndon Baines Johnson Library, Austin, Texas.

[42] Survey 11, 3. Folder "Prosecuting Attorneys Working File," Box 116. Commission on Obscenity and Pornography Records, Lyndon Baines Johnson Library, Austin, Texas.

[43] Survey 42, 5. Folder "Prosecuting Attorneys Working File," Box 116. Commission on Obscenity and Pornography Records, Lyndon Baines Johnson Library, Austin, Texas.

in a similar vein, another prosecutor hoped for "mandatory retirement of Supreme Court justices who are senile and whose sex drives apparently is satisfied only by permitting pornography."[44]

Everything about this post-*Roth* status quo would seem to be a gift to those involved in the business of producing and selling stag films. If the immediate postwar years saw the circulation of films continue on much as before, then we might expect that a de facto easing of regulations on top of that might encourage expansion of these programs, at last allowing those involved to make a living away from the gaze of the policeman. If the only significant change in this period was to the regulatory environment, then the classic stag program should have persisted into the 1960s and beyond, even flourished, making life easier for both the audiences and the dealers that served them.

It is certainly true that, by 1970, erotic films were available to a much wider audience than they had been before, and they were every bit as graphic as anything seen by secret audiences in the previous decades. But aside from the reach and character of the films, the very means by which they were sold, shown, and seen would represent a significant departure from the practices which I have documented up to this point. Some of this may be attributed to the legal climate, but that was not the only factor at work.

In fact, the ease in regulations was, if anything, no help at all to the kind of stag screenings that had been the norm up to this point. Just as the very legal foundation of obscenity was being eroded, the classic stag show, the staple of pornographic film production and exhibition, suddenly began to lose its relevance. Often one-man operations, these tiny distributors wouldn't entirely disappear even by the end of this period, but the decline in their fortunes was acknowledged even by the most sympathetic observers.

One small-time distributor who could serve as an illustration of this trend was a man named John Nasser, who, by the mid-1960s, has gotten in well over his head. A resident of Terre Haute, he exemplified the slump that this field of endeavor found itself in. Nasser was a character on the fringes of society who made most of his official living working at a race track and running poker games. Since the 1930s, he had been showing stags to various gatherings throughout west-central Indiana, having obtained the prints from a group operating along a route stretching from Peoria to Danville, Illinois. At the peak of his business, he

---

[44] Survey X, 5. Folder "Prosecuting Attorneys Working File," Box 116. Commission on Obscenity and Pornography Records, Lyndon Baines Johnson Library, Austin, Texas.

claimed to have had 104 separate audiences that he would regularly screen films for, encompassing different lodges, civic groups, and other types of informal gatherings. By the 1960s, however, he seems to have been beset by a terminal case of bad luck: only two of his regular screening outlets remained, and he was on the verge of going out of business. (The only reference to Nasser that I could find in the local press from this time was a 1962 classified ad in the "lost and found" section of the *Terre Haute Tribune,* imploring the reading public's help in recovering "several hundred dollars" he'd lost downtown on the previous Monday morning.[45])

Part of this appears to have been caused by Nasser's falling out of political favor in Terre Haute. Eugene Slabaugh and George Huntington of the Kinsey Institute had met with and interviewed Nasser in the 1960s; in a 1965 conversation between the two researchers, Huntington declared that he was competing for a shrinking share of the market with a rival in town who benefited from social connections that the older man did not have. Huntington surmised that this man was "probably being backed financially and is currently receiving some political support from either an assistant or deputy fire chief in Terre Haute who is a former commander of the VFW."[46] But this alone couldn't account for his failures. Quite apart from local competition, Huntington and Slabaugh acknowledged that a real change in the habits of the men who had made up Nasser's audience had come about, and he was ill-equipped to adjust to it. They note specifically his inability to understand that the audience of the 1960s was not the same as the one he had catered to during the war, or even shortly thereafter.

> The reasons he's being cut out of the business is that he can't adjust to the times and is unable to realize ... that the market is changing. You're going from all 16mm shows of one-hour duration in various clubs to a lot of 8mm private viewing things, and these are films to be sold ... and this guy can't get on to the idea that it's possible to sell a film for $15 to $20 that you buy for seven-and-a-half dollars. He wants to get $50 [or] $75 out of this film and he can't stay in business. He can't compete.[47]

Though there were still opportunities to project stags for groups of men in the 1960s, these were losing ground to other types of exhibition; traditional stag shows had become a smaller slice of the pie. Nasser's way of doing business—to

[45] *Terre Haute Tribune,* September 19, 1961, 15.
[46] George Huntington and Eugene Slabaugh in discussion, 1966, Kinsey Institute.
[47] Ibid.

say nothing of the price he demanded for screenings and sales of prints—seems to have become ossified in the 1930s, when 16mm was the format of choice. Nasser seemed to be at a loss, without any plan to adapt to changing conditions.

But the change in the economies of pornographic film affected more than just the luckless Nasser; as Huntington and Slabaugh saw it, the entire landscape for stag film distributors and exhibitors really had changed. Another stag dealer discussed by the pair, Hansel Aldridge of Anderson, Indiana, seems to have been a much more prudent businessman; unusually for a man of his position, he owned his own optical printer, which he used to create new copies of existing films (he never produced any original titles of his own), and took special measures to protect his investment in case of legal trouble. Huntington explained the situation to Slabaugh:

> Now Aldridge has a backlog, has stored a set of 70 master negatives on film, which he is storing and is not going to use. He stored these as a sort of safety factor if he ever is arrested and his material is confiscated; this material is stored in a separate place. And he can pay his fine and come back out and start up his business again with no problem, with no initial investment again.[48]

Even as fastidious as he was, however, he wasn't able to make a proper living printing, renting, or showing films, thanks to the thinness of the market. As Huntington put it, "Aldridge still hangs onto his machinist's job, despite the fact that he, hands down, has the largest outlet of films, and is making what is a borderline-to-a-good living in dealing with [erotic] material, both film, still photos, cartoon books, or what will you. I think he can handle anything, but he can't get all the bread he needs this way."[49] Though probably very few minor stag dealers got rich from their activities before the war, by the middle of the 1960s it seems as though it had become nigh impossible to make the barest living from stags. That the fortunes of both Nasser and Aldridge appeared to be heading in the same direction, despite the evident gulf in business acumen between the two, illustrates that, by the mid-1960s, there was very little future in an enterprise of this scale.

To what may we attribute this general decline? Ruling out the possibility that sexually charged moving images had lost their sway over the eyes, brains, and other parts of the audience which had previously patronized the classic stag

---

[48] Slabaugh audio notes, 1965, Kinsey Institute.
[49] Huntington and Slabaugh discussion, 1966, Kinsey Institute.

show, we must agree with Huntington that they were seeking similar material elsewhere. But where? Perhaps we might look to the setting-place of much of twentieth-century film history, the public, mainstream, and commercial movie theater. It has been suggested that, from the late 1940s on, greater tolerance of nudity and sexual themes in theatrical exhibition may also have diverted some members of this audience.

The years after the war saw films with relatively strong sexual imagery making their way to the movie theater. As I pointed out in an earlier chapter, consolidation of public film exhibition into the greater mainstream industry required uniform standards of content, which meant the total exclusion of eroticism from commercial movie theater screens. The last attempt to test this consensus had occurred at the Princess theater in 1923 (referred to in Chapter 1), which met with harsh disapproval from other exhibitors in the trade press. For the following quarter century, no theater owner would suggest or even hint at the possibility of screening stag films at his establishment. It is true that sporadic raids and arrests for showing so-called obscene films did happen in commercial theaters before (and during) the war, but none of the reports that I found involved pornography per se; most often, these were features, either exploitation movies or European art films.

But by the late 1940s, a newfound tolerance for films featuring either some nudity or a more blatant sex appeal can be found. This was largely the work of theatrical exhibitors, themselves suddenly reeling from changes in their basic business model. The *Paramount* decision (which had smashed the studios' vertically integrated control over production, distribution, and exhibition of films), competition from television, and the dispersal of a significant portion of the audience to the suburbs, to name only the most prominent factors, had disrupted the relatively stable model that had served mainstream film exhibition exceptionally well over the last few decades. Such pressure led exhibitors to court audiences and taste cultures curious about non-Hollywood cinema, resulting in the expansion of, for example, the market for arthouse and foreign movies.

This, famously, cultivated a commercial space for the great classics of postwar modernist film, but the search for alternatives to Hollywood led many exhibitors to place their bets on less-elevated fare as well. Eric Schaefer has demonstrated that burlesque and nudist films enjoyed a resurgence in the years immediately following the war. Burlesque films had stepped into the gap left by the traditional exploitation picture, then on the wane. Appearing as both features and short subjects, these films centered on one or more striptease performances, often pointedly alluding to the type of act that might have been common on the vaudeville stage during the turn of the previous century. In fact, the men who brought this genre to prominence—J. D. Kendis, Willis Kent, and Dan and Louis Sonney are names that recur often in these kinds of studies, though there were certainly others—pitched these films as an almost nostalgic call-back to a comparatively sexually innocent era. Schaeffer contends that "ten years and the intervention of the war had established some distance between burlesque's controversial status in the 1930s and the postwar market. This distance allowed the exploiteers to construct burlesque as a bygone form of entertainment despite its resurgence on the nightclub and theater circuits."[50] (This is an early appearance of the germ of nostalgia that would grow into a full-blown subcultural taste for pre-1970s pornography, of the sort the David Church finds in the current "remarketing of stags" to appeal to "the more general allure of vintage-ness."[51])

Nudist films, conversely, wouldn't mount a sustained comeback until the early 1950s, when the first feature-length treatments of that theme would be released;[52] but it would seem that their appearance on theater screens (some of which, following another of Schaefer's hypotheses, may have been "cobbled together from older material"[53]) might have been an early sign that exhibitors had found a way to appeal to audiences with a taste for more explicit fare.

But even the lure of nudity in and of itself does not seem sufficient to have skimmed off of the audience for stag shows. While it is undeniable that the general tendency of popular and cinematic culture was toward a more frank, stylized, or even *outre* portrayal of sexuality, there were larger structural factors at work. The collapse of the classic stag program can more readily be explained not by assuming that its audience was necessarily lured away to other kinds of erotic entertainment, but by examining the conditions which supported that kind of exhibition, which were themselves in a state of decay.

The audience for these shows, as seen in many examples across the preceding chapters, was composed primarily of men who had some kind of already-existing association with each other, often related to worklife or some manner of civic organization. These forms of association were in a state of slow

---

[50] Eric Schaefer, *Bold! Daring! Shocking! True!: A History of Exploitation Films, 1919–1959* (Durham, NC: Duke University Press, 1999), 307.

[51] David Church, *Disposable Passion: Vintage Pornography and the Material Legacies of Adult Cinema* (New York: Bloomsbury Academic, 2016), 37.

[52] Schaefer, *Bold!*, 299–302.

[53] Ibid., 299.

disintegration after the war. The postwar years saw a drop—at first gradual, though ultimately rather steep—in membership among civic groups, including the great lodges which would have hosted many of the stag shows of the previous era (Robert Putnam has demonstrated that this trend affected nearly every civic and professional association[54]). Related to this is the flight of a significant part of the population from the cities and into suburbs. This undercut opportunities for after-hours work-based socialization among men, since fewer and fewer laborers lived near their places of employment, but also, more generally, were both a cause and symptom of a general trend toward privacy and domesticity in social life. Putnam cites a study of the changing community life in Lexington, Massachusetts, as it evolved from a small country town to a bedroom community to make the point that, after postwar suburbanization, "work-based ties now compete with place-based ties rather than reinforcing them. If your co-workers come from all over the metropolitan area, you must choose—spend an evening with neighbors *or* spend an evening with colleagues. (Of course, tired from a harried commute, you may well decide to just stay at home by yourself.)"[55]

Certainly, these social ties did not disappear completely overnight and similarly, stag shows based on these kinds of associations would still occur in the 1950s and beyond. The first lines of this very book describe such an incident, and the diligent researcher can find news reports of raids on stag shows taking place into the late 1960s. But these isolated incidents were regarded as passe even then. The President's Commission concluded in its final report that "the market for 'traveling road shows' of hard-core stag films [had] dramatically declined during the 1950's and became relatively rare in the 1960's. By 1970 only a few operators put on stag shows for groups of 50 to 200 people." The report did allow that for "some parts of the country, however, the traditional form of 'stag show' has retained some viability"[56] but by this time, even those had become so rare as to be remarkable.

As both this audience and style of exhibition dried up, pornographic films would survive, and even flourish, in other contexts. The next two decades would see stags finally come up from the underground, finding a broader audience than anyone would have dared predict. This was accomplished not

---

[54] Robert Putnam, *Bowling Alone: The Collapse and Revival of American Community* (New York, NY: Touchstone Books, 2001), Appendix III.

[55] Ibid., 214.

[56] *Technical Report of the Commission on Obscenity and Pornography, Volume III* (Washington, DC: U.S. Government Printing Office, 1971), 190–1.

by an incorporation into the mainstream of commercial, theatrical cinema, but via the accelerated development of other types of distribution and exhibition. The producers and sellers of these films were able to adapt to the changing circumstances by concentrating their business on other markets. In fact, the focus of their efforts rode the coattails of those same trends which were responsible for the dissolution of the traditional stag show; rather than trying to remain viable as a form of entertainment for an audience of acquaintances, the marketers and distributors of postwar pornographic films chose instead to turn to the solitary viewer as their main customer. Already-existing audiences which had constituted themselves via an association from work, or neighborhood, or civic membership were no longer as viable as they had been, and a newer type of distributor, one dedicated to finding and marketing to individual consumers, was coming into being. The screening of pornographic film would, in this era, turn from a communal ritual into a private pleasure.

Most of what seems to have been brand new during this time were, at the root, simple improvements to already-existing infrastructure. As always, those innovations which proved to have the greatest impact were those that extended established practices. Mail order is one such example.

Films had been distributed by mail since the earliest days of consumer-grade film, even before the debut of 16mm. As we have seen earlier, it didn't take long for sellers of adult films to join the game, soliciting customers via print ads and mailing all manner of explicit footage. By the 1950s, however, these operations had become more sophisticated, in part because these same retailers had learned to market their materials with a bit more finesse.

After the war, direct mail marketing had become a widely utilized means of not only advertising goods to consumers but, more importantly, of harvesting information about them so as to more effectively convince them to buy more in the future. The methods in use in the Eisenhower era may seem crude in comparison to those of the present day, when the recording, storage, and exploitation of personal data are the very gears which turn whole sectors of the economy. Nevertheless, these early methods of targeted advertising were still significantly more complex than what had come before, and the distributors of adult material would profit immensely by their adoption.

Though something of a tangent to my main topic, an understanding of these new strategies of direct marketing will explain much about the changes in spectatorship of pornographic films in the 1950s and 1960s. It is fortunate that the men who established these practices were only too happy to share their stories, resulting in whole shelves of writing explaining exactly how to peddle one's wares in the most efficient fashion. One particularly generous figure was Walter Weintz, a copywriter and ad man who, decades after his career had peaked, revealed his secrets in a memoir recounting its highlights.

Along with another man named Frank Herbert, Weintz had used direct mail to drive up the subscription numbers of *Reader's Digest*, pulling it out of a postwar slump. Important to a campaign such as this, Weintz insisted, was very specific attention paid to the language of the appeal. So he and his team, for example, would begin by "offering prospective customers a special introductory bargain," available only to new subscribers.[57] They would add further incentives to potential customers by including "free" gifts, such as "a copy of *Getting the Most Out of Life*, a book of *Digest* article reprints."[58] Inducements of this type they called "action devices," the "action" they hoped to inspire being new orders. He regarded these kinds of tricks as creative adaptations of methods which had been used to move sales in other business environments, particularly retail.

> Retail stores fill the Sunday supplements with "cents off" coupons—which are simply another form of "hot potato." And they use premiums on every conceivable kind of product: "Buy one product get another free" is a universally-used offer. Once the principle is grasped, it is easy enough—or at least it becomes easier—to apply it for any product you may be selling.[59]

The refinement of mail-order copywriting was not a radical innovation, but merely the extension of marketing logic to a different realm of communication— from the face-to-face to the written.

What was something of a departure from traditional practice was the means by which these sellers identified their target consumers and, from them, shaped a market for their product. This was done through the collection, aggregation, and indexing of information about customers, based on a variety of factors— often broad demographic categories such as age, income level, and occupation, but also behavioral traits, such as past spending and consumption habits. This information could then be used as a basis for crafting narrow appeals to each particular group. As with his copywriting tips, Weintz illustrated this strategy with practical examples, coming this time from the world of politics. In a 1950

---

[57] Walter Weintz, *The Solid Gold Mailbox: How to Create Winning Mail-Order Campaigns, by the Man Who's Done It All* (New York: John Wiley & Sons, 1987), 36.
[58] Ibid., 38.
[59] Ibid.

campaign for Ohio Senator Robert Taft, who was fighting an uphill re-election battle in the face of an expensive counter-offensive from the state's powerful labor unions, Weintz decided to craft the most specific direct-mail push possible. He did this by writing a number of different test letters, each focused on a different political concern but closing with an identical appeal for a monetary contribution to the campaign; the letter which received the greatest response (ironically, the same one which most enthusiastically touted the Senator's sponsorship of the union-busting Taft-Hartley act) became the template for the wider mailings sent out throughout the remainder of the campaign, especially those destined for the blue-collar cities which were presumed to be the challenger's natural constituency. Taft sailed to victory.[60]

While neither the Taft campaign nor the *Readers Digest* marketing team invented these methods, their cases provide a lucid example of exactly how efficient and effective the process had become at this time. Richard Viguerie, who would later perfect these techniques in his mission to revive the right in the 1970s and beyond, said of the Taft campaign that "this is the first documented case in American political history in which direct mail was used to bypass the establishment (in this instance the union bosses) and go directly to the constituents (the union workers themselves), producing a victory based on conservative principles."[61] This is the very function of "direct" in direct mail— to send a field-tested, fine-tuned appeal to a specific individual, rather than a diffuse message from the top down that would have to first meet the approval of certain gatekeepers before it could be heard. Seen in this way, the advantages of this approach to pornographers are readily apparent.

Due to the ambiguous legal status of the material on offer, dealers in adult films who did business by mail had every incentive to take their trade directly to the customer. The means by which they not only found those potentially interested in such fare, but stoked their curiosity to the point where they would place an order, were virtually identical to those used by Weintz and Herbert. Adult film dealers adopted these early on; Mary Tager, a retired mail-order seller of short nude and striptease films, testified before the Kefauver Committee that she had purchased address lists as a way to find new customers as far back as

---

[60] Ibid., 82–3.
[61] Richard Viguerie, *America's Right Turn: How Conservatives Used New and Alternative Media to Take Power* (Chicago, IL: Bonus Books, 2004), 89.

1950.[62] But by the end of the 1960s, the use of direct mail marketing had become much more advanced. The case of Saul Resnick, profiled in an internal memo as part of the investigation by the President's Commission on Obscenity, illustrates how the same methods used to sell Robert Taft could also be used to sell dirty movies.

Resnick, proprietor of an adult film concern called Cameo Distributors, Inc., was in many ways typical. He did not disdain print advertising, and was known to buy space in men's magazines such as *Escapade*, *Gent*, *Men's Real Adventures*, to name just a few. These were not insignificant investments; the Commission's memo notes that the price per inch of these publications ranged from $28 in *Men's Action* all the way up to $112 in *Country Wives*. But these ads served a dual function: first, and most obviously, they initiated contact between his outfit and the potential customer, and was the first step in what, ideally, would be

Figure 4.1 Mailer from Mondo Films, one of the distribution outfits owned by Saul Resnick. (From folder "Saul Resnick," Box 20, Commission on Obscenity and Pornography Records, Lyndon Baines Johnson Library, Austin, Texas.)

[62] *Subcommittee to Investigate Juvenile Delinquency*, 316–17.

a completed sale. The more important result of this first encounter, however, was that Resnick had now obtained the mailing address of someone who had demonstrated not only an interest in his products, but was sufficiently motivated to take action—i.e., fill out a form and mail it in—to obtain it. Resnick now also knew what particular product line appealed to this particular prospective customer, and would tailor any future correspondence accordingly.

Resnick also purchased mailing lists, after the fashion of Tager. However, Tager, according to her testimony, simply bought her lists from a general dealer who offered only limited precision in terms of the demographics of the addresses he sold. Asked by the committee if the lists "were really just compilations of names and addresses without any specification that they be people who purchased nude photographs," Tager admitted that "there would be no actual way of knowing. You would only have … their word that they were buyers of merchandise that would be similar to what you were selling."[63] Resnick, meanwhile, worked with sellers who had much more actively curated their lists, having refined their techniques over many years. One of these, a man named Floyd Clemens, frequently sold lists to Resnick, and claimed to have assigned names to different lists based on their preferred type of product: prosthetics, film, lingerie, paperbacks, and so forth.[64]

Resnick's mailings followed the field-tested principles of persuasion used by the *Readers Digest* marketers. One mailing, which purported to be a letter from a woman called "Crystal," pitches the recipient an "introductory offer" of some films at a discount price.[65] Another, subsequent "Crystal" ad makes the same claim, specifically worded to appeal to a new customer. "I ran my little ad, for good people like yourselves who will have a crack (at my lower prices) and at seeing some of the finest quality stag films I ever filmed! Loaded with adult Action! Take advantage of my Get Acquainted Prices. I do want to make you a long term repeat satisfied customer."[66]

Resnick was also willing to make use of the "action device," usually in the form of a short sample film. Costing between $1 or $2 and measuring 26 feet,

[63] Ibid., 317.
[64] "Memorandum for File: Floyd Clemens (Mailing List Broker)," August 12, 1969, Folder "Floyd Clemens," Box 19. Commission on Obscenity and Pornography Records, Lyndon Baines Johnson Library, Austin, Texas.
[65] "Hello, Friend; Thanks for answering our little ad.," Folder "Saul Resnick," Box 20, Commission on Obscenity and Pornography Records, Lyndon Baines Johnson Library, Austin, Texas.
[66] "Hello Friend; Thanks for answering my little ad.", Folder "Saul Resnick," Box 20, Commission on Obscenity and Pornography Records, Lyndon Baines Johnson Library, Austin, Texas.

these would be offered in the initial print ads, as an enticement to buy more full-length films later on. While not quite in the same category as the free book offered by Weintz, it was in a similar tradition, in that it would both bring to the fore customers willing to spend money and bait them to continue with an actual item, as opposed to more innuendo-laden ad copy. As Weintz wrote, albeit in a very different context, "The difference between a *physical, tangible* valuable *object* and a vaguely worded *offer* was all-important."[67] Resnick was a serious businessman, and saw no reason not to avail himself of the latest techniques in salesmanship; his overall success, while not quite on the scale of *Readers Digest*, was a testament to their effectiveness.

The value of the address went beyond just a direct sale, however. Resnick also used the names he collected in trades with other dealers. Of the 25,000 names he had accumulated as of 1969, approximately one-sixth had been obtained from his fellow distributors via sale or trade of mailing lists; Resnick claimed to know of distributors who boasted of 50,000 names.[68] By circulating lists of names among other dealers, Resnick would have verified, after the fashion of Weintz, that the addresses he was contacting belonged to men who had purchased adult materials via the mails in the past, and were thus likely to do so again. His main reason for doing this was of course to find as many paying customers as possible, but he also sought to minimize the number of customers who were indifferent to his appeal. Sending out letters cost money, and it was natural that he would not wish to waste resources on those for whom explicit films held no interest.

But even worse than simple lack of response was active hostility. Many households objected to what they saw as the intrusion of pornography into their very homes, either because of a general moral objection to the material in and of itself, or because of concern that it might be intercepted by any children or teenagers in the house.

As befits an era in the midst of a moral panic over juveniles' exposure to sexuality of any sort, the latter scenario was the stuff of nightmares. As early as 1958, a UPI wire story would warn readers:

> Each day several thousand teenage youths in every part of America receive similar lurid solicitations in the family mail. They are the product of a new and flourishing racket which the Post Office Department has tried in vain to smash.

---

[67] Weintz, *Solid Gold Mailbox*, 37–8, emphasis in the original.
[68] "Memorandum: Saul Resnick," September 12, 1969, Folder "Saul Resnick," Box 20, Commission on Obscenity and Pornography Records, Lyndon Baines Johnson Library, Austin, Texas.

Figure 4.2 Mailer from Margin Films, another of the distribution outfits owned by Saul Resnick. (From folder "Saul Resnick," Box 20, Commission on Obscenity and Pornography Records, Lyndon Baines Johnson Library, Austin, Texas.)

Postal inspectors estimated that direct mail advertisements for pornography are flooding the country at a rate of 50 million pieces a year. A large proportion of this obscenity goes to children in their early teens who get on the sucker lists by writing away for cowboy pictures, model airplanes, camping knives and other items which are offered in innocent-looking ads ….

For the adult customer or the older teen-ager who has access to a home movie projector, there are 8mm "stag films" at prices ranging up to $75 which depict "sexy sirens in ACTION." The advertisements intimate—in language that cannot be quoted in a family newspaper—that the movies show actual boudoir scenes, including a wide variety of perversions.[69]

For their part, distributors themselves seemed to want to avoid putting their material in front of both adults who objected to pornography on principle and

---

[69] "Fifty Million Pieces of Pornography Flood Mails Annually, Most Aimed at Teenagers," *Capital Journal*, February 19, 1958, 11.

juveniles generally, or at least this is what they claimed publicly. Chris Warfield, a man in Los Angeles who was "in the business of supplying pictures or films of pretty girls through the mail," told an interviewer from the Obscenity Commission that he "advocates strict penalties under a new law for indiscriminate mailings,"[70] and took steps to alert the recipient to the content of his mail before opening by including "a standard notice on the outside of each envelope warning that it contains 'adult' material"[71] (though this warning could also function as a form of advertising as well). He was far from alone in this practice, with most mail-order proprietors insisting that the ensuing bad publicity would not be worth the trouble in the end. Assuming Warfield's sentiments were genuine, it is interesting to note that pornographers of this era did not share the libertarian orientation of many of their successors in the industry. Given the real danger that obscenity enforcement posed to their businesses and themselves, this may seem counterintuitive. But whatever retrospective meaning may be attached to their work now, and whatever they may have been accused of at the time, they did not consider themselves to be engaging in subversive behavior. In contrast to later pornographers like Larry Flynt, who, perhaps self-servingly, styled themselves as free-speech crusaders, dealers like Resnick and others of that generation regarded themselves simply as businessmen meeting a consumer demand in exchange for a modest remuneration. Thus, when asked their opinion on the matter, those engaged in the business of adult entertainment generally registered no ideological opposition to obscenity laws, and often would declare themselves in favor of regulation of some kind.

Certainly, there was a self-serving element to this as well. So long as content of adult material was regulated to a legible degree, established pornographers could rely on the built-in advantages they already enjoyed to maintain their position in the market: generally high-quality products, an established system of distribution, an active mail-order operation, and a network of reliable retail outlets could all be used to crowd out any potential competitors. With no brakes on what could legally be portrayed in a film (or magazine, paperback novel, etc.), they were vulnerable to ambitious competitors, who could potentially attract the attention of an audience through sexually audacious imagination alone.

---

[70] "Memorandum For File RE: Chris Warfield (Los Angeles HO.4 2220)," December 15, 1969, Folder "J Sampson Reading File," Box 33, Commission on Obscenity and Pornography Records, Lyndon Baines Johnson Library, Austin, Texas.

[71] Ibid.

Atlanta's Mike Thevis, a dealer in erotic films and books, admitted as much to a researcher from the Johnson Commission; as he saw it, "competition would increase enormously if all laws were dropped. A lot of potential entrants into the field stay out, he believes, because it borders on illegality."[72] What, at first glance, seems to be pure timidity on the part of various distributors of adult material actually served a dual function; this ought to remind the scholar of commercial pornography that the boundaries producers and sellers felt were worth transgressing, were less a matter of ideological conviction—the protection of the innocent, the spread of sexual libertinage, the sanctity of the home—than a simple question of business.

These complications aside, mail order remained popular as a way for distributors and aficionados of pornographic film to find each other. In fact, it apparently became popular enough to inspire a general worry, on the part of regular customers, over the possibility of dealing with dishonest brokers. This concern was evidently such that 1967 saw the publication of sex researcher Glenn Thompson's *Sex Rackets*, which purported to advise the potential customer on how to avoid scams. Most of the rip-offs described by Thompson in his book amount to either blatant false advertising, catalogs and ads worded to seem to promise more than they could deliver, or distributors simply taking the money and sending nothing in return. As he put it:

> The man who places a numbers bet or an illegal wager on the horses, only to have his bookie skip town when he hits it big, is in no position to sue. And neither is the man whose overactive fantasy and imagination lets him read in to advertising what is not clearly there. He may think he is ordering something highly prurient and obscene, but if the advertiser delivers only legal nudes, he cannot sue because he expected to receive illegal sex action films.[73]

Like most books promising to address the truth about pornography from this period, its value is less factual than artifactual, though that it was published at all would seem to suggest that more people were indeed ordering sexually explicit items (and, since the book purportedly advises the reader on how to safely acquire "illegal sex action films," it can be assumed that fewer and fewer potential customers were being dissuaded by legal proscription).

---

[72] "Memorandum To: Files FROM: Paul Bender," June 27, 1969, Folder "Mike Thevis," Box 21, Commission on Obscenity and Pornography Records, Lyndon Baines Johnson Library, Austin, Texas.

[73] Glenn Thompson, *Sex Rackets* (Cleveland, OH: Century Books, 1967), 122 *sic*.

While mails had become more efficient as a means of distribution, other opportunities to see adult films outside of one's private home were coming to the fore in this era. Single-viewer peep booths would become much more prominent, advancing significantly beyond the first tentative experiments during the war; recall, in the previous chapter, Frank Healy's attempt to load a Panoram machine with a 16mm striptease reel at Detroit's Olympic Recreation Room. Despite these failures and the ensuing legal repercussions, a surprising number of arcade managers tried to replicate this method, with at least several of them meeting with the same results. An early example occurred in 1954, when Leonard Lenit, the operator of the Super Arcade in downtown Chicago, was arrested for "displaying lewd film." Lenit wasn't the only one to try this even in that city, as the *Tribune* noted that his "Super Arcade is one of several S. State st. spots where obscene pictures have been shown in peep movie machines."[74] This practice was not unique to Chicago, either; historian Peter Alilunas has documented a wave of arrests occurring across the United States beginning in the early 1950s, all for some variation on the charge of "operating indecent peepshows." Arcade proprietors were also arrested or cautioned in San Francisco and Washington DC during the 1950s, mostly for showing non-hardcore striptease films of the like produced by Joe Bonica, William H. Door, and, in another echo from the war years, W. Merle Connell, who had been one of those initially arrested as a part of the Hertzwig ring.[75] He concludes from this that this kind of unsanctioned use of the now-obsolete machines (the Soundies Corporation had ceased operations in 1947) was a fairly common practice, a claim which seems to me to be credible. Only through their misuse were Panorams ever to be successfully adopted by exhibitors.

Despite unwelcome attention from the authorities, the coin-op business was profitable enough to attract investment from many different entrepreneurs. A number of different businessmen realized, evidently simultaneously, that real profits could be found in the ownership and control of a fleet of machines, which would then be leased to bookstores, bars, or other sites where men tended to gather in public. Though some of these investors may have also been involved in ancillary industries—the production of films, ownership of bookstores, etc.— control of the booths themselves was the cornerstone of their operation.

---

[74] "Obscene Films Seized in Raid at 500 S. State," *Chicago Tribune*, July 23, 1954, 37 *sic.*

[75] Peter Alilunas, *Smutty Little Movies: The Creation and Regulation of Adult Video* (Oakland: University of California Press, 2016), 46.

Development and growth of adult bookstores in recent decades would prove to be a key to the success of the new style of peep booths. In contrast to the machines found within, the sudden proliferation of just these kinds of bookstores would prove to be a genuine innovation in the distribution of stag films, both directly and indirectly. Adult bookstores were the result of an emergence of a kind of print culture which served up material with a relatively high degree of sexual frankness. For all of the harassment from police, prosecutors, and judges that stag movies and those associated with them had received from the beginning of the century on, it was not films but print culture—books, magazines, comics, and other printed works—that had more often been at the forefront of legal battles over alleged obscenity. A perusal of the papers of the New York Society for the Suppression of Vice, for example, will show far more entries in the monthly reports concerned with salacious reading material than with their film equivalents. Similarly, most of the celebrated, precedent-setting obscenity trials of the twentieth century concern books, such as the 1933 *Ulysses* case, or the much later (and successful) prosecutions of Samuel Roth and Ralph Ginzburg. Probably this had something to do with the fact that printed works require no special technological dependencies. To watch a stag film, one needs a film projector and the skills to operate it; to read a book, it is enough that one is merely literate. Seen that way, it is no surprise that the guardians of morality would direct their resources to the fight against the spread of literary smut than of any other sort.

However, it is also true that print culture, perhaps in part because of these battles and their attendant publicity, was able to find and exploit a market for these kinds of works, and thus to establish a relatively stable commercial ecosystem. This in turn would be more likely to successfully withstand future legal challenges. Roth may have gone to prison for trading in obscenity but, as Jay Gertzman points out, only a few years later he would be released into a world that had seen the flourishing of the marketplace for erotic literature, both antique and modern.[76] A side effect of this was the establishment of stores devoted exclusively (or, depending on local laws, sometimes merely predominantly) to the sale of adult books and magazines.

Though printed items usually made up the bulk of the items for sale, it was the rare adult bookstore which didn't diversify its holdings to include all

---

[76] Jay A. Gertzman, *Bookleggers and Smuthounds: The Trade in Erotica, 1920–1940* (Philadelphia: University of Pennsylvania Press, 1999), 283–5.

kinds of adult-oriented products. A mix of attractions was the order of the day; the offerings at one Denver-area bookstore, inspected by the President's Commission, act as something of a Platonic ideal of these type of places: "In addition to the pinball machine, telephone, cigarette machine, and change booth, approximately 30 magazines, 8-10 movies, and 10-15 paperback books are displayed. These materials … are sold by the cashier."[77] (Obviously, there were exceptions to this arrangement; another Denver bookstore "on the edge of the skid row section" was shown to have been "more limited in its entertainment offerings," with only a pinball machine and some semi-private film booths to bait the customer.[78])

As we have seen, stag films were often found for sale at these places, and this increased availability of films directly to the consumer (typically on 8mm or Super 8 rather than 16mm) grew the home-viewing market even more. But even the presence of print materials, especially periodicals, was a boost to home viewers, as these usually carried ads for mail-order film offerings. But for customers who had no access to a projector, or who wished to watch such films away from their domestic habitat, the booths near the back of the store were the real attraction.

According to legend, it was an encounter with a modified peep machine, after the fashion of those described above, which launched the career of the first serious peep-booth entrepreneur. Martin Hodas, a seller of jukeboxes, pinball games, and other coin-operated amusements, claimed to have found a roadside arcade in New Jersey that had outfitted a row of Panorams with some striptease films.[79] He took this idea back to New York City, where he was soon able to place his own modified design in adult bookstores across town. Filmmaker Larry Revene, who shot some of the pornographic loops and shorts which would eventually play in these machines, writes that Hodas soon had trouble "supplying enough units as quickly as the burgling market demanded. The next problem was the glut of quarters that had to be emptied constantly to keep the machines from jamming."[30]

---

[77] "Marketing Analysis: Denver," Section IV, 40, October 31, 1969, Folder "Mail-Out T&D Effect," Box 83. Commission on Obscenity and Pornography Records, Lyndon Baines Johnson Library, Austin, Texas.

[78] Ibid., Section IV, 39.

[79] Amy Herzog, "In the Flesh: Space and Embodiment in the Pornographic Peep Show Arcade," *The Velvet Light Trap*, No. 62 (Fall 2008), 31–2.

[80] Larry Revene, *Wham Bam $$ Ba Da Boom! Mob Wars, Porn Battles, and a View from the Trenches* (Hudson Delta Books, 2013), 68.

Imitators came fast on Hodas's heels. Mike Thevis, already manufacturing his Cinematics model of peep machine for non-sex films, quickly placed the machines in his chain of Atlanta-based adult bookstores. Thevis is alleged to have passed this idea on to Ruben Sturman, who followed suit by adapting the concept to a design of his own. "Instead of relying on a stand-up machine, Sturman's company placed two coin-operated 8mm projectors in a small booth with a screen and door that could be locked. A customer deposited a quarter to see one or two minutes of a twelve-minute 'loop,' a film that could run continuously."[81] He moved these into his vast chain of adult bookstores across the United States, and also started a company, Automated Vending, to build and service machines.

In contrast to the modified Panorams encountered earlier, which had been rather haphazardly placed in bars or arcades, the strategy of Sturman, Thevis, and (after a few years of leasing machines to outside bookstores) Hodas of placing these machines in their own stores was much more ambitious and rational, from a business standpoint. By controlling the manufacturing and maintenance of their devices, as well as the sites that they occupied, they made sure that each one of the quarters put into the slots landed in their pockets. Commenting on Sturman's case, Eric Schlosser points out that "booths cost almost nothing to maintain. New loops cost about $8 each, an expense that could be amortized by the coins of two or three customers. The projectors were durable and cheap. An average-sized store earned at least $2,000 a week from its peep booths, and a large store could easily earn five times that amount."[82] Hodas eventually moved to eliminate the cost of purchasing the film from the books, opening his own bare-bones studio for shooting his own loops in the late 1960s, creating a kind of small-time vertical integration of production, distribution, and exhibition.[83]

The proliferation of peep show booths into an ostensibly a public space was yet another example of the way in which pornographic films had come into open view. Both the stores and the sellers of the films shown within were reasonably free of police harassment (though this would certainly vary greatly depending on local circumstances), owing in large part to the uncertain legal climate referred to above. The men in charge of these businesses were aware of this confusion

---

[81] Eric Schlosser, *Reefer Madness: Sex, Drugs, and Cheap Labor in the American Black Market* (Boston, MA: Houghton Mifflin, 2003), 129.

[82] Ibid., 130.

[83] Richard F. Shepard, "Peep Shows Have New Nude Look," *New York Times*, June 9, 1969.

and intended to exploit it. "The law is very vague on obscenity," Hodas told the *New York Times* in 1969, though he also admitted that he wasn't taking any chances with regard to the content of the films he would screen. "The idea is not to give them any reason to think a film's obscene. As long as there's no auto-eroticism or sexual contact, it's all right."[84] Thevis, too, was generally hesitant to display anything that might earn him too much attention. An investigator from the Johnson Commission reported that "Thevis does not try to be a 'leader' in explicit content … Thevis changes his content to keep up with the times after judicial decisions have made it safe to do so. He has got more explicit stuff in his files, and will use it when it appears advisable."[85] (Though he was referring specifically to his printed wares in this quote, I think that it is reasonable to assume that his attitude here extended to the films shown in his stores.)

Thus, it is not surprising that, according to the evidence I could find, the films screened in peep booths were slightly less explicit than some others that might have been for sale to home viewers. A Johnson Commission investigator reporting on a pair of Denver-area stores found, for example, that the films on display confined to either striptease acts or mild lesbian activity.[86] An earlier report from the California Attorney General's office surveyed many peep booths in the state, and found that the "films usually feature a single female. They range from strip-teases to extended close-ups of undulating shaven genitals simulating sexual intercourse."[87] Unsimulated sex acts are mentioned only sparingly in any contemporary reports; in another Johnson Commission study of peep arcades in San Francisco, only one was found to feature explicit, hard-core sex, while offerings at other sites were consistent with the material described above.[88] One arcade manager even admitted that he was "careful to only order one-girl films, so as not to offend any of the patrons"[89] This is in keeping with the peep booth tradition; Alilunas says that the films that had been shown in modified Panorams probably didn't even feature nudity, for example,[90] so the unwillingness of

---

[84] Ibid.

[85] "Subject: Visit with 'Pornographer,' Thevis, Atlanta, Ga., June 24, 1969", 2, Folder "Mike Thevis," Box 21. Commission on Obscenity and Pornography Records, Lyndon Baines Johnson Library, Austin, Texas.

[86] "Marketing Analysis: Denver," Section IV, 39.

[87] Thomas C. Lynch, *A Report to the California Legislature on Obscenity: The Law and the Nature of the Business* (California Department of Justice, 1967), 88.

[88] "San Francisco Erotic Marketplace," 55. Folder "Traffic and Distribution," Box 136. Commission on Obscenity and Pornography Records, Lyndon Baines Johnson Library, Austin, Texas.

[89] "San Francisco Erotic Marketplace," 50.

[90] Alilunas, *Smutty Little Movies*, 45.

these somewhat-public screenings to leap to the avant-garde of graphic sexual representation might be evidence of a certain running reticence on behalf of their exhibitors. Hodas and Thevis both understood that it often makes more business sense to chase trends than to set them, and given that the films they screened were among the earliest to be shown in a public space, this was likely a well-founded caution.

Whatever the nature of the material screened within, the coin-op peep booths of the 1960s were among the first entries of stag films into a public setting. However, these steps out of the private realm of the club, fraternity, or workingman's gathering were still tentative, enough so that some qualities of the presentation were changed. The most notable of these was that, despite the new apparatus's situation within public space, the peep booth experience was one that was intended solely for the private, individual viewer. Obviously, the machines of the 1960s were constructed in such a way as to assume that the space it would occupy was at a premium; the average adult bookstore could only fit so many onto the premises, resulting in a booth that offered a tight fit. But other details built into its construction suggest that the overall presentation was intended to preserve and reinforce the viewer's solitude.

Ironically, these measures sometimes came at the cost of the viewer's privacy. An observer from the President's Commission, studying a pair of bookstores in Denver, observed of the patrons that they "appeared to be seeking personal satisfaction in viewing the movies. The exact nature of such satisfactions apparently varied from pleasure in viewing nude females to something more physical (a number [unrecorded] of patrons were observed with an open trouser fly as they exited the arcade.)."[91] Initially, it seems as though masturbation in the booths was at least tolerated in some locations. One of the Denver establishments featured booths that could certainly have been exploited for this purpose. "The extremely weak light and the black curtains and booth frames create a situation which would certainly allow private actions such as masturbation."[92] However, there was also a strong imperative to discourage this behavior, and to especially discourage homosexual activity; it was as though the price of allowing such films out into the streets was the expectation of a corresponding restraint on the spectator's behavior. Los Angeles, for example, would soon forbid the use of privacy curtains in booths; a state legislative report noted initially that the

[91] "Marketing Analysis: Denver," Section V, 51. Box 83.
[92] Ibid., 39.

"machines, the floor and the surrounding area in the enclosure were found to be caked with sexual emissions. This was found to violate certain local health and sanitation standards and the enclosures were removed in an effort to avoid this problem."[93] Likewise, at another store in Denver, the booths were arranged in such a way—a "booth in use" light, prominent signage prohibiting more than one customer per booth, brightly colored curtains—so as to be "not conducive to masturbation or homosexual contact."[94]

The ultimate effectiveness of these measures is impossible to know. But the overall drift is clear—booths were intended for an audience of one. Limits on what could be portrayed in films themselves had been relaxed, but the communal appreciation of erotic images, in whatever capacity, had been sharply curbed.

As businesses based in California (and, to a somewhat lesser extent, New York) had stepped into the void left by the small-timers of the Midwest, so too would these same regions pioneer new forms of public exhibition of adult films. Earlier in this chapter I documented the way in which the general temperature of movies shown in theaters had risen, beginning with the exhibition of nudist and burlesque films, which then cleared the path for nudie-cuties and sexploitation. During this time, hard-core stags continued to lead a parallel existence, still banished from public screens but available to those who sought more explicit thrills and were willing to look. It's only at the end of this period, and the end of my story, that hard core at last crept into theaters and out of the underground completely—advertised openly, and available to any adult willing to buy a ticket.

By 1967, San Francisco and Los Angeles would see the opening of the first storefront theaters dedicated to 16mm "beaver" shorts. Just skirting the edge of hard core, these films were little more than an even-more-explicit take on the "art studies" genre of film, consisting of a series of shots of a single nude woman striking suggestive poses. Schaefer links this kind of film to its antecedents in "the tradition of home and arcade films shot on and exhibited with 16mm equipment."[95] As theaters devoted to sexploitation films tended to project only 35mm, and peep booths were moving to 8mm, storefronts stepped in as venues for both a certain kind of content and a certain kind of format. "That 16mm production was relatively anonymous and inexpensive and that sexploitation

---

[93] Lynch, *Report to the California Legislature*, 89.

[94] "Marketing Analysis: Denver," Section V, 41. Box 83.

[95] Eric Schaefer, "Gauging a Revolution: 16mm Film and the Rise of the Pornographic Feature," *Cinema Journal*, Vol. 41, No. 3 (2002), 7.

films were somewhat more daring ... seems to have given 16mm filmmakers and other low-end operators reason to push acceptable theatrical limits and make and show inexpensive beaver films."[96] 16mm projectors could be had for a reasonably low cost (certainly relative to a 35mm setup), and the theaters were usually simple converted commercial spaces, often not licensed as theaters at all. Costs of the film, whether rented or produced in-house, were also manageable, and the final product was typically a no-frills affair indeed, relying on straightforward nudity and sexual forwardness for its "attraction," rather than any of the effects that could only be generated by a more elaborate production.

The escalation of ever-more-explicit content did not end here, resulting in an all-out arms race between virtually all filmmakers operating at the time. "But the 16mm producers were pushed into a position of innovation to stay a step ahead of traditional 35mm sexploitation, which, in turn, had been forced into greater explicitness by the arrival of the beavers and increasingly sexy Hollywood fare."[97] Schaefer contends that, while outmaneuvering its more mainstream competition in explicitness was an important advance, equally as decisive was the development of more coherent narratives within the context of the "beaver" film, as well as the expansion of these movies to feature-length (albeit very often on the short side; running times within squinting distance of an hour were not uncommon).

The eventual result of this was the hard-core narrative feature. Combining the narrative elements of sexploitation (ultimately derived from mainstream cinema in general) with the unsimulated sex and nudity of the beaver shorts, these movies would become a legitimately important part of the commercial moviegoing landscape in the 1970s and 1980s, albeit one that would never attain the prestige of the major studio productions, or even the quasi-respectability of unapologetic genre pictures. By the end of the 1960s, this form had just begun to emerge, first appearing in San Francisco, and then in New York, with theaters devoted to pornographic features soon springing up at all points in between.

These developments have been addressed in greater depth elsewhere, and I see no need to belabor this history any more than I have. But I do think it is important to emphasize an aspect of the exhibition conditions of the new beaver films—and of their hard-core feature descendants—which I feel has been undertheorized, relative to its broader importance. Like the films which were

---

[96] Ibid., 8.
[97] Ibid., 12.

sent through the mails to the domestic viewer, like those which unspooled within the coin-op peep booths, these works were intended for the lone spectator. If this orientation toward the individual was not a feature of the film itself, it could be discerned from the very arrangement of the exhibition situation.

This is admittedly a counterintuitive assertion. Unlike the other two forms of exhibition reviewed in this chapter, the viewer of the theatrical sex film was almost invariably in the presence of others during a screening, and in a much more open, public space. The similarity between the experience of watching a mainstream film in a multiplex and a pornographic film in a theater would surely be close enough to lure the spectator to a collective experience of the work, or so one would think.

But observations made of the new adult theatrical scene at the time militate against this interpretation. That this was a form of exhibition intended for individual spectators appears to be borne out by the findings of the Johnson Commission, which noted that its patrons were, as with peep booths, mostly single men. The commission devoted several pages to a study of these new theaters, and a census of the audiences among several houses in disparate geographic locations found that a mean average of 88 percent of all attendees were men on their own.[98] While many theaters at the time made efforts to appeal to couples as a means of improving their general image—Arlene Elster, manager of San Francisco's Sutter Cinema, insisted to the *New York Times* that "couples and younger people" were a growing segment of her audience[99]—this seems to have been successful only in limited circumstances. The author of the commission's report wrote that couples tended to visit the theaters only on weekends (and even then they made up but 3 percent of the total audience), and thus were likely not regular patrons during the week. Local variables such as the overall class and age of the potential pool of viewers may have been a factor as well; looking at the breakdown of their census of individual theaters, only the college town of Amherst, Massachusetts, showed a significant portion of the crowd made up of couples (25 percent versus 70 percent for single men), whereas theaters in midtown New York City, Los Angeles, Chicago, Atlanta, and Kansas City found single men making up more than 90 percent of their

---

[98] Charles Winick, "Some Observations on Characteristics of Patrons of Adult Theaters and Bookstores," in *Technical Report of the Commission on Obscenity and Pornography, Volume IV: The Marketplace: Empirical Studies* (Washington, DC: US Government Printing Office, 1969), 234.

[99] William Murry, "The Porn Capital of America," *New York Times*, January 3, 1971, section SM, 8.

crowds.[100] As the Commission concluded, the "group attendance at movies or in bookstores is not important in terms of numbers. The typical patron is clearly a solo male who seems typical of his community or area and does not appear deviant or marked by stigmata."[101] While outliers could certainly be found in particular circumstances, we are probably safe to generalize theatrical adult films as an activity for individual men.

Once inside the theater, said men tended, according to the commission's study, to continue in their solitude, keeping to themselves even more than they might have done in other situations. Strangers were given a wider physical berth than usual, as the commission observed: "In most adult theaters, however, the customers tend to sit further apart than do movie goers at conventional theaters."[102] The theaters themselves seemed to operate in such a way as to encourage this behavior in their spectators, arranging their seating to create more distance between them (the commission: "Some theaters have designed their interiors in such a way as to maximize privacy, perhaps in response to customers' requests."[103]) and to preserve anonymity of the members (the commission again: "Some more expensive adult theaters keep the lights dim for a few minutes after the program ends, so that it is possible to get out before the lights go on."[104]). In a much less subtle gesture, it was not uncommon for police officers, undercover or otherwise, to be seeded amongst the crowd, presumably to discourage homosexual activity.[105]

For their part, a majority of spectators interviewed by the commission were in favor of measures to encourage privacy, some most emphatically so. One man, whose feelings were characterized as "fairly common," said "I avoid sitting next to or touching anyone—it's like going to the toilet, you want to be by yourself … Maybe it's the shame of it, a secret, dirty pleasure."[106] Another man's sentiments conveyed a disdain for having to so much as notice his neighbors, and anxiety that they might notice him. "People in the audience are not tortured and sensitive looking, like the kid in *Midnight Cowboy*, they look uncomfortable. Some of them look around and I don't like the idea that they're looking at me."[107] Most

[100] Winick, "Some Observations," 234–5.
[101] Ibid., 243.
[102] Ibid., 241.
[103] Ibid., 250.
[104] Ibid., 241.
[105] Ibid., 250.
[106] Ibid.
[107] Ibid.

of the other interviewees expressed similar opinions, apparently preferring to remain as alone as their counterparts in the peep booths, or in a basement rec room before their home projectors.

As much as the new adult theaters may have superficially resembled the movie houses that had dominated commercial exhibition for more than half a century, it was not clear that they served the same social function. The commission's report, not generally given to musing on the historical sociology of cinema, acknowledged that mainstream film fans had a fairly stable set of reasons for going to the theater, including its proximity to "the courtship activities of young people and the recreational sharing of married couples,"[108] as well as the more prosaic pleasures of appreciation of particular actors, directors, and subjects. "Attendance at adult movies does not seem to be related to such functions, for the most part."[109]

I would suggest that, in fact, the new wave of adult films and, more precisely, their conditions of sale and exhibition, had hardly any social dimension at all. Each of the three outlets for pornographic movies that rose to prominence in the 1960s—domestic projection, peep booths, and storefront theaters—encouraged solitary consumption. Either by the physical arrangement of the exhibition, the various regulations governing their operation, the ways in which spectators were addressed by the distributors, or many other factors, pornographic cinema became a completely individualized pursuit.

To find this tendency put into its purest expression, we must return to the Supreme Court. Earlier, I demonstrated the way in which certain decisions, mainly *Roth* and *Redrup*, influenced the way in which obscenity was defined and regulated. While exerting a more ineffable social influence, these also had consequences for the way in which police and prosecutors executed obscenity claims (the consequence often being that they didn't). This in turn influenced what producers and distributors of adult films, of any kind, were able to do; the cover of an expanded view of the First Amendment was a definite factor in pornography's turn to the public audience.

In the years since the *Roth* decision the Supreme Court had been called to weigh in on a number of important obscenity cases. In *Memoirs v. Massachusetts* (1966), the Court reaffirmed the importance of the "no redeeming social value" test for potentially obscene works; *Ginsberg v. New York* (1968) brought out the

---

[108] Ibid., 251.
[109] Ibid.

opinion that regulation of the marketing of questionable materials for minors was lawful, regardless of whether or not said material was ruled too obscene for adults to possess. But of the major 1960s Court decisions regarding obscenity, the one that is most crucial to understanding the assumptions which undergirded the new kinds of adult movies is 1969's *Stanley v. Georgia*. Unlike previous cases which involved producers of erotic material, this one dealt instead with its consumers and spectators, and acted as a kind of renegotiation of the terms under which citizens were allowed to legally own, read, or watch it. Although the legal reasoning for which the case is famous would apply to any medium, it is only appropriate that this one deals specifically with film.

At stake in the decision was the Georgia state obscenity law, which had recently expanded to criminalize the possession of obscene materials. Robert Eli Stanley was one of the first to be swept up in this law when Atlanta police, searching his home for evidence related to another crime, found three reels of 8mm film, later determined to be obscene. Stanley's appeal to the Supreme Court on First Amendment grounds was successful, but, as before, a reading of the text of the decision reveals that, though it seemed to be staking out a space for complete individual autonomy, definite constraints were implied as well.

The decision to free Mr. Stanley, as articulated in the ruling by Justice Marshall, rested on the court's recognition that the films in question were in his private possession, and for his own private use. This, as Marshall pointed out, was a salient difference between this case and one such as *Roth*, which "dealt with the power of the State and Federal Governments to prohibit or regulate certain public actions taken or intended to be taken with respect to obscene material."[110] "Public action" is the important phrase here—throughout the decision, the Court tacitly affirmed the principle that the state has the right to regulate and proscribe obscenity in public life, including by restricting the sale or distribution of certain materials; indeed, this had been the consistent position of the court since *Roth*. However, by restricting the enjoyment of pornographic films to himself only, Stanley necessarily placed himself beyond the considerations of the state, and could not be prosecuted. The privacy of the ultimate personal realm, that of the mind and imagination, was extended by the court to cover one's immediate domestic and physical space, making all of these the proper fiefdom of the sovereign individual. "If the First Amendment means anything, it means that a

---

[110] *Obscenity and Pornography Decisions of the United States Supreme Court*, Maureen Harrison and Steve Gilbert, eds (Carlsbad: Excellent Books, 2000), 152–3.

State has no business telling a man, sitting alone in his own house, what books he may read or what films he may watch. Our whole constitutional heritage rebels at the thought of giving government the power to control men's minds."[111] This consideration overruled even the importance of obscenity as a legal concept. The court did not dispute that obscenity was not entitled to free speech protections, and did not weigh in on whether or not Stanley's films met the standard required to be regarded as obscene; nevertheless, the decision explicitly ranked the state's duty to prosecute obscenity below that of an individual's right to regulate their own reading (or, in this case, viewing) as they pleased, and the right to behave as they saw fit within private space. Summing up the state of Georgia's arguments for prosecution in one sentence, Marshall rhetorically asked, "If the State can protect the body of a citizen, may it not, argues Georgia, protect his mind?"[112] In their *Stanley* decision, the court answered the question squarely in the negative.

The immediate relevance of this to the post-stag wave of pornographic films of the 1960s and 1970s is obvious; although technically the court acknowledged that prosecution of the sale and distribution of pornography was within constitutional limits, in practice freeing potential customers from the fear that they might find themselves in legal trouble could only encourage those curious about explicit material to investigate. This would help to build a customer base for producers, thus bankrolling more films, books, magazines, and other kinds of smut. But as much as legal decisions act as catalysts for certain types of development and change, they just as often function as official recognition of a certain prevailing social consensus. In this case, I think that *Stanley* served as notice that, by 1969, sexual expression had become a matter of individual autonomy, subject to one's free choice.

This orientation toward individualism, here grounding certain ideas about conduct in the sexual realm, was becoming the conventional wisdom throughout American society by this time, here finding its codification in legal precedent. Such a rich, confident expression of that idea issuing from the bench rang like a clarion, announcing the hegemony of individualist libertarianism in social life that would last for the ensuing several decades. The engine of Stanley's victory was not an arbitrary move toward sexual tolerance for its own sake, but rather a re-thinking of the relationship between the citizen and society, and the responsibilities one had for the other. Brenda Cossman has written about

---

[111] Ibid., 154.
[112] Ibid., 152.

the way in which the concepts of citizenship have changed in the modern era, culminating in the notion of "citizenship as self-governance." In contrast to earlier periods, in which individuals were understood to be at the mercy of obviously coercive measures from the state, the late postwar time saw a devolution of authority over the individual to the individual themselves. Any one person's flourishing—or languishing—was, in this scheme, no longer the responsibility of any social or state apparatus, but of that person alone. Reviewing some of the earlier scholarship on this question, Cossman finds an association between the decline of Fordist-era social democracy and the re-focusing of social life on the individual. In her reading, there exists a definite coincidence between "a heightened emphasis on self-governance with the decline of the welfare state and the emergence of the neo-liberal state; as governments retract from the provision of social goods and services, individuals are called upon to become responsible for themselves and their families."[113] Cossman further contends that this individualization, self-discipline, and responsibilization have been extended to the realm of sexuality as well.

A consequence of this was a revision of exactly what behavior could be regarded as sexually deviant, or, more precisely, how sexual behavior of any sort may potentially come to be regarded as such. The imperative to keep one's sexuality private and properly regulated is the highest one, while the particular character of that sexuality is no longer as important as it once might have been. As examples of those who run afoul of this new arrangement—"bad sexual citizens," as she calls them—Cossman invokes the specters of welfare mothers and deadbeat dads, whose failure to properly discipline themselves sexually have brought about inconvenient consequences not only for themselves but for their children, and, significantly, for their fellow tax paying citizens, as their reliance on public provision casts them as a burden on society as a whole. Under the new, individualized regime of sexual citizenship, the state is fully justified in subjecting them to its full coercive powers, and inviting itself to regulate their lives.

While this new order finds some citizens in sudden violation of its rules of decency, it also offers blanket pardons to others.

> Sexual subjects once cast as outlaws or strangers, such as lesbians and gay men, are being brought into the folds of, and reconstituted in the discourse of, this new

---

[113] Brenda Cossman, *Sexual Citizens: The Legal and Cultural Regulation of Sex and Belonging* (Redwood City, CA: Stanford University Press, 2007), 13.

privatized and self-disciplined citizen. The reconstitution of outlaws as legitimate subjects in law has occurred within this dominant modality of citizenship in which the sexing of citizenship and the disruption of heteronormativity is accompanied by the privatization of sex.[114]

So-called traditional modes of sexual propriety, then, are no longer in and of themselves essential to this concept of citizenship; heteronormativity itself is negotiable in the new regime of the private, individual regulation of the self.

Although she doesn't mention the *Stanley* decision, Cossman's ideas seem to me to be a sensible elaboration of much of what the Court wrote in that case. In the recent past, as demonstrated by the dozens of cases of police busts at stag screenings that I've referenced throughout this book, obscenity—a deviation from healthy sexuality properly understood—was sufficient for coercive state action. By 1969, Justice Marshall dismissed this entirely, explicitly arguing that obscenity is not a concern of the state if it is enjoyed privately, lobbing the ball back to the individual as the ultimate arbiter of what is sexually permissible. For a variety of reasons, I would not suggest that stag film spectators and, say, gay men and lesbians were regarded as precisely interchangeable "sexual outlaws" before the 1960s; but it remains true that both were thought to be in violation of standards of sexual propriety, and thus found themselves frequently at the receiving end of coercive actions from those working on behalf of the state and civil society (if not always to the same extent or severity). But the rehabilitation of each of these into "legitimate subjects" (again, to varying degrees) occurred at around the same time, and this was, in all cases, contingent on their ability to assimilate their sexual behavior into the realm of the private. *Stanley* was an articulation of this imperative.

As much as that decision had announced the rules for how pornographic materials might be viewed from that point forward, it was also describing the situation as it then existed. As we have seen, all of the important ways in which adult movies were being distributed and exhibited in 1969 presupposed an individual consumer, as though the new wave of producers and exhibitors had anticipated the court's decision and brought themselves into conformity with its pronouncements ahead of time. The men in charge of the vast mail-order operations of this period not only assumed a spectator with access to sufficiently private domestic space but deliberately tailored its pitch to individuals, based

---

[114] Ibid., 15.

on their particular proclivities. Peep booths were built specifically to house one person, and this solitude was enforced by regulations as to the size and shape of the booth (as well as by bookstore attendants in person, if necessary). Even the new movie theaters devoted to adult films served spectators who were discouraged from interacting with each other any more than necessary. That a situation so closely resembling the mainstream commercial movie theater, the very space in which was cultivated the sense of almost subconscious collectivity that fueled the great mass art of the twentieth century, could be reconfigured as a gathering place for the lonely crowd is a testament to how far the process had come by the end of the 1960s.

Contrast this state of affairs with what had occurred during the peak of the stag era. As I demonstrated in previous chapters, the classic stag show was almost by necessity a social event. It was the rare screening that wasn't made up of people who knew each other via some previous association, whether through work, or membership in a civic organization, or some other connection to the larger social world. The need for secrecy almost demanded such a thing, as a sense of who may or may not be trusted was essential to keeping oneself out of trouble with the law. Once this ecosystem became no longer viable, pornographic films sought out new audiences in different circumstances, this time as consumers and individuals, rather than communities. In a sense, the new kinds of pornographic films available at this time didn't "replace" stag shows; while the material on screen may have seen superficial resemblance in terms of sexual frankness, the new modes of exhibition weren't in any way replicating the function of the old ones. Seen this way, stag screenings cannot be said to have "evolved" into domestic viewing, peep booths, or hard-core films in theaters, as these are simply essentially different experiences.

This is only a general picture of how this period progressed, and exceptions may be found. There were certainly individual viewers of films before the war (many of these probably supported the various mail-order operations), and stag shows still occurred well into the 1970s. And even the general tendency toward solo consumption in the post-stag era took on different forms of expression as the years went on. Even in the late 1960s, there was a budding sense of social feeling among a few of the spectators at adult movies found by the President's Commission. While most of those interviewed expressed disdain for the rest of the audience, there were some who, at least in their own imaginations, found something reassuring about being part of a communal experience, and expressed this with disarming intimacy. One middle-aged respondent claimed to "enjoy the feeling that the people in the theater are turning on at the same time," while another said that he liked to "think about what the other guys in the theater are thinking … I wonder if they are seeing the same thing I am. It's a nice feeling. In my mind's eye, I become closer to the other people there, but in safety." Yet another took these identifications with the other men in the audience to what could be thought to be its logical conclusion. "I can feel my penis moving forward with every scene where there is a girl undressed. I wonder if the men in the audience also feel horny the same way I do. There are dozens or maybe hundreds of men, each one of whom is getting an erection at the same time."[115]

Examples of homosociality crossing over into homoeroticism are familiar to scholars of adult exhibition, particularly in the 1970s and beyond. Use of adult theaters as cruising sites would become a regular practice after the turn of the decade, as the many chronicles of this activity can attest. Most notable among these is Samuel R. Delany's *Times Square Red Times Square Blue*, which mixed his reminiscences of visits to the various New York adult theaters with a more detached, almost anthropological overview of the social value of the relationships, of all kinds, that he made there with the other men who frequented the same venues. His encounters were often sexual in nature, but not exclusively so. But what was important about these exhibition sites for Delany was that they fulfilled the potential for certain kinds of connection which were excluded from one's everyday social role.

> They were encounters whose most important aspect was that mutual pleasure was exchanged—an aspect that, yes, colored all their other aspects, but that did not involve any sort of life commitment. Most were affable but brief because, beyond pleasure, these were people that you had little in common with. Yet what greater field and force than pleasure can human beings share?[116]

Delany later referred to these kinds of meetings as "interclass contact," and contrasted this with the sort of relationships one would build within the confines of work life, family, or other public engagements (which he presciently called "networking").

Delany allowed that "contact" of this sort is not limited to the adult theater, and is in fact the natural consequence of a kind of ideally ordered urban life. "It is the discussion that begins with the person next to you at the bar. It can be the

---

[115] Winick, "Some Observations," 250.
[116] Samuel R. Delany, *Times Square Red Times Square Blue* (New York: New York University Press, 1999), 56.

conversation that starts with any number of semiofficial or service persons—mailman, policeman, librarian, store clerk or counter person."[117] However, adult theaters for him were a privileged area for this kind of social possibility. This found its highest expression in a New York City which was, at one time, more conducive generally to such potential, only to be done in by the ravages of AIDS, crack, and Manhattan real estate speculation.

This is the most optimistic outcome for the post-stag spectators, one in which they must still encounter pornographic exhibition as individual sexual citizens, but are allowed enough sexual outlawry to occasionally permeate the various class barriers in which they and their neighbors are contained. This is the farthest possible distance from the traditional social role of stag screenings, which sought instead to strengthen connections within already existing groups through the shared pleasure of forbidden films. Just as Delany allowed for the possibility of interclass contact outside of the adult theater, so too was group solidarity in the stag era celebrated and reinforced in countless other ways not involving a surreptitiously procured collection of reels and a projector. By the time of Delany's writing, social unity of that sort seemed not only impossible, but undesirable; he even explicitly contrasts the freedom of interclass contact with the supposedly stultifying nature of group cohesion:

> The small-town way to enjoy a big city is to arrive there with your family, your friends, your school group, your church group, or—if you are really brave—your tour group, with whom you associate (these are all preselected network groups) and have fun, as you sample the food and culture and see the monuments and architecture. But the one thing you do not do is go out in the street alone and meet people.[118]

Stag films could be said to have survived in some form after 1970, inasmuch as a sufficiently motivated spectator could still see short, plotless, anonymously shot sex films; in fact, he could do so more easily then than at any other time in history. However, the stag parties his fathers and grandfathers attended were rapidly growing obsolete, due in some part to changes in technology and obscenity law, but mostly to changing patterns of public association, which saw the slow decline of the civil society which supported these kinds of screenings. The very idea of indulging in such pleasures with anyone from his place or work,

---

[117] Ibid., 123.
[118] Ibid., 156.

church, or club would have been anathema, as alien to him as the ghostly, black-and-white images of nude women with hair and makeup current to the 1930s. Pornographic films continue to be made up to the present day, and spectators (in the United States at least) no longer fear the knock at the door, so long as they obey the command that the door remain closed.

Conclusions and Directions
for Further Research

The post-stag pornographic films which were developed in the 1960s would seem to share many similarities with early cinema, or at least with its mythology. The early storefront theaters of San Francisco are of course reminiscent of the first nickelodeons (a fact noted in passing by Schaefer[1]), peep booths have an obvious parallel with early single-viewer machines such as the Mutoscope (as pointed out in a 1963 report by the California Attorney General[2]). As the new adult theaters began showing hard-core features increasing in length and narrative complexity, it must have been tempting to see a movement similar to that of the transition from the "cinema of attractions" of the pre-1907 period to the early longer narrative works of Griffith, De Mille, and others. In this view, pornographic films in the 1970s were undergoing a period of accelerated evolution, transforming into a mature movie culture with features at the center. The stag period could then be regarded as one of perpetual childhood, as if the "cinema of attractions" had never ended. For decades, almost no technical advances were made, and development of general formal qualities was nonexistent, or at least haphazard and hopelessly varied from one film to the next. Even the means of exhibition stayed the same from the very earliest days—there is very little qualitative difference between the screening that sent Sam Efrus to jail and any one of the stag shows that John Nasser would have put on in, say, 1960—as though all assembled were recreating a form of historical exhibition, after the fashion of Civil War reenactors.

---

[1] Eric Schaefer, "Gauging a Revolution: 16mm Film and the Rise of the Pornographic Feature," *Cinema Journal*, Vol. 41, No. 3 (Spring 2002), 8.
[2] Thomas C. Lynch, *A Report to the California Legislature on Obscenity: The Law and the Nature of the Business* (California Department of Justice, 1967), 88.

But to read an overdetermined historical parallel into all of this would be irresponsible. Stag films were not some embryonic earlier stage of the hard-core feature, nor is the history of the stag period to be regarded as that of a progression toward the new exhibition trends of the 1960s. If I have accomplished anything in the previous pages, I would hope that I have established that the underground exhibition of pornographic films should be regarded as its own type of film culture, one which operated largely beneath the notice of the wider society, but which was still susceptible to its currents. It mostly disappeared after 1970, and has only a tenuous connection to the landscape of moving image pornography that arose afterward. The so-called golden age of pornographic cinema— encompassing the works of such high-profile auteurs as Mitchell brothers, Gerard Damiano, Alex de Renzy, Radley Metzger, Wakefield Poole, as well as countless other more obscure filmmakers—is at least as interesting historically (and vastly more interesting aesthetically) as the stag era, but they are of such a different character from the old stags that I think to assume any essential continuity between them is specious.

That said, the purveyors of the new wave of hard-core films were only too happy to claim stag films as part of their lineage. So the Peekarama theater, located in downtown San Francisco, proudly advertised "STAGS to STAGGER The Imagination" as their fare.[3] Probably some of this was a means of differentiating their films from traditional sexploitation, but others used stags as direct artistic inspiration.

Schaefer provisionally suggests that the hard-core feature had its (possible) coming-out party at the Alex De Renzy's Screening Room theater with the debut of Michael Benveniste and Howard Ziehm's *Mona the Virgin Nymph*. De Renzy of course would soon release his own hard-core films (and later, videos) as the years went on. At some point during 1970, his initial, quasi-documentary features would come out, including one film called *A History of the Blue Movie*. Consisting of several vintage stags cut together in (alleged) chronological order (broken up only by a very beaver-ish modern-day interlude near the end), De Renzy's documentary functions as something of a precursor to the books that would be published a few years hence, and which would act as something of a first draft of the history of pornographic films, such as Gilmore's *Sex and Censorship*, Di Lauro and Rabkin's *Dirty Movies*, and Knight and Alpert's

---

[3] *San Francisco Examiner*, July 13, 1970, 24.

Playboy's Sex in Cinema. Like these, De Renzy's *History* professes to have a serious purpose, but seems designed to simply take advantage of the post-*Roth* legal consensus protecting the public screenings of images of hard-core sex— albeit in restricted circumstances, and (in practice) depending very much on location. De Renzy would shortly thereafter turn to narrative features, dropping any educational pretense entirely. After 1970, the main attraction of the stag film—the realistic depiction and documentation of hard-core sex acts—had taken its place alongside story, character, causality, and all the other trappings of classical narrative cinema. In the ultimate example of truth in advertising, the copywriters behind the ads for *Mona* would, according to Schaefer, write that the film "makes so-called stag movies passe."[4]

The stag film, of course, did not disappear. Though now superseded by other forms of exhibition, the classic stag film, now almost exclusively found on 8mm or Super 8mm, was still sold openly, either from adult book shops or, as always, by mail. Slade claims that, at the peak of pornographic feature production in the early 1970s, 100 35mm features were being produced per year, while "8mm shorts rose to about 500 annually."[5]

Schaefer points out that there was in fact considerable overlap between the two formats; while the new stags were still "short films—virtually always in color and sometimes with sound—they often employed stars from the burgeoning hardcore feature arena and supplemented their films with glossy, full-color magazines and fliers."[6] Furthermore, production and distribution of stags became a profitable enough venture that many tiny studios were founded at this time, now perfectly able to do business in the open, some of which still exist in some form in the present day. "Among the companies with the most widely circulated home movies of the 1970s and early 1980s were Blazing Films, Lasse Braun, Collection, Color Climax, Diplomat Films, Expo Film, Limited Edition, Pretty Girls, Swedish Erotica, and The VIP Collection."[7]

But this was not to last. It is something of a commonplace that the sudden availability of hard core on the VHS and Betamax formats led directly to the emergence of the home-video market as a whole; this is overstated, as there were

---

[4]   Schaefer, "Gauging a Revolution," 17.
[5]   Joseph Slade, *Pornography and Sexual Representation: A Reference Guide, Volume I* (Westport, CT: Greenwood Press, 2001), 81.
[6]   Eric Schaefer, "Plain Brown Wrapper: Adult Films for the Home Market, 1930–1969," in *Looking Past the Screen: Case Studies in American Film History and Method*, ed. Jon Leis and Eric Smoodin (Durham, NC: Duke University press, 2007), 221.
[7]   Ibid.

other commercial and institutional forces at work in the creation of this new sector. But while pornography on video may not exactly have been the midwife to one type of exhibition culture, it is beyond dispute that it was the undertaker for another. As David F. Friedman recalled: "Adult video viewing at home began replacing adult theater attendance, seriously affecting not only [the Friedman-owned] Pussycat [theater chain] but all X-rated movie houses across the nation. The production of adult pictures on film declined sharply. It was difficult to find enough playable 35mm features to maintain the weekly booking policies."[8]

Production and sale of stags on Super 8mm and 8mm declined for the same reason, and in tandem with all types of home film exhibition. Perhaps a snapshot of the changing fortunes of the relevant amateur production equipment—"By 1981, the sale of Super 8 cameras had dropped to about 200,000 units per year, from 600,000 in 1977, while video camera shipments had risen to 200,000"[9]— might serve as a proxy for the collapse of the 8mm format as a whole.

This is the point at which I shall definitively conclude the narrative part of my history, as the scope of my overall inquiry does not extend to the home video market (please see Peter Alilunas's *Smutty Little Movies: The Creation and Regulation of Adult Video,* which bravely ventures into this formidable area of moving image history). Even the features and stag reels available for over-the-counter purchase are only mentioned here by way of an epilogue.

While I hope that the preceding narrative has made a genuine contribution to the understanding of a variety of historical questions—about pornographic movies in general, about the margins of amateur filmmaking, about the business practices of early stag film entrepreneurs, about the conventions of mass journalism, about the record-keeping practices of the FBI—there are as many issues which I have not been able to properly address.

Most frustratingly, I have been able to turn up only limited information on the production of stag films, particularly before 1950. I mean "production" in a narrower sense than I have used it throughout this work, where it has often meant to encompass everything up to and including the development of raw stock and manufacture of projection prints from a reversal positive print. While clues about that stage of production were somewhat forthcoming, I do regard it as something of a disappointment that I was unable to find out more

---

8　David F. Friedman, "The Pussycat Theatre—What's in a Name?" *Something Weird Video Blue Book* (1997), 41.

9　Alan Kattelle, *Home Movies. A History of the American Industry, 1897–1979* (Nashua: Transition Publishing, 2000), 247.

about the processes that led up to that point—finding performers, inventing scenarios, lighting, editing, and so forth. The information I did find—such as the reminiscences in Ries's suicide note, the various news articles quoted throughout—was often tantalizingly vague, leading only to further questions. The few attempts at writing the history of stag film production have been unsatisfying, to say the least, usually amounting to little more than a sequence of unsubstantiated claims of the sort that I discussed in my introduction.

Again, this is largely a by-product of the secretive nature of stag films, and may never be fully resolved. In addition, my own approach in this volume may have been particularly unsuited to finding a satisfactory solution. My strategy has been to attempt to answer questions with an aggregation of particular incidents, and then try to tease out from those a responsible generalization which might have a kind of broad explanatory power for the wider world of stag films (e.g., suggesting that the business practices of stag producers were becoming more sophisticated based on the arrests of Arnild, Hertzwig, Ries, and their circle). It has occurred to me during the completion of this book that this might be ill-suited to address the questions I have above about stag production, since the possibility exists that there in fact was no typical system for shooting these films. Selling them, distributing them, publicizing them (to the extent that this was done), and arranging for their screenings all required some interaction with established entities, a meeting-halfway of some existing social practice, and thus a submission to certain rules of exchange. Shooting these films, done as they were in absolute secrecy, was a nearly anarchic situation, conceptually. Candy Barr alleged that her scenes in *Smart Aleck* were performed under threat of violence;[10] the pseudonymous "Joan" interviewed by Thompson claims to have done her films voluntarily and regarded the whole experience with mild boredom;[11] Slabaugh and Huntington suggested that a not-insignificant number of films shown to stag audiences were in fact privately produced, true home movies intended for no other audience than their makers (Slabaugh: "I have the feeling that the single films, those that don't cross into any series, you're going to have a high proportion of films that were not meant for the commercial market. Probably 60 % of your single films ... were, I feel, not

---

[10] Skip Hollandsworth, "Candy Barr," *Texas Monthly*, September 2001; accessed at https://www.texasmonthly.com/articles/candy-barr/.

[11] Dave Thompson, *Black and White and Blue: Adult Cinema from the Victorian Age to the VCR* (Toronto: ECW Press, 2007), 92.

intended for the commercial market. They're on by accident."[12]). Between these three scenarios—none of which can be independently verified (though Barr's case at least can be traced back to the testimony of an identifiable person)—is a vast spread of different production situations, none of which may be perfectly harmonized with the other. It doesn't tax credibility to assume that, for as long as they remained underground, the shooting phase of stag films may have been the only one to never feel the touch of rationalization or systematization, at least not on a wide scale. It's hard to even speculate on how the great majority of these films were made.

One possible way to at least address this question, if not fully answer it, might be with recourse to micro-histories. While I realize that I am proposing a research program which would be even more labor-intensive than my own (and not necessarily more likely to produce results), I would be curious to see what may be learned by sustained investigation of a single stag film. Are there any works for which era or location of production may be hypothesized? Can any of the performers be positively identified? As with so much more of what's required to construct a worthy history of the oldest pornographic movies, this would necessarily be a collaborative effort; archives would have to be scoured for common copies of titles, scholars would need to consult with film collectors (who are typically scholars themselves, credentialed as such or not), questions about landmarks would have to be crowdsourced.

Slabaugh's attempts at granular description of the films under his care (mentioned in my introduction) seems to have been the closest thing to a project such as this. Noted in the records he left behind are the incidence of repeat performers between different films—certainly ripe subjects for further investigation—as well as location for some films. It is not known exactly what this latter attribution is based on, or how certain Slabaugh was in assigning them. Access to any notes he may have made during this process, or to any records explaining the chain of custody of the films themselves would be immeasurably useful here, but this is of course easier said than done as there is no guarantee that these still exist (if they existed at all in the first place). Still, if his efforts perhaps can't be entirely replicated, they can serve as an inspiration and a starting point.

Perhaps it may be useful as well to begin the research process on the other end of the trail, that is, with the names of people known to have been involved with stag movie production. I have obviously uncovered some of these in

---

[12] Huntington and Slabaugh discussion, 1966, Kinsey Institute.

Figure 5.1 Pat Waring at the Flamingo Club in Arizona, three years after her arrest with the Ries group. (Ad in the Tucson *Arizona Daily Star*, December 22, 1947, page 9.)

the preceding pages, and have found many others who didn't make it into the narrative itself. This is certainly no easy task, but performers' names did occasionally make the news. One person I was not able to fit into my main story was Pat Waring, arrested in the dragnet that followed the arrest of the Ries group, accused of posing for lewd pictures.[13] She denied this, and I was not able to turn up any evidence as to whether or not she was able to beat the charge.

What is especially interesting about Waring, however, is that she led a relatively public life afterward. She worked as a dancer in clubs, and her appearances were heavily advertised (during 1947, she was billed on multiple occasions as "Miss Oomph '48"). She appears in ads and news stories about upcoming performances throughout the 1940s and into the 1950s, indicating that, whatever trouble she may have been involved with in California, the whiff of scandal didn't seem to follow her afterward. This could have been the case for any number of reasons: she may have been acquitted of her charges, the films she (maybe) appeared in may have been burlesque or striptease instead of hard-core movies, or the circles she traveled and worked in—to say nothing of her audiences—simply didn't care about her past adventures, if they were even aware of them. Further investigation of her role in the Ries arrest would answer these questions, as well as possibly dig up other leads to those who may have associated with that circle as well. Waring is an uncommon case in that she left something of a paper trail, but such a close investigation of even those who seemed to be only supporting players in the world of adult films could yield unexpected results.

Finally, I would be curious to know what, if anything, may be said about stag movies from a stylistic or formal perspective now that some basic assumptions can be made about how they were distributed and shown. In what way were the films' (assumed) viewing situation incorporated into the strategies used to present the content?

Most claims made about the content of stag movies in other works seem to focus most often on thematic concerns (such as the way in which the zeitgeist creeps into the frame, e.g., a performer impersonating Adolf Hitler appears in a Second World War film), the way in which "national character" determines the material on screen (Di Lauro and Rabkin, for example, spend a chapter making the case that different national audiences preferred different fetishes[14]), or, in

---

[13] "2 More Held in Lewd Picture Inquiry, 2 More Freed," *Los Angeles Times*, April 6, 1945, 6.
[14] Al Di Lauro and Gerald Rabkin, *Dirty Movies: An Illustrated History of the Stag Film, 1915–1970* (New York: Chelsea House, 1976), 90.

the case of many feminist analyses, a kind of psychoanalysis of the image. Can a firmer historical grounding, one which reliably situated these films within a social context, contribute to an analysis of their content in any way? By "content" here I refer not only to the people, things, and actions photographed—the "pro-filmic event"—but formal tactics used to make these legible and even, at the risk of sounding perverse, the style?

Constructing a historical account of style and aesthetics in stag movies would be a big job indeed. A genealogy of style in any kind of expression would seem to depend on a common system of interaction among artists, in this case filmmakers, even if amateur ones. Such a genealogy would purport to explain the product of a community of producers—however broadly we may define "community"—which had a mechanism for seeing each other's films, directly interacting with each other, publishing and reading about advances in the field, and so forth. This was of course the case for all of the great national studio cinemas, and also for amateurs (thanks to *Movie Makers*, the Amateur Cinema League, and other organs), and even for other types of small-scale production, such as industrial films. No matter how prosaic and disdainful of ornamentation a publicly released film might have been, it still would be under some expectation to conform to basic stylistic norms at least. Did stag movies exist within something analogous to this kind of community of producers? Would it have been necessary for them to follow a sort of stylistic template?

I'm not so sure that they would. For one thing, I'm skeptical that such a thing as an aesthetic norm existed for stag movies, given the wide variety of quality (and even coherence) on display (the likely diversity of production scenarios, which I referred to above, would seem to be an argument against this as well). At the extreme end, there are titles which are truly primitive, featuring the most basic set-ups and often lacking in even the most elementary sense of narrative or spatial continuity—these might better be classified with the most functional amateur films, such as footage of birthday parties.

Others, however, were carried off with at least a modicum of skill, and even visual interest, but then it seems strange to assume that the competence on display in these cases was in any way an answer to other stag movies, and more likely came about as a response to the norms of other types of cinema, such as Hollywood releases or art films.

I realize that a concern for the proper appreciation for the aesthetics of stag movies may seem to be a bit much. I don't wish to inflate my claim on this matter past the point of common sense. In most important ways, I agree with Patricia

Zimmerman when she claims that any aesthetic observations of amateur films—and stag movies are exactly that—can and should be a part of a broader symptomatic, historical critique.

> Because their visual form is almost always positioned as "other" than the more developed cinematic languages of narrative or documentary, amateur films are often categorized as a series of cinematic failures infused by a quaint naivete and innocence, a kind of primitive cinema that failed to evolve a more complex semiotic structure. Amateur films more often than not lack form, structure, style, and coherence of normative visual tropes, precisely because they occupy psychic realms and psychic fantasies that are themselves unformed and forming. These various "lacks" and "insufficiencies," if you will, are exactly what make amateur film such a complicated social document, where the larger political world collides with psychic terrains, where invisibility vies with visibility.
>
> However, I would argue that this alterity of amateur film instead forces us to analyze these films not as artistic inventions ... but as a series of active relationships between the maker and the subject, between the film and history, between representation and history, between the international and the local, between reality and fantasy, between the real and the imaginary. Amateur films are records of marginal practices, but they are also registers of complicated social, historical, national, and psychic discourses.[15]

That said, I would like to second the call made by Joe Rubin to extend the consideration of stylistic factors to adult cinema, asking only that it be stretched just slightly further back into history in order to cover stag movies as well. In many ways, Rubin's argument is much more grounded than is my own; he is able to point to skilled directors like de Renzy, Wakefield Poole, and Bob Chinn as evidence for the stylistic potential of the adult film, and thus can challenge scholars of moving image pornography—most of whom likely began as fans of cinema in general—to give aesthetic concerns the same weight for those mentioned above as they would for Sirk, Fassbinder, or Welles.[16]

That Rubin makes a positive case for the artistic qualities of the X-rated feature might seem to bring my attempted parallel up short—after all, he is at pains to point out that "X-rated films were well photographed, professionally

---

[15] Patricia Zimmerman, "Morphing History Into Histories," *The Moving Image*, Vol. 1, No. 1 (Spring 2001), 112–13.

[16] Joe Rubin, "Fading Flesh: Personal Reflections on the Quest to Preserve Hardcore Cinema," in *Porno Chic and the Sex Wars: American Sexual Representation in the 1970s*, ed. Carolyn Bronstein and Whitney Strubg (Amherst: University of Massachusetts Press, 2016), 352.

lit, and generally made with the same care and attention as any comparably budgeted feature film of the era," and rails against the notion that "filmmakers creating X-rated movies were motivated almost solely by a desire to depict sex acts and that all other aspects of the film were merely window dressing."[17] This last point in particular could credibly be made against a number of stag shorts. However, in the very next paragraph, he borrows a term from Ted McIlvenna, the founder of the Institute for the Advanced Study of Human Sexuality, to describe the films he's defending—"erotic folk art." That, to my mind, is a much more fitting description of even the lowliest stag than it is of the work of any of the above-named directors. Stag films were a form practiced by (mostly) nonprofessionals, who sought to capture on film that which hadn't found its way onto public cinema screens, and thus had no established conventions of cinematic presentation. How they sought to adopt and adapt various conventions in order to make this material both legible and appealing to the senses of the spectator—in whatever situation they imagined that spectator would encounter the work—is, to my way of thinking, an avenue worth pursuing, and I hope that my own much more mundane, trainspotting chronicle will have made that pursuit somewhat more likely.

[17] Ibid.

References

Archival Sources

Federal Bureau of Investigation (Freedom of Information Act [FOIA]): Obscene File, administrative file.

Kinsey Institute, Bloomington, Indiana: audio recordings, Eugene Slabaugh and George Huntington, 1965–6.

Lyndon Baines Johnson Library, Austin, Texas: Records of the President's Commission on Obscenity and Pornography.

Wisconsin State Historical Society, Madison, Wisconsin: John Saxon Sumner Papers, 1901–61.

Published Sources

Akron Beacon Journal. "County Squad Raids Obscene Film Show." July 20, 1929, 5.

Akron Beacon Journal. "Raid 'Peep Show,' Arrest Operator." November 20, 1942, 8.

Akron Beacon Journal. "Norwat Goes Free on Picture Count." December 18, 1942, 35.

Alilunas, Peter. *Smutty Little Movies: The Creation and Regulation of Adult Video*. Berkeley: University of California Press, 2016.

Arizona Daily Star. "Truth Is Beauty, Beauty, Truth." May 27, 1925.

Asbury Park Press. "800 Reels of Indecent Films Bring Three-Year Sentence." April 25, 1931, 1.

Ashbee, Henry Spencer. *Forbidden Books of the Victorians, Volume I*. London: Odyssey Press, 1970.

Bach, Steven. *Marlene Dietrich: Life and Legend*. New York: Da Capo, 2000.

Bakersfield Californian. April 26, 1945, 20.

Baltimore Sun. "2 Accused of Possessing Obscene Film Give Bail." February 10, 1928, 3.

Baltimore Sun. "1,000 Taken in Raid on Obscene Movie." September 24, 1931, 7.

Baltimore Sun. "7 Are Fined in Film Case." July 16, 1943, 5.

Battle Creek Enquirer. "Driver Jailed, Fined on 2 Charges Here." May 20, 1950, 2.

Berube, Allen. *Coming Out under Fire: The History of Gay Men and Women in World War II*. Chapel Hill: University of North Carolina Press, 2010.

Bougie, Robin, ed. *Cinema Sewer: The Adults-Only Guide to History's Sickest and Sexiest Movies, Volume 5*. Godalming: FAB Press, 2015.

Brooklyn Daily Eagle. "House Painter Accused of Having Indecent Film." November 9, 1940, 2.

Brownlow, Kevin. *Behind the Mask of Innocence*. New York: Knopf, 1990.

Camper, Fred. "Some Notes on the Home Movie." *Journal of Film and Video* 38, no. ¾ (Summer–Fall 1986): 9–14.

Capital Journal (Salem, OR). "Fifty Million Pieces of Pornography Flood Mails Annually, Most Aimed at Teeners." February 19, 1958, 11.

Charles, Douglas. *The FBI's Obscene File: J. Edgar Hoover and the Bureau's Crusade against Smut*. Lawrence: University Press of Kansas, 2012.

Chicago Tribune. "Naughty Dances and Snappy Film End Club's Life." June 29, 1920, 1.

Chicago Tribune. "Obscene Films Seized in Raid at 500 S. State." July 23, 1954, 37.

Church, David. *Disposable Passions: Vintage Pornography and the Material Legacies of Hardcore Cinema*. New York: Bloomsbury Academic, 2016.

Chute, David and Kevin Allman, "Wages of Sin: An Interview with David F. Friedman," *Film Comment* (July-August, 1986).

Cincinnati Enquirer. "Fifty Persons Arrested." March 4, 1933, 14.

Cincinnati Enquirer. "Prejudice Is Charged." March 9, 1933, 18.

Cincinnati Enquirer. "Sentences." February 15, 1941, 22.

Cossman, Brenda. *Sexual Citizens: The Legal and Cultural Regulation of Sex and Belonging*. Redwood City, CA: Stanford University Press, 2007.

Courier-Journal, December 5, 1932, 2.

Courier-News (Bridgewater, NJ). "Big 'Smoker' Is Raided." February 25, 1939, 12.

Croughton, Amy H. "Some Say." *Courier-News (Bridgewater, NJ)*, April 25, 1933, 6.

The Daily Democrat, June 10, 1896, 8.

Delany, Samuel R. *Times Square Red Times Square Blue*. New York: New York University Press, 1999.

Democrat and Chronicle (Rochester, NY). "Alleged Exhibitor Fights Charge of Showing Obscene Films in Raided Garage." June 27, 1925, 19.

Democrat and Chronicle (Rochester, NY). "Obscene Matter Measure Passed." March 25, 1927, 37.

Democrat and Chronicle (Rochester, NY). "Distribution of Obscene Films Charged in Arrest of Elmira Pair." May 3, 1939, 16.

Democrat and Chronicle (Rochester, NY). "Jury Finds True Bills on 16 Cases." May 19, 1939, 23.

Democrat and Chronicle (Rochester, NY). "Films at Smoker Lead to Arrest." January 17, 1944, 13.

Democrat and Chronicle (Rochester, NY). "Court Orders Obscene Films to Be Destroyed." December 11, 1945, 17.

Democrat and Chronicle (Rochester, NY). "U.S. Judge Rules Questioned Film Can Be Delivered." December 20, 1953, 6B.

Des Moines Register. "Students Held after 'Obscene' Film Show." December 4, 1932, 2.

Detroit Free Press. "'Indecent' Film Plot Is Exposed." December 8, 1923, 22.

Detroit Free Press. "Union Stag Party's Movies Not Obscene, Jury Decides." July 18, 1939, 4.

Detroit Free Press. "Police Confiscate Films as Indecent." February 14, 1943, 10.

Detroit Free Press. "Dance in Nude Charge Lands Nine in Court." September 26, 1944, 7.

Detroit Free Press. "Four Seized in Raid on Theater." October 13, 1948, 1.

Di Lauro, Al and Gerald Rabkin. *Dirty Movies: An Illustrated History of the Stag Film, 1915–1970*. New York: Chelsea House, 1976.

Doherty, James. "Reports Drop in Sex Crimes; 1,713 This Year." *Chicago Tribune*, December 31, 1953, 11.

Elmira Star-Gazette, July 23, 1938, 12.

Elmira Star-Gazette, December 12, 1938, 16.

Elmira Star-Gazette. "Two Charged with Mailing Art Films." May 3, 1939, 8.

Elsaesser, Thomas, ed. *Early Cinema: Space, Frame, Narrative*. London: British Film Institute, 1990.

Enticknap, Leo. *Moving Image Technology: From Zoetrope to Digital*. New York: Wallflower Press, 2005.

Exhibitors Herald. "Popular Pictures and Sun Corp Move." May 25, 1918, 34.

Exhibitors Herald. "'Film Smoker' Is Success." February 9, 1924, 45–6.

Exhibitors Herald. "Protests against Film Smoker." February 23, 1924, 59.

Exhibitors Herald and Moving Picture World. "Government Quizzes Two Film Cutters for Indecent Film." December 1, 1928, 42.

Fahey, James J. *Pacific War Diary, 1942–1945*. Boston, MA: Houghton Mifflin, 2003.

Fernett, Gene. "Itinerant Roadshowmen and the 'Free Movie' Craze." *Classic Images*, no. 88 (1982): 12.

Film Daily. February 27, 1940, 10.

Film Daily. "Barry Asks Sen. Wheeler to Retract Lewd Charge." October 24, 1941, 1.

Fresno Bee The Republican. "Reedly Man Is Arrested, Lewd Pictures Seized." March 8, 1938, 9.

Fussell, Paul. *Wartime: The Experience of War, 1939–1945*. New York: Oxford University Press, 1989.

The Geneva Times, April 27, 1900.

Gertzman, Jay A. *Bookleggers and Smuthounds: The Trade in Erotica, 1920–1940*. Philadelphia: University of Pennsylvania Press, 1999.

Gibson, Pamela Church, and Roma Gibson, eds. *Dirty Looks: Women, Pornography, Power*. London: British Film Institute, 1993.

Gilbert, James. *A Cycle of Outrage: America's Reaction to the Juvenile Delinquent*. New York, NY: Oxford University Press, 1988.

Gilmore, Donald H. *Sex and Censorship in the Visual Arts, Volume II*. San Diego, CA: Greenleaf Classics, 1970.

Gomery, Douglas. *Shared Pleasures: A History of Movie Presentation in the United States*. Madison: University of Wisconsin Press, 1992.

Green, Abel, and Joe Laurie, Jr. *Showbiz: From Vaude to Video*. New York: Henry Holt and Company, 1951.

Gubern, Roman. *La imagen pornografica y otras perversiones opticas*. Barcelona: Editorial Anagrama, 2005.

Gunning, Tom. *D.W. Griffith & the Origin of American Narrative Film: The Early Years at Biogaph*. Urbana: University of Illinois Press, 1991.

Hammond Times (Hammond, IN)."Purveyor or Obscene Films Outwitted by Investigator [*sic*]." July 1, 1948, 13.

Harrison, Maureen, and Steve Gilbert. *Obscenity and Pornography Decisions of the United States Supreme Court*. Carlsbad: Excellent Books, 2000.

Harrison, Paul. "Hollywood." *Wilkes-Barre Times Leader*, September 5, 1938, 1.

Hartford Courant. "Police Raid Movie, Arrest Exhibitor." September 27, 1942, 7.

Hearings Before the Subcommittee to Investigate Juvenile Delinquency of the Committee on the Judiciary, United States Senate, Eighty-Fourth Congress, First Session, Pursuant to S. Res. 62 Investigation of Juvenile Delinquency in the United States. Washington, DC: Government Printing Office, 1955.

Herald and News (Klamath Falls, OR). "Boys See Obscene Films, Arrested." October 16, 1950, 12.

Herbert, Stephen, and Luke McKernan, eds. *Who's Who of Victorian Cinema: A Worldwide Survey*. London: British Film Institute, 1996.

Herzog, Amy. "In the Flesh: Space and Embodiment in the Pornographic Peep Show Arcade." *The Velvet Light Trap*, no. 62 (Fall 2008): 29–43.

Higham, Charles. *The Life of Marlene Dietrich*. New York: Norton, 1979.

Hiner, Jack. "Memo to the Boss: Teen-Agers Jam Theater for Lewd 'Strip' Films." *The Star Press*, January 1, 1947, 1.

Hollansworth, Skip. "Candy Barr." *Texas Monthly*, September 2001. Accessed at https://www.texasmonthly.com/articles/candy-barr.

Home Movies, November, 1942, 238.

Horak, Jan-Christopher. "Out of the Attic: Archiving Amateur Film." *Journal of Film Preservation* 56 (June 1998): 50–3.

Horak, Jan-Christopher. "The Strange Case of *The Fall of Jerusalem*: Orphans and Film Identification." *The Moving Image* 5, No. 2 (2007): 26–49.

The Houston Herald. "The Screen." May 11, 1933, 4.

Independent Record (Helena, MT). "Baltimore Scandal." February 15, 1940, 6.

Indiana Gazette. "Sex Crimes Draw Activity." April 22, 1940, 2.

Indiana Gazette. "Four Held for Obscene Films." July 28, 1943, 12.

International Photographer. "Toy Projectors Big Holiday Factor." November, 1930, 33–4.

International Photographer. "Hollywood Film's Sound Studio Will Stamp Its Own Flexo Records." October, 1930, 37.

International Photographer. "Mickey Mouse Makes Bow to 16mm." June, 1932, 25.

Jones, James. *Whistle*. New York: Delta Trade Paperbacks, 1999.

Kattelle, Alan. *Home Movies: A History of the American Industry, 1897–1979*. Nashua: Transition Publishing, 2000.

Kendrick, Walter. *The Secret Museum: Pornography in Modern Culture*. Berkeley: University of California Press, 1997.

Kingsport Times (Kingsport, TN). "'Stag' Party." February 12, 1940, 8.

Knight, Arthur and Hollis Alpert. "The History of Sex in Cinema, Part Seventeen: The Stag Film." *Playboy*, November, 1967, 178.

Koszarski, Richard. *An Evening's Entertainment: The Age of the Silent Feature Picture 1915–1928*. Berkeley: University of California Press, 1990.

Lansing State Journal. "Padlock Theater, Confiscate Films." October 15, 1948, 4.

Levine, Lawrence. *Highbrow/Lowbrow: The Emergence of Cultural Hierarchy in America*. Cambridge, MA: Harvard University Press, 1990.

Levinson, Capt. Edwin B. "Operation and Maintenance of Projectors in the Field." *Business Screen* VII, no. 1 (December 1945): 64.

The Literary Digest. "Wise Mabel." March 2, 1918, 75.

Los Angeles Times. July 4, 1937, 8.

Los Angeles Times. "Sentence in Mail Case Suspended." March 22, 1938, 28.

Los Angeles Times. "Immoral Film Causes Arrest." July 20, 1943, 6.

Los Angeles Times. "Lewd-Photo Raids Net 18 with Mass of Evidence." April 4, 1945, 7.

Los Angeles Times. "Complaints Pouring in on Lewd Photo Charges." April 5, 1945, 7.

Los Angeles Times. "2 More Held in Lewd Picture Inquiry, 2 More Freed." April 6, 1945, 6.

Los Angeles Times. "Jury Indicts Man for Obscene Films." April 7, 1946, 15.

Los Angeles Times. "Hollywood Man and Wife Found Dead in Chicago." September 16, 1947, 2.

Los Angeles Times. "Blue Movies." October 25, 2007, http://latimesblogs.latimes.com/thedailymirror/2007/10/blue-movies.html.

Lynch, Thomas C. *A Report to the California Legislature on Obscenity: The Law the Nature of the Business*. California Department of Justice, 1967.

Mason City Globe-Gazette (Mason City, IA). "In Extortion Plot?" November 23, 1936.

Mendes, Peter. *Clandestine Erotic Fiction in English, 1800–1930: A Bibliographical Study*. Aldershot: Scholar Press, 1993.

Miami Daily News Record. "Bizzell Wars on D.D.M.C." December 11, 1932, 1.

Milwaukee Journal. "Builders' Stag Party Raided." February 4, 1928, 2.

Milwaukee Journal. "Action Would Not Be Legal, Wengert Says." February 8, 1928, 1.

Milwaukee Journal, February 6, 1954, 1–2.

Minneapolis Star. "First Instance of Faked Photo Racket in City." November 25, 1936, 5.

Minneapolis Star. "Shop Owner Held for District Court." November 30, 1944, 13.

Minneapolis Star. "Dillon Hints City May Be Lewd Photo Center." December 6, 1944, 15.

Minneapolis Star. "'Professor' and Lewd Books Held." December 8, 1944, 1.

Minneapolis Star. "Lewd Book Probe Hits Stag Films." December 9, 1944, 1.

Minneapolis Star, January 12, 1945, 13.

Moreck, Curt. *Sittengeschichte des Kinos*. Dresden: Paul Aretz, 1926.

Morning Call (Allentown, PA). May 18, 1943, 24.

Motion Picture Herald. "War Knocks Out the 'Juke-Box' Movie Line." December 27, 1941, 67.

Motion Picture Herald. "Seeking Licenses for Sound Machines." June 27, 1942, 54.

Motion Picture Herald. "Drive against Obscenity Started in Los Angeles." July 18, 1942, 39.

Mount Carmel Item. "Drive On to Rid Mails of Obscene Films." April 29, 1925, 4.

Movie Makers, June, 1938, 310.

Movie Makers, March, 1942, 99.

Movie Makers, June, 1942, 225.

Movie Makers, November, 1942, 443.

Movie Makers, January, 1943, 3.

Movie Makers, February, 1943, 53.

Moving Picture News, April 8, 1911, 19.

Moving Picture News. "Operators' Union of Washington D.C." December 16, 1911, 6.

Moving Picture World, January 20, 1912.

Mundy, J. H. "Obscene Film." *The Star Press*, January 2, 1946, 6.

Murray, William. "The Porn Capital of America." *New York Times*, January 3, 1971. Section SM, 8.

New York Clipper, October 19, 1907, 971.

New York Times. "Raid on Film Show Lands 81 in Cells." December 1, 1922.

New York Times. "Court Releases 292 Seized at a Show." April 29, 1934, 16.

News-Review (Roseburg, OR). "Love Scenes Too Filthy for Jury; Picture Halted." November 23, 1928, 1.

Oakland Tribune. "Man Arrested for Having Obscene Film." September 13, 1928, 48.

Oakland Tribune. "1000 Fight to Flee Raid on Lewd Show." November 8, 1938, 3.

The Observer. "When the French Started Making Dirty Movies." November 3, 1996.

Oshkosh Daily Northwestern. "Having a Good Time at Road School." February 2, 1929, 10.

Palladium-Item (Richmond, IN). "10 Arrested Where 65 See Obscene Films." March 15, 1951, 17.

Palm Beach Post. "Hollywood Party Is Ended in Court." March 1, 1931, 1.

Pasadena Independent. "Lewd Movie Maker Called 'Vulture.'" December 22, 1958, 25.

Philadelphia Inquirer. "2 Held as Police Raid Obscene Film Exhibit." July 3, 1930, 2.

Philadelphia Inquirer. "Wife Asks Divorce from Du Pont Aide." October 17, 1935, 3.

Philadelphia Inquirer. "Denounces Wife as 'Gold Digger.'" October 18, 1935, 5.

Philadelphia Inquirer. "Racy Books and Films Seized after Arrest." January 20, 1937, 4.

Philadelphia Inquirer. February 19, 1939, 14W.

Philadelphia Inquirer. "2 Men Arrested in Gambling Raid." February 21, 1942, 6.

Philadelphia Inquirer. "100 Seized By Raiders at Smoker." March 23, 1942, 19.

Philadelphia Inquirer. "Four Held after Raid on Lewd Show." November 21, 1942, 19.

Philadelphia Inquirer. "Arrests Bare Lewd Film Ring Here." July 28, 1943, 25.

Philadelphia Inquirer. "12 Convicted for Staging Lewd Show." July 29, 1943, 21.

Philadelphia Inquirer. "3 Cameramen Fined for Obscene Films." September 28, 1943, 12.

Pittsburgh Post Gazette. "Slovak Hall Movies Held Too Snappy." April 27, 1939, 15.

Pittsburgh Post Gazette. "142 Are Arrested in Pictures Raid." April 18, 1942, 4.

Pittsburgh Post Gazette. "City, County Stag Raids." January 1, 1944, 9.

Pittsburgh Post Gazette. "Year in Prison Imposed." May 5, 1944, 15.

Pittsburgh Press. "70 Arrested in Liquor Raids." February 5, 1944, 1.

Pittsburgh Press. "Obscene Movies Charge Holds 3." January 15, 1949, 15.

Popular Mechanics, April, 1940, 42.

Popular Mechanics, May, 1940, 39.

Popular Mechanics, June, 1940, 43.

Pryluck, Calvin. "The Itinerant Movie Show and the Development of the Film Industry." *Journal of University Film and Video Association* 35, no. 4 (Fall 1983): 11–22.

Putnam, Robert. *Bowling Alone: The Collapse and Revival of American Community.* New York, NY: Touchstone Books, 2001.

Read, Paul and Mark-Paul Meyer. *The Restoration of Motion Picture Film.* Oxford: Butterworth-Heinemann, 2000.

Reno Gazette-Journal. "'Indecent' Films Reno Bound Seized." September 13, 1928, 8.

Revene, Larry. *Wham Bam $$ Ba Da Boom! Mob Wars, Porn Battles, and a View from the Trenches.* Hudson Delta Books, 2013.

Roepke, Martina. "Tracing 17.5mm Practices in Germany (1902–1908)." *Film History* 19, no. 4 (2007): 348–9.

Ross, Steven J. *Working Class Hollywood: Silent Film and the Shaping of Class in America.* Princeton, NJ: Princeton University Press, 1988.

Rubin, Joe. "Fading Flesh: Personal Reflections on the Quest to Preserve Hardcore Cinema." In *Porno Chic and the Sex Wars: American Sexual Representation in the 1970s,* edited by Carolyn Bronstein and Whitney Strub, 349–57. Amherst: University of Massachusetts Press, 2016.

St. Louis Post-Dispatch. "Obscene Films Seized in Home Movie Raid." September 27, 1940, 29.

Samuel, O. M. "New Orleans, L.A." *Variety,* December 7, 1907, 31.

Samuel, O. M. "New Orleans, L.A." *Variety,* May 5, 1908, 35.

San Bernardino County Sun. "So-Called Obscene Films Too Bad for Federal Grand Jury." November 24, 1928, 2.

San Francisco Examiner. July 13, 1970, 24.

San Mateo Times. "Police Raid Naughty Film." March 28, 1942, 1.

Santa Ana Register. "Ross Pleads Own Case before Jury." March 17, 1938, 1.

Schaefer, Eric. *Bold! Daring! Shocking! True!: A History of Exploitation Films, 1919–1959.* Durham, NC: Duke University Press, 1999.

Schaefer, Eric. "Gauging a Revolution: 16mm Film and the Rise of the Pornographic Feature." *Cinema Journal* 41, no. 3 (2002): 3–26.

Schaefer, Eric. "Plain Brown Wrapper: Adult Films for the Home Market, 1930–1969." In *Looking Past the Screen: Case Studies in American Film History and Method*, edited by Jon Leis and Eric. Smoodin, 201–26. Durham, NC: Duke University Press, 2007.

Schatz, Thomas. *Boom and Bust: American Cinema in the 1940s*. Berkeley: University of California Press, 1999.

Schlosser, Eric. *Reefer Madness: Sex, Drugs, and Cheap Labor in the American Black Market*. Boston, MA: Houghton Mifflin, 2003.

Sheaffer, Louis. *O'Neill, Son and Playwright*. Boston, MA: Little, Brown, 1968.

Sheaffer, Russell. "Smut, Novelty, Indecency: Reworking a History of Early-Twentieth-Century American 'Stag Film.'" *Porn Studies* 1, no. 4 (2014): 346–59.

Shepard, Richard F. "Peep Shows Have New Nude Look." *New York Times*, June 9, 1969.

Shteir, Rachel. *Striptease: The Untold History of the Girlie Show*. New York: Oxford University Press, 2005.

Sklar, Robert. "Oh Althusser!: Historiography and the Rise of Cinema Studies." In *Resisting Images: Essays on Cinema and History*, edited by Robert Sklar and Charles Musser. Philadelphia, PA: Temple University Press, 1990.

Slade, Joseph. *Pornography and Sexual Representation: A Reference Guide, Volume I*. Westport, CT: Greenwood Press, 2001.

Slade, Joseph. "Eroticism and Technological Regression: The Stag Film." *History and Technology* 2, no. 1 (March 2006): 27–52.

Snyder, Thomas D., ed. *120 Years of American Education: A Statistical Portrait*. Washington, DC: Center for Education Statistics, 1993.

Something Weird Video Blue Book. Something Weird Video, 1997.

The Star Press (Minneapolis, MN) "Obscene Films." July 24, 1938, 8.

Star Tribune (Minneapolis, MN). "Raiders Find Lewd Photos, Books Cache." December 2, 1933, 3.

Star Tribune (Minneapolis, MN). "Lewd Picture Sift Spreads." December 10, 1944, 8.

Star Tribune (Minneapolis, MN). December 14, 1944, 12.

Star Tribune (Minneapolis, MN). December 21, 1944, 8.

Stevenson, Jack. "Blue Movie Notes: Ode to an Attic Cinema." In *Fleshpot: Cinema's Sexual Myth Makers & Taboo Breakers*, edited by Jack Stevenson, 7–16. Manchester: Headpress/Critical Vision, 2002.

Stone, Melinda, and Dan Streible. "Introduction: Small-Gauge and Amateur Film." *Film History* 15, no. 2 (2003): 123–5.

Streible, Dan. "Children at the Mutoscope." *Cinemas* 141 (2003): 91–116.

Streible, Dan. *Fight Pictures: A History of Boxing and Early Cinema*. Berkeley: University of California Press, 2008.

Strub, Whitney. *Perversion for Profit: The Politics of Pornography and the Rise of the New Right*. New York: Columbia University Press, 2011.

Swanson, Dwight. "Home Viewing: Pornography and Amateur Film Collections, a Case Study." *The Moving Image* 5 (2005): 136–40.

Tampa Times. "Charges Motion Pictures Obscene." August 13, 1938, 2.

Tampa Tribune. "Film Called Indecent; Gore Is Fined $600." August 28, 1946, 15.

Tampa Tribune. "Theater Man Fined." April 6, 1949, 9.

Technical Report of the Commission on Obscenity and Pornography, Volume III. Washington, DC: U.S. Government Printing Office, 1971.

Technical Report of the Commission on Obscenity and Pornography, Volume IV: The Marketplace: Empirical Studies. Washington, DC: U.S. Government Printing Office, 1971.

Tepperman, Charles. *Amateur Cinema: The Rise of North American Moviemaking, 1923–1960.* Oakland: University of California Press, 2015.

Terre Haute Tribune, September 19, 1961, 15.

Thompson, David. *Black and White and Blue: Adult Cinema from the Victorian Age to the VCR.* Toronto: ECW Press, 2007.

Thompson, George Raynor and Dixie R. Harris. *The Signal Corps: The Outcome (Mid-1943 through 1945).* Washington, DC: Office of the Chief of Military History, U.S. Army, 1966.

Thompson, Glenn. *Sex Rackets.* Cleveland, OH: Century Books, 1967.

Uricchio, William. "Archives and Absences," *Film History* 7, no. 3 (Autumn 1995): 256–63.

Variety. "Stag Burlesque Raid." March 27, 1907, 5.

Variety. "But One 'Cooch' Dancer." March 14, 1908, 4.

Variety. "Police Censor 'Troc's' Bill." March 14, 1908, 4.

Variety. "Chicago Police Keeping Watch on Dive Keepers." April 4, 1908, 6.

Variety. "Clubs and Club Agents." December 10, 1910, 29.

Variety. "Hunting 'Cooch' Reels." January 7, 1916, 27.

Variety. "Carnival Crimes." April 28, 1922, 7.

Variety. "'Girl Shows', Carnival's Ruination; Not So Many Now but All Must Go." September 8, 1922, 7.

Variety. "Burlesque Over the Years." January 14, 1925, 47.

Variety. July 5, 1932, 36.

Variety. July 31, 1935, 18.

Variety. "509 Club Det., Fined for 'Obscene' Shows." October 14, 1942, 45.

Variety. "Dirty Jukepix Burns Det. Cops." February 17, 1943, 3.

Viguerie, Richard. *America's Right Turn: How Conservatives Used New and Alternative Media to Take Power.* Chicago: Bonus Books, 2004.

Wallace, Irving. "All This Is Hollywood, Too!" *Modern Screen*, February, 1941, 34–5, 87–9.

Washington Times, December 9, 1911, 12.

Waugh, Thomas. *Hard to Imagine: Gay Male Eroticism in Photography and Film from Their Beginnings to Stonewall*. New York: Columbia University Press, 1996.

Waugh, Thomas. "Homosociality in the Classical American Stag Film: Off-Screen, On-Screen." In *Porn Studies*, edited by Linda Williams, 127–41. Durham, NC: Duke University Press, 2004.

Weintz, Walter. *The Solid Gold Mailbox: How to Create Winning Mail-Order Campaigns, By the Man Who's Done It All*. New York: John Wiley & Sons, 1987.

Williams, Linda. *Hard Core: Power, Pleasure, and the Frenzy of the Visible*. Berkeley: University of California Press, 1989.

Williams, Linda. "'White Slavery' versus the Ethnography of 'Sexworkers': Women in Stag Films at the Kinsey Archive." *The Moving Image* 5, no. 2 (Fall 2005): 107–34.

Wollenberg, H. H. *Fifty Years of German Film*. New York: Arno Press & The New York Times, 1972.

Woodward, Bob and Scott Armstrong. *The Brethren: Inside the Supreme Court*. New York: Simon and Schuster, 1979.

Zimmerman, Patricia. "Morphing History into Histories: From Amateur Film to the Archive of the Future." *The Moving Image: The Journal of the Association of Moving Image Archivists* 1, no. 1 (2001): 108–30.

Index

9 781501 386473